NATIONAL
GEOGRAPHIC

THE
OLD
WEST

STEPHEN G. HYSLOP

NATIONAL GEOGRAPHIC
WASHINGTON, D.C.

CONTENTS

PRECEDING PAGES: **Page 1:** Portrait of Iowa warrior Wash-ka-mon-ya (Fast Dancer), by George Catlin, 1844; pages 2–3: "The Oregon Trail," by Albert Bierstadt, 1869. OPPOSITE: Texas Rangers, late 1800s.

The Louisiana Purchase and the Contest for the West

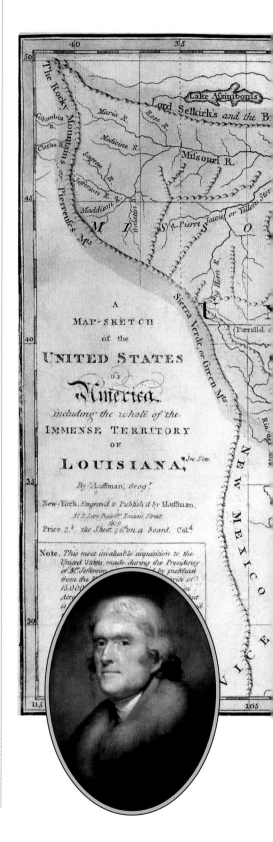

O n July 4, 1803, President Thomas Jefferson announced a momentous deal that altered the scope and destiny of the nation he helped found in 1776. The announcement, published in a Washington, D.C., newspaper on Independence Day, revealed that the United States had reached an agreement in Paris to purchase from France "sovereignty over New Orleans, and the whole of Louisiana." As claimed by France, Louisiana covered a vast area extending from the Mississippi River to the headwaters of its western tributaries, including the Missouri and Arkansas Rivers, originating in the Rocky Mountains. In later years, when that territory had been fully explored and mapped, its area would be calculated at over 500 million acres, obtained for $15 million, or barely 3 cents an acre. "You have made a noble bargain for yourselves," said the French foreign minister Talleyrand to Jefferson's negotiators in Paris, "and I suppose you will make the most of it."

The Louisiana Purchase would be hailed for doubling American territory at the stroke of a pen. Yet this historic deal did not give the U.S. undisputed possession of Louisiana in full. The treaty did not define that territory or its boundaries, except to say that what the U.S. obtained by purchase was of the same extent as when "France possessed it." The only areas that France possessed by right of occupancy were those places where French colonists had settled, including promising towns along the Mississippi such as St. Louis and Baton Rouge and the strategic port city of New Orleans, which in itself was worth millions because it gave the U.S. control of maritime trade between the Mississippi Valley and distant Atlantic ports by way of the Gulf of Mexico. Populous New Orleans would serve as the nucleus for the state of Louisiana, admitted to the Union in 1812, and St. Louis would

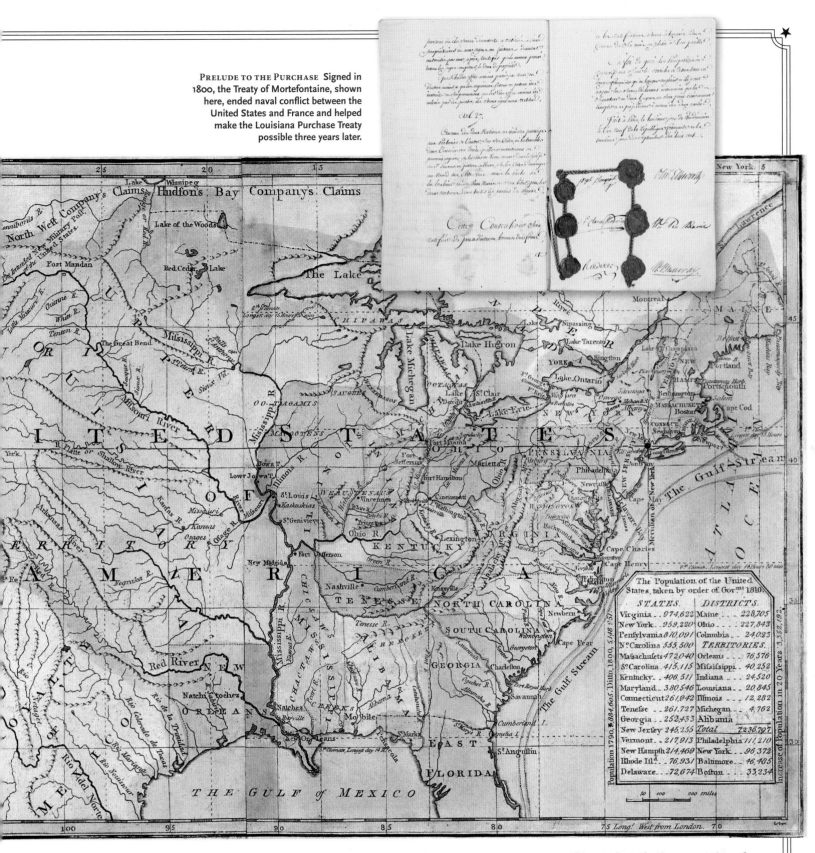

Signed in 1800, the Treaty of Mortefontaine, shown here, ended naval conflict between the United States and France and helped make the Louisiana Purchase Treaty possible three years later.

The Population of the United States, taken by order of Gov.mt 1810.

STATES.		DISTRICTS.	
Virginia	974,622	Maine	228,705
New York	959,220	Ohio	227,843
Pensylvania	810,091	Columbia	24,023
N.º Carolina	555,500	**TERRITORIES.**	
Massachusets	472,040	Orleans	76,576
S.º Carolina	415,115	Mississippi	40,252
Kentucky	406,511	Indiana	24,520
Maryland	380,546	Lousiana	20,845
Connecticut	261,942	Illinois	12,282
Tenesse	261,727	Michegan	4,762
Georgia	252,433	Alabama	
New Jersey	245,255	Total	7,236,797
Vermont	217,913	Philadelphia	111,210
New Hampsh.	214,469	New York	96,372
Rhode Isld.	76,931	Baltimore	46,405
Delaware	72,674	Boston	33,234

Population 1790, 3,884,665. Ditto, 1800, 5,148,051.

Increase of Population in 20 Years 3,352,092.

50   100   200 miles

GRAND BARGAIN This map shows the "immense territory of Louisiana," as purchased from France in the historic deal secured in 1803 by President Thomas Jefferson (inset). The population figures at lower right, based on the 1810 census, exclude the many Indians of various tribes that occupied most of the Louisiana Territory, a small part of which became the state of Louisiana in 1812.

VAST CLAIM Standing at the mouth of the Mississippi in 1682, La Salle claims Louisiana for France in a chromolithograph designed for the Louisiana Purchase Exposition in 1903, celebrating the centennial of that deal. Claims to vast areas by explorers like La Salle were seldom honored by rival nations unless reinforced by settlements of the sort French colonists established at New Orleans and elsewhere in the Mississippi Valley.

help foster the settlement of Missouri, which achieved statehood in 1821. But the bulk of the Louisiana Territory took far longer for the U.S. to secure and organize because it was occupied by tribes that were not under American authority and would not be part of the American nation any time soon. (Not until the 20th century would Indians be assured of American citizenship or acknowledged as Native Americans.)

Louisiana was christened in 1682 by the French explorer La Salle, who after venturing down the Mississippi to its mouth, claimed in the name of King Louis XIV the entire area drained by that river and "all the rivers which discharge themselves therein." La Salle's extravagant claim extended to all the "nations" and native people within that huge expanse, much of which he never explored. Later French traders and soldiers gave France a more substantial claim to Louisiana by venturing up the Missouri and other western tributaries of the Mississippi and forging economic and diplomatic ties with various tribes. French officials were sometimes politely addressed by those Indians as "father" (a term Indians also applied to tribal chiefs), but that did not make them French subjects or entitle French emperor Napoleon Bonaparte to sell their territory to the U.S.

Jefferson acknowledged that Indians had "rights of occupancy in the soil, and of self-government." Land they occupied could not rightfully be taken by American officials or citizens, he concluded, unless tribes abandoned it or ceded it by treaty. Before his presidency ended, Jefferson initiated treaty talks with Osage Indians living west of St. Louis, who were among the first of many tribal groups within the area purchased from France to cede land to the U.S. in exchange for cash or goods. As late as the 1890s, U.S. commissioners would purchase some 15 million acres from various tribes in Oklahoma Territory for about a dollar an acre on average. Tribal leaders were pressured into selling and received less than the land was worth, but by making such deals with western tribes the government acknowledged that much of the territory obtained from France in 1803 remained Indian property until tribes relinquished it.

In sum, what Jefferson purchased beyond the Mississippi Valley and its valuable French settlements was a problematic claim to an immense tract of Indian country—a claim that would take explorers, soldiers, and settlers nearly a century to secure fully at great cost. That price would be paid not just in dollars but in blood as Anglo Americans clashed with Indians and other frontier inhabitants and competitors. Among those who contested America's western claims were not only various Indian nations but also two European nations that had long vied with France in North America: Great Britain—which remained at odds with its former American colonists over the disputed U.S.-Canadian border, among other issues—and Spain, which rejected the Louisiana Purchase and retained control of Florida and the Southwest, from Texas to California.

Spain had received Louisiana from its ally France in 1763 before returning it in 1800 on condition that it not be ceded to any other nation—a pledge Napoleon violated. Furthermore, Spain denied that Louisiana extended westward across the Great Plains to the Rockies. The Spanish explorer Coronado had been the first European to traverse the Plains, in 1541, and Spanish traders had followed in his wake. Spaniards were the original colonizers of the West, and in competing for control of that region the U.S. would have to contend with their long-standing claims.

AMERICA'S FIRST COWBOYS

★

Spanish colonists introduced to America not only cattle and horses but also the art of herding cattle on horseback, performed by cowboys called vaqueros. Many of the vaqueros who rode herd along the Spanish frontier that stretched from California to Texas were Indians or mestizos. In California, Franciscan padres trained Indians they converted to tend large herds of cattle that supported the missions. Some of those vaqueros later went to work for private ranchers whose free-roaming animals were rounded up periodically to be branded or slaughtered.

Even vaqueros who were not of Spanish heritage spoke Spanish. From them and their language, Americans derived such terms as lasso, lariat, rodeo, chaps, mustang, vamoose, calaboose, stampede, and many other words in the cowboy lexicon. Vaqueros also introduced cowboy attire, such as bandanas and ponchos, and cowboy cuisine, including chili, beans, and other chow consumed by buckaroos (a word derived from "vaqueros"). Some vaqueros became banditos, as did a number of American cowboys. Indeed, the English term "cow-boy" was long applied to men who stole cattle as well as to those who herded them. Americans who settled in Texas in the early 1800s referred to ranch hands as vaqueros. Not until after the Civil War did cowboy become a common and complimentary term there.

RIDING HERD Vaqueros in California tend cattle, introduced there by Spanish colonists who arrived in 1769. By the early 1800s, cattle formed the basis of California's economy.

A NEW ERA A bird roughly resembling an eagle, symbolizing the American nation, flies over New Orleans with a banner promising prosperity in a picture produced soon after the Louisiana Purchase was announced in 1803. A busy port controlling access to the Mississippi, New Orleans was the single greatest prize Jefferson obtained from France.

SPANISH PRECEDENTS

I n 1598, nine years before English pioneers settled Jamestown in Virginia and 22 years before Pilgrims landed at Plymouth, Juan de Oñate founded Spanish New Mexico, the first enduring European colony in the American West. That colony came to grief in 1680 when Pueblo Indians—who occupied multistory dwellings of great antiquity when Oñate and his colonists arrived—rebelled against the heavy demands placed on them by Spanish officials and missionaries. Pueblos killed many of the colonists, forcing the survivors to flee to El Paso. Ranches lay abandoned, and horses there dispersed and were taken by tribes such as the Apache and Comanche whose people learned to ride mustangs—an innovation that transformed the lives of Plains Indians.

CONQUISTADORES Spaniards of Coronado's expedition attack the Zuni pueblo of Hawikuh in 1540. Zunis and other Pueblos later resisted the Spanish colonists who founded New Mexico in 1598 and drove them out in 1680. Not until the colonists returned and lessened their demands on Pueblos did they gradually come to terms with the New Mexicans.

Spaniards regained control of New Mexico in the 1690s, but officials and priests eased the burdens of colonization on Pueblos, who retained their distinct communities and ceremonies while joining Spanish troops in campaigns against tribes that raided their colony. Spanish New Mexico was one of the few places in the early West where Euro Americans reached a durable accommodation with Indians on whose land they settled. By 1800, its population was about 40,000, with Pueblos constituting nearly half that number. Many of the Spanish colonists were partly of Indian ancestry. As one New Mexican wrote, Pueblos in appearance were "hardly distinguishable from ourselves."

Two other Spanish colonies west of the Mississippi, Texas and California, were colonized originally by Franciscan priests who established missions among Indians, and by soldiers who manned forts called presidios that guarded the northern frontier of New Spain (as Mexico was known officially). Many missions built in Texas in the late 1600s and early 1700s were abandoned because of attacks by hostile tribes, epidemics among Indians gathered there, or a lack of converts. Several enduring missions, however, arose near the presidio of San Antonio de Béxar, which was founded in 1718 and helped protect missionaries and their converts as well as settlers. By the early 1800s, the town of San Antonio had nearly 1,500 inhabitants, who came from as far away as the Canary Islands. Another 2,000 or so settlers lived in smaller villages or on scattered ranches where cowboys called vaqueros tended longhorns, which came to symbolize Texas and its cattle trade.

The Spanish colony of Alta California was inaugurated in 1769 when soldiers and Franciscans arrived from Baja California and founded a presidio and mission at San Diego. Urged on by their energetic leader, Father Junípero Serra, padres forged a chain that grew eventually to 21 missions extending up the coast from San Diego to Sonoma, north of San Francisco Bay. Although some California Indians became devout Christians and acquired useful skills, the Franciscans faced stiff opposition to their efforts, both from Indians who forcefully resisted conversion and from disheartened converts who ran off at the risk being pursued by troops. Tragically, missions intended to save Indians became breeding grounds for disease, decimating tribes like the Chumash of the central coast, who impressed Spaniards at first contact with their well-crafted houses and boats. Chumash confined at missions built in the late 1700s would later stage a determined revolt.

Like Spanish Texas, Alta California never had more than a few thousand colonists. Many were descendants of those who arrived in 1776 under Juan Bautista de Anza, a dynamic Spanish officer who led a party of

FOUNDING FATHER Standing at the altar, Father Junípero Serra celebrates Mass in 1770 at newly founded Monterey, which became the capital of Spanish and later Mexican California. The original colonists of Alta California included Serra (inset) and his fellow gray-robed Franciscans, Spanish troops, and mission Indians who accompanied them from Baja California.

240 men, women, and children overland from Sonora. They suffered only one casualty on their grueling five-month trek from Tubac in what is now Arizona, which they left in October 1775, to Monterey, the capital of Spanish California. That loss occurred early in the journey when a woman "successfully gave birth to a very lusty boy," in Anza's words, before dying the next day. As his colonists neared the snowcapped Santa Rosa Mountains in southern California at year's end, he reported, one man suffered so severely from exposure that "in order to save his life it was necessary to bundle him up for two hours between four fires." But Anza's party revived when they reached the coast and found the winter weather springlike and the hillsides green from fresh rains. Some of them went on to found a presidio overlooking San Francisco Bay, where a town arose called Yerba Buena, from which modern-day San Francisco evolved. Others were among the first settlers of San Jose, at the lower end of the bay. Many in Anza's party were mestizos (partly Indian), and several of the pioneers who founded Los Angeles in 1781 were of African heritage.

Prominent Spanish colonists often prided themselves on their pure Spanish ancestry. Yet tolerance for those of other races or of mixed race was a trait that people on the frontier of New Spain had in common with colonists on the frontier of New France, which included French settlements up around the Great Lakes and down along the Mississippi. French trappers and traders who ventured beyond Quebec, the core of New France, often married Indians, which gave them closer ties to tribes they dealt with. Early Spanish colonists in America often did likewise because most of them were men. Had France and Spain remained the dominant colonial powers in the West, as they were in the mid-1700s, that tradition of intermingling with native people might have persisted. But beginning in 1754, with the outbreak of the French and Indian War, the momentum shifted to British and soon-to-be American colonists, who proliferated along the eastern seaboard and advanced westward as families, settling on tribal land and pressing for the removal of Indians.

COLONISTS IN CAPTIVITY

............................★............................

Indian tribes often adopted captives they took. Women and children were more likely to be adopted than men, who feared for their lives when seized. In late 1607, Capt. John Smith of the Jamestown colony was captured by warriors sent by Chief Powhatan, who ruled a confederacy of tribes in Virginia. Smith thought he was about to be executed when Powhatan's daughter, Pocahontas, seemingly saved his life. Powhatan may have intended for her to intercede on Smith's behalf, for the chief then offered to "esteem him as his son" if Smith paid him ample tribute, including "two great guns." Smith went free and never made that payment.

In 1755, during the French and Indian War, a colonist with a similar name, James Smith, was clearing a road for British troops in Pennsylvania when he was captured and claimed by a warrior of the Caughnawaga (Kahnawake)—Iroquois who had embraced Christianity and settled in Quebec among the French, whom they supported while other Iroquois backed the British. Smith was forced to run a gauntlet of warriors who clubbed him and was taken to a Caughnawaga village, where he was stripped and immersed in a river by women he feared were trying to drown him. He was then dressed as a member of the tribe and initiated by a chief, who spoke though an interpreter: "My son, you are now flesh of our flesh, and bone of our bone. By the ceremony which was performed this day, every drop of white blood was washed out of your veins."

COLONIZER John Smith survived captivity in Virginia and later surveyed New England.

THE EXPANSIVE AMERICANS

British colonists were not always at odds with Indians. Like Spanish and French colonists, they too sometimes traded with native people and sought to convert them to Christianity. Some British traders settled among the Cherokee and other tribes of the southern woodlands and married Indian women. And some descendants of those unions achieved prominence among the so-called Five Civilized Tribes (Cherokee, Creek, Chickasaw, Choctaw, and Seminole), which adopted European technology and customs, including ownership of black slaves by wealthier members of those tribes.

Conscientious British colonial leaders such as William Penn, a Quaker who founded Pennsylvania in 1681, tried to uphold treaties that reserved adequate land for tribes and barred colonists from encroaching on them. In a letter he addressed to Indians of Pennsylvania, Penn wished that "we may always live together as neighbours and friends." That dream of a peaceable kingdom in America was soon shattered, however, because settlers in Pennsylvania and other eastern colonies were too numerous to be held back. By 1750, there were over a million British colonists in

FRIENDLY PERSUASION
In a painting by Benjamin West, William Penn spreads his arms to welcome Lenape (Delaware) Indians to a parley in Pennsylvania in 1683 that yielded a peace treaty. Such treaties did not stop white settlers from later displacing eastern tribes. Many of the Delaware ended up on reservations west of the Mississippi.

America—more than ten times as many settlers as in the French and Spanish colonies north of Mexico combined. Fear of encroachment by land-hungry settlers led many tribes east of the Mississippi to side with France in the war against Britain that began when French and Indian forces clashed in western Pennsylvania with troops led by George Washington of the Virginia colonial militia, who suffered defeat at Fort Necessity on July 4, 1754. Among the few tribes to back the British in the grueling conflict that followed were the powerful Iroquois of upper New York, but they too feared encroachment and many of them would later oppose American colonists when they rebelled against Britain.

The seeds for that American Revolution were sown during the French and Indian War, from which the British emerged triumphant in 1763. Although they won Canada from France—which relinquished any claim to land east of the Mississippi and ceded the remainder of Louisiana to Spain—the British soon found themselves

PONTIAC'S WAR Portrayed as a menacing figure in this early American engraving, Chief Pontiac of the Ottawa rallied tribes below the Great Lakes to continue fighting the British after the French conceded defeat in 1763. Pontiac may have taken part in the battle that claimed General Braddock's life in 1755. His Ottawas were among the most determined foes of British troops and American colonial forces.

embroiled in a punishing conflict with tribes of the Great Lakes region, led by Chief Pontiac of the Ottawa, who refused to bow to Britain after the French had yielded. "You think yourselves masters of this country, because you have taken it from the French," a Shawnee chief allied with Pontiac said to British officials after the uprising ended. The French could not surrender that country to the British, the chief added, for "it is the property of us Indians."

British authorities hoped to avoid further Indian wars by enforcing a proclamation in 1763 that prohibited settlement west of the Appalachians. Yet that order was defied both by settlers and by colonial officials who hoped to win independence from Britain and profit from westward expansion. Washington, Jefferson, Patrick Henry, and Benjamin Franklin were among those who invested in companies that sought to obtain land concessions from tribes on the frontier and sell the property to settlers.

The restless, adventurous character of frontier Americans in that revolutionary era was personified by Daniel Boone, who was born in Pennsylvania in 1734 and came of age in western North Carolina, where he served in a militia company guarding against Indian attacks. While campaigning against the French and Indians in 1755, Boone met John Finley, who had traded with tribes west of the Appalachians and told him of the plentiful game to be had there. In the late 1760s, they set out with others on long hunts over the mountains into the woodlands of Kentucky, where they took pelts from bears and bison, which could still be found east of the Mississippi. Boone and his fellow long hunters were forerunners of the buckskin-clad mountain men who later trapped beaver in streams flowing from the Rockies. Indeed, the land Boone entered beyond the Appalachians was the original American West and nurtured the venturesome spirit that later propelled pioneers across the continent.

In 1775, Boone began clearing a trail from southwestern Virginia into Kentucky. Known as Boone's Trace or the Wilderness Road, it traversed Cumberland Gap—an inviting pass through the Appalachians that was threaded by some 300,000 pioneers over the next few decades, many of whom claimed homesteads in Kentucky or Tennessee. For Boone and those who settled near his Kentucky stronghold, Fort Boonesborough, the American Revolution against Britain mattered less than their own struggle against Indians who opposed their intrusions. The fighting was not incessant, for settlers and Indians sometimes met peacefully and exchanged goods. But trade too could cause conflict. The trans-Appalachian pioneers were mostly subsistence farmers and hunters who had little to sell other than the corn whiskey they distilled—liquor that wreaked havoc when used by unscrupulous parties to gull Indians into making bad bargains or deceptive treaties. Even treaties concluded fairly with chiefs often ignited battles when applied to tribes whose leaders had not been party to them.

After the Americans won independence, tribes living in the Northwest Territory, north of the Ohio River, formed a confederacy to resist further intrusions and land cessions and were

CUMBERLAND GAP

Situated where Virginia, Kentucky, and Tennessee meet, Cumberland Gap was an inviting corridor through the Appalachians for Americans seeking homes beyond those mountains. Land speculator Richard Henderson organized the Transylvania Company and in 1775 secured a controversial treaty with Cherokee chiefs, who sold their claim to a large area west of Cumberland Gap. Henderson assigned Daniel Boone to blaze a trail through the gap that settlers could follow. At first, that narrow Wilderness Road could only accommodate people using packhorses to haul their goods, but by the 1790s it was wide enough to convey settlers in wagons to Kentucky and Tennessee, which were largely populated by way of Cumberland Gap.

The 1775 treaty did not protect those pioneers from Indians who resented intrusions on their territory. Some prominent Cherokee leaders opposed the deal, among them a chief called Dragging Canoe, who reportedly warned that the land purchased by Henderson would become "a dark and bloody ground." The United States refused to recognize such treaties between land companies and Indian tribes, but that did not stop settlers from pouring through the gap—or Indians of various tribes from targeting them. Among the victims was Capt. Abraham Lincoln, grandfather of the future president. A friend of Daniel Boone, Captain Lincoln left Virginia with his wife and five children in 1782 and crossed Cumberland Gap to settle in Kentucky, where he was killed in an Indian attack two years later. He died within sight of his youngest boy, Thomas, who later conferred his father's name on his son, born in a log cabin in Kentucky in 1809.

AMERICAN PATHFINDER Daniel Boone, with a rifle at his shoulder, leads settlers through Cumberland Gap in this painting by George Caleb Bingham.

aided in opposing the U.S. by British officers holding forts around the Great Lakes. In October 1791, warriors led by Chief Little Turtle of the Miami inflicted a staggering defeat on American forces near the upper Wabash River, killing or wounding some 900 men. Like later victories for Indians such as the Battle of the Little Bighorn, however, this triumph was short-lived. Shocked by the debacle, the U.S. fielded a stronger army under Maj. Gen. Anthony Wayne, which crushed the confederacy in battle at Fallen Timbers in 1794 and forced its leaders to cede much of what became the state of Ohio.

One incentive for Jefferson to conclude the Louisiana Purchase was his hope that tribes remaining east of the Mississippi would accept treaties removing them beyond that river. His plan to set aside the trans-Mississippi West as a vast Indian reserve was doomed, however, for white settlers were no more willing to accept the Mississippi as a barrier to expansion than they had been to halt at the Appalachians in 1763. Moving west was regarded by Americans as their birthright, and many did so more than once—among them Daniel Boone, who left Kentucky with family members to settle in distant Missouri several years before the U.S. claimed it as part of the Louisiana Purchase.

What westering Americans like the Boones encountered beyond the Mississippi was a land of relentless competition, where European powers as well as expansive Indian tribes like the Comanche and Sioux believed that what they gained by might was theirs by right. In that contentious arena, claims staked by nations or individuals counted for little unless they were forcefully upheld. Securing those claims required not only strength but also patience, persistence, and a willingness to come to terms with competitors who might serve better as friends than foes. In 1803, when Jefferson concluded his purchase and commissioned the Lewis and Clark expedition—the first great American venture in the wider West—he made sure that the explorers he set to that task were determined, well armed, and capable of standing up to the challenges awaiting them. Yet he also supplied them amply with gifts for tribal leaders and gave them good advice for negotiating Indian country. "In all your intercourse with the natives," he urged, "treat them in the most friendly & conciliatory manner which their own conduct will admit." ■

AMERICAN ADVANCES
U.S. troops in blue overwhelm their Indian foes in the Battle of Fallen Timbers on August 20, 1794. A crushing defeat for a tribal confederacy whose leaders included Chief Little Turtle of the Miami and Chief Blue Jacket of the Shawnee, the battle helped clear the way for the settlement of Ohio, which became a state in 1803. In that same year, the Louisiana Purchase was concluded and the American flag was raised over New Orleans (opposite).

CHAPTER ONE

1803–1846

WESTWARD EXPANSION

AMERICAN PROGRESS An allegorical figure representing American Progress holds a telegraph wire in her hand in this patriotic print based on an 1872 painting by John Gast. The early days of America's westward expansion, when wagons began crossing the Plains, are portrayed at left; later developments such as the advent of railroads appear at right.

WESTWARD EXPANSION

Returning from their historic expedition across the continent, Meriwether Lewis and William Clark were descending the Missouri River with their Corps of Discovery in August 1806 when they met two American trappers named Joseph Dickson and Forrest Hancock, heading upriver by canoe in pursuit of beaver pelts. The pair had started out two years earlier and had little to show for their efforts. Nonetheless, they said they were "determined to proceed." Lewis gave them "a short description of the Missouri . . . and pointed out to them the places where the beaver most abounded." A few days later at a Mandan Indian village in what is now

North Dakota, they were joined by John Colter, a valued member of the corps, who had received permission from Lewis and Clark to accompany the trappers up the Missouri.

In the annals of American exploration, Dickson and Hancock would amount to little more than a footnote. Yet they and others like them did more to expand their nation over the next 40 years than all the explorers sent out by the government. To be sure, official expeditions such as those led

by Lewis and Clark (1804–06), Zebulon Pike (1806–07), and John C. Frémont (1842–46) did much to promote westward expansion, but that historic advance was largely accomplished by unheralded pioneers like Dickson and Hancock, acting on their own initiative. Born in Pennsylvania in 1775, Dickson moved to Tennessee before migrating again to a homestead across the Mississippi from St. Louis. He and his wife had several children, but that did not stop him from heading

1803 President Thomas Jefferson concludes the Louisiana Purchase and plans an American expedition to the Pacific, to be launched in 1804 by Meriwether Lewis and William Clark.

Andrew Jackson

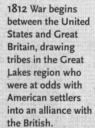

1812 War begins between the United States and Great Britain, drawing tribes in the Great Lakes region who were at odds with American settlers into an alliance with the British.

1821 Mexico achieves independence from Spain and assumes the boundary that Spain negotiated with the U.S. in 1819 under the Adams-Onís Treaty, giving Mexico possession of territory extending from Texas westward to California.

Spanish North America, 1814

1815 American forces led by Maj. Gen. Andrew Jackson defeat British troops at New Orleans in a battle fought before word arrives that the U.S. and Great Britain have come to terms.

1822 Missouri merchant William Becknell brings trade goods in wagons to New Mexico, inaugurating the Santa Fe Trail as a wagon road.

off in 1804 with Hancock, who had settled in Missouri with Daniel Boone and his kin. Among the traits exhibited by mountain men, as such venturesome trappers were known, was a stubborn self-assurance that could make them quarrelsome. Dickson fell out with his partners along the Yellowstone River and turned back, but Hancock continued on with Colter, who at some point in his journeys came upon a sulfurous geological hot spot later known as Colter's Hell.

Within a few decades of the Lewis and Clark expedition, trappers, traders, and settlers would go a long way toward fulfilling Thomas Jefferson's dream of an American "empire of liberty" spanning the continent. In the Northwest, mountain men competed with British trappers sent out by the Hudson's Bay Company and found a better way to the Pacific coast than Lewis and Clark's route up the Missouri. That new path developed into the Oregon Trail, a wagon road that would bring American settlers to Oregon in substantial numbers and bolster America's claim to that country. In the Southwest, which passed from Spanish to Mexican control in 1821, settlers from southern states poured into Texas and far outnumbered its Hispanic residents, while traders from Missouri pioneered the Santa Fe Trail, which exposed New Mexico first to American enterprise and later to American

> "I AM PERSUADED NO CONSTITUTION WAS EVER BEFORE SO WELL CALCULATED AS OURS FOR EXTENSIVE EMPIRE & SELF GOVERNMENT."
> —THOMAS JEFFERSON

occupation. Before the United States could take possession of the distant West, however, it had to tighten its grip on the near West between the Appalachians and the Mississippi, where tribes clinging to their homelands faced a foe so hard and tough he was called Old Hickory.

THE JACKSONIAN ERA

Born in 1767, Andrew Jackson took part in the American Revolution as a youngster and later prospered as a lawyer, planter, and slave owner in Tennessee before winning fame as a general during the War of 1812. His greatest victory came against the British at New Orleans in January 1815, but an earlier triumph at Horseshoe Bend in Alabama, where he crushed an uprising by Creek Indians called Red Sticks, set the tone for his subsequent efforts to secure the frontier for American settlers. He was rivaled in that regard by William Henry Harrison, who stripped tribes below the Great Lakes of territory through treaties and armed force and like Jackson was later elected president.

But no one did more than Old Hickory to expand the American nation at the expense of Indian nations. In 1818, he invaded Spanish Florida and began a long-lasting conflict against Seminole Indians and fugitive black slaves they harbored. That campaign brought Florida within America's

Oregon Trail emigrants

1843 Nearly a thousand people join the Great Migration on the Oregon Trail and become the first American settlers to reach the Columbia River in wagons.

1846 President James Polk concludes a treaty with Great Britain giving the U.S. control of Oregon up to the 49th parallel and leads the nation into war with Mexico after fighting erupts along the disputed Texas border.

1830 President Andrew Jackson secures passage of the Indian Removal Act in Congress and sends commissioners to press southern tribes to give up their land and migrate beyond the Mississippi to Indian Territory.

1836 Texas emerges as an independent republic after rebel forces under Sam Houston defeat Mexican troops led by Antonio López de Santa Anna at San Jacinto.

Sam Houston

1845 The U.S. annexes Texas and sends an expedition led by Capt. John C. Frémont to California, where he will back American settlers in their Bear Flag Revolt against Mexico.

grasp and helped propel Jackson to a massive presidential victory in 1828. A champion of the common man—meaning white men of little means, who had recently gained the same voting rights as wealthy property owners—he opened large areas for white settlement by removing southern tribes to Indian Territory (later Oklahoma). The forceful removal of the Cherokee on their Trail of Tears was Jackson's way of fulfilling what journalist John O'Sullivan called America's "manifest destiny to overspread the continent allotted by Providence for the free development of our yearly multiplying millions."

Reelected in 1832, Jackson remained influential after he left the White House. In 1844, he urged James Polk of Tennessee to campaign for president and press for the annexation of Texas, which had broken free from Mexico. When Jackson died in 1845, President Polk was about to admit Texas as a state. That fateful step would lead to war with Mexico and transform what had been an infant republic struggling against the British Empire when Jackson was a boy into a continental empire in its own right, extending to that glittering land of promise called California. ■

BUFFALO HUNTER Wearing a buckskin outfit of the sort favored by mountain men, a hunter scans the horizon for bison in this painting by Alfred Jacob Miller, an artist who accompanied a caravan of fur traders to the Rocky Mountains in 1837.

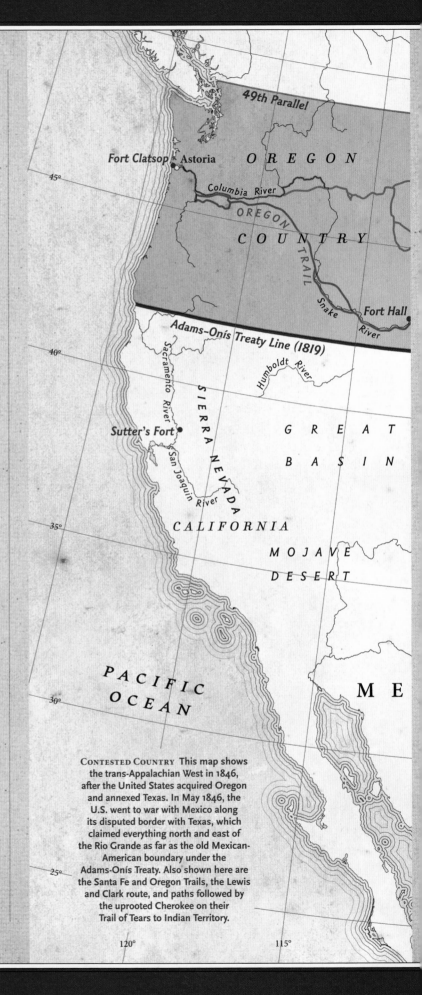

CONTESTED COUNTRY This map shows the trans-Appalachian West in 1846, after the United States acquired Oregon and annexed Texas. In May 1846, the U.S. went to war with Mexico along its disputed border with Texas, which claimed everything north and east of the Rio Grande as far as the old Mexican-American boundary under the Adams-Onís Treaty. Also shown here are the Santa Fe and Oregon Trails, the Lewis and Clark route, and paths followed by the uprooted Cherokee on their Trail of Tears to Indian Territory.

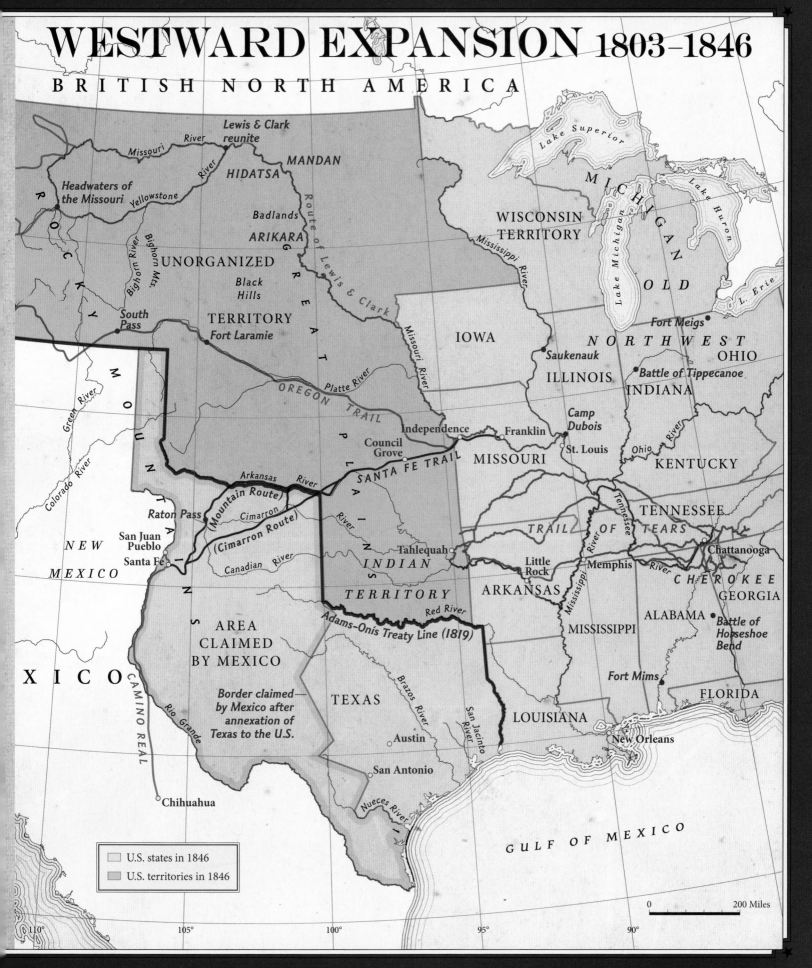

WESTWARD EXPANSION 1803–1846

BRITISH NORTH AMERICA

Lake Superior

Lake Huron

Lake Michigan

L. Erie

MICHIGAN

WISCONSIN TERRITORY

OLD

Fort Meigs

NORTHWEST

OHIO

Mississippi River

IOWA

Saukenauk

ILLINOIS

Battle of Tippecanoe

INDIANA

Camp Dubois

Ohio River

Missouri River

Independence

Franklin

St. Louis

MISSOURI

KENTUCKY

Council Grove

SANTA FE TRAIL

Tennessee River

TENNESSEE

TRAIL OF TEARS

Chattanooga

Lewis & Clark reunite

MANDAN

HIDATSA

Missouri River

Yellowstone River

Route of Lewis & Clark

Badlands

ARIKARA

Black Hills

UNORGANIZED

TERRITORY

Headwaters of the Missouri

Bighorn River

Bighorn Mts.

ROCKY

South Pass

Fort Laramie

OREGON TRAIL

Platte River

GREAT PLAINS

Arkansas River

(Mountain Route)

Raton Pass

Cimarron

(Cimarron Route)

Canadian River

River

INDIAN

TERRITORY

Tahlequah

Little Rock

Memphis

Mississippi River

CHEROKEE

GEORGIA

Green River

Colorado River

MOUNTAINS

NEW MEXICO

San Juan Pueblo

Santa Fe

XICO

CAMINO REAL

Rio Grande

AREA CLAIMED BY MEXICO

Border claimed by Mexico after annexation of Texas to the U.S.

TEXAS

Brazos River

Austin

San Antonio

Chihuahua

Nueces River

Adams-Onís Treaty Line (1819)

Red River

ARKANSAS

MISSISSIPPI

ALABAMA

Battle of Horseshoe Bend

Fort Mims

FLORIDA

San Jacinto River

LOUISIANA

New Orleans

GULF OF MEXICO

U.S. states in 1846
U.S. territories in 1846

0   200 Miles

110°   105°   100°   95°   90°

LEWIS AND CLARK EXPEDITION

Charting a Path to the Pacific

In early 1803, President Thomas Jefferson made plans for American explorers to span the continent by ascending the Missouri River, crossing the Rockies, and reaching the Pacific. Intended to enhance knowledge of the West and its tribes and promote trade, the historic expedition took on added significance that year when the Louisiana Purchase was concluded. Jefferson instructed Capt. Meriwether Lewis, who had been his personal secretary before taking charge of the expedition, to inform tribes along the Missouri that Americans were now "sovereigns of the country, without however any diminution of the Indian rights of occupancy . . . henceforward we become their fathers and friends." As Jefferson conceded privately, the United States was "miserably weak" in the West and had few troops to spare

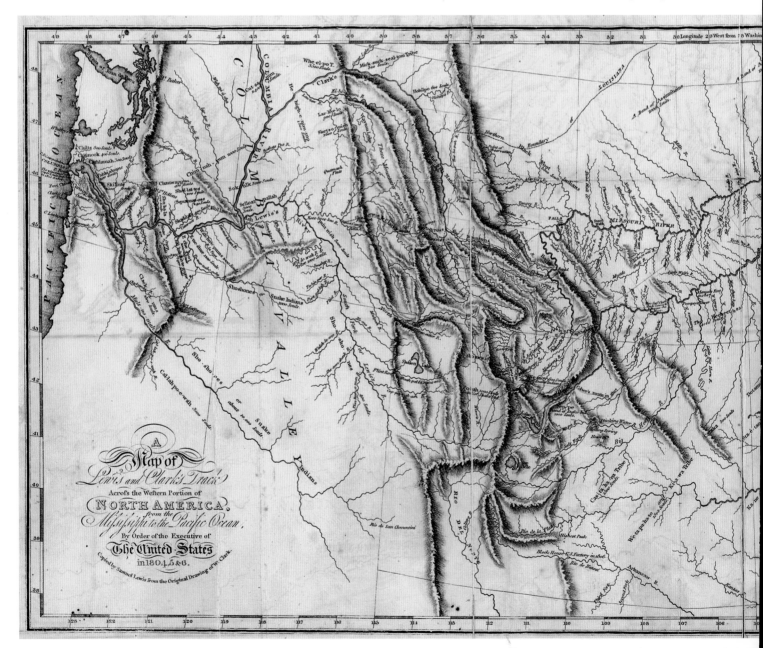

if tribes there chose to defy their new "fathers." Lewis wisely shared command of the hazardous expedition with his fellow Virginian and former Army colleague, William Clark, who had battled Indians in Ohio but also had a knack for appeasing tribal leaders.

Lewis and Clark began by recruiting 29 men for their Corps of Discovery, including venturesome Americans like John Colter of Kentucky as well as Frenchmen familiar with the Missouri and its tribes like interpreter George Drouillard, who was half Indian and adept at sign language.

LEADERS William Clark (above left) was 33 and Meriwether Lewis (above right) 29 when they set out with their corps.

In May 1804, the Corps of Discovery left Camp Dubois, near St. Louis, and headed up the Missouri in two row-boats with sails—called pirogues—and a larger keelboat, which was also equipped with a sail but often had to be rowed, poled, or towed upstream by men with ropes in hand. The keelboat was loaded with tobacco, beads, and other gifts for Indi-ans, but few were encountered until August when the explorers met a band of Teton or Lakota Sioux—the powerful western branch of that tribe who ranged far out onto the Plains in decades to come while the Dakota, or eastern

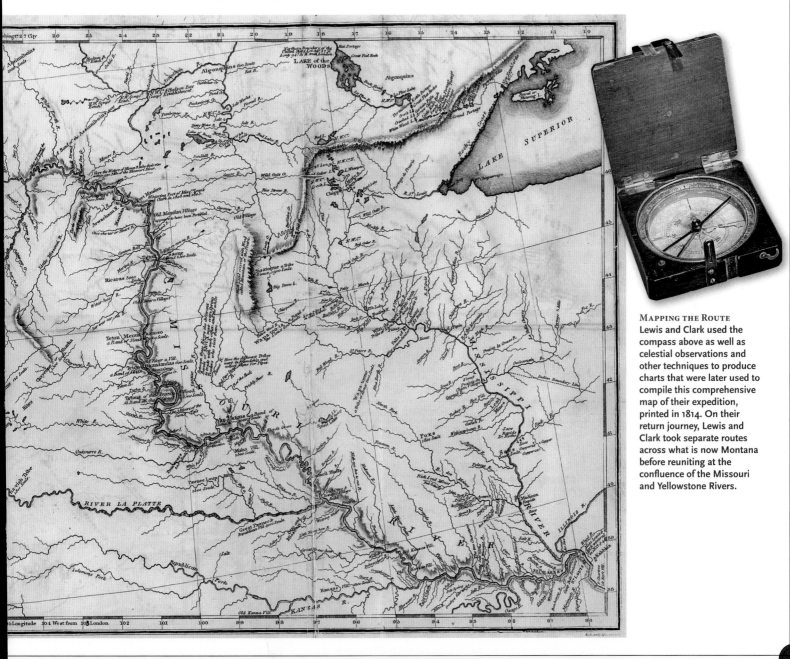

MAPPING THE ROUTE
Lewis and Clark used the compass above as well as celestial observations and other techniques to produce charts that were later used to compile this comprehensive map of their expedition, printed in 1814. On their return journey, Lewis and Clark took separate routes across what is now Montana before reuniting at the confluence of the Missouri and Yellowstone Rivers.

Sioux, inhabited the woodlands and prairie between the upper Mississippi River and the Missouri River. The Lakotas encountered by Lewis and Clark had obtained guns and other trade goods that gave them power over their neighbors and feared that Americans might weaken their position by trading with tribes upriver. One chief tried to prevent the explorers from proceeding until they brandished weapons and induced him and his warriors to back off.

Lewis and Clark hoped to counter the worrisome Sioux by winning over three tribes to their north—the Arikara, Mandan, and Hidatsa—who lived in permanent villages and raised crops to supplement the game they hunted. They welcomed the explorers

NEAR THEIR GOAL Lewis and Clark sit side by side, with Sacagawea behind them, in this view of the corps at the mouth of the Columbia, produced by Frederic Remington a century later. The sage grouse below was drawn by Clark in his journal in March 1806, around when they began their return journey.

and their gifts and offered favors in return, including invitations to sleep with women that were declined by the leaders but accepted by their followers, among them Clark's black slave York. "These people are much pleased with my black servant," wrote Clark. "Their women very fond of caressing our men &c." These seemingly obliging tribes were reluctant to defer to the Americans, however, and defy the Sioux. The Arikara and Sioux were rivals but not yet bitter enemies. They sometimes clashed but also traded with each other and banded together to hunt or raid. During the winter, while the corps was lodged nearby, the Mandan came under attack by Sioux and Arikara warriors but turned down Clark's offer to help them retaliate. "My father, the snow is deep and it is cold," a tribal chief told him; "our horses cannot travel through the plains, those people who have spilt our blood have gone back." The chief suggested postponing any reprisal until the snow melted in the spring, but by then the explorers would be on their way to the Pacific.

Across the Rockies

Before continuing up the Missouri in the two pirogues and six canoes in early April 1805, Lewis and Clark sent several men downriver in the keelboat with reports and natural specimens for Jefferson and added to their corps the French-Canadian trader Toussaint Charbonneau along with his Indian wife, Sacagawea, and newborn son. Captured several years earlier by Hidatsas from a Shoshone band near the Rockies, Sacagawea proved vital to the explorers when they reached the headwaters of the Missouri in August. They desperately needed horses to cross the Rockies, and Sacagawea guided them to her band, who supplied them with mounts. Grueling weeks on mountain trails followed before they encountered hospitable Nez Perce Indians along the Clearwater River in late September, boarded canoes, and descended to the Columbia River. "Ocean in view!" Clark wrote when they reached the Columbia's broad estuary in November. "O! the joy."

After spending a dreary winter at Fort Clatsop, an outpost they built near the Pacific, the explorers eagerly embarked on their return journey. In July 1806, the corps divided, with Lewis leading nine men on a northerly route that brought

BIOGRAPHY

SACAGAWEA'S JOURNEY
CIRCA 1787–1812

Abducted as a girl from her Shoshone band by Hidatsa warriors around 1800, Sacagawea was later purchased by Toussaint Charbonneau and became one of his two Indian wives. She bore her first child, Jean Baptiste, in February 1805 and carried him in a cradleboard as they accompanied Lewis and Clark. When the canoe she was in nearly capsized, she saved "almost every article indispensable to our enterprise," Lewis reported. She later helped guide the explorers to her Shoshone village (inset) and served as interpreter. Recognizing Chief Cameahwait there as her brother, she embraced him "and cried profusely." Her presence reassured many tribes they met with, Clark wrote, for "a woman with a party of men is a token of peace."

At the explorers' winter camp, Sacagawea told them she had traveled a great way "to see the great water." She then accompanied them to the Pacific, where she marveled at the ocean and the remains of a whale. She and Charbonneau left Lewis and Clark when they returned to the Mandan and Hidatsa villages in 1806. It was probably Sacagawea whose death trader John Luttig recorded when he wrote that the "wife of Charbonneau" had died of fever in December 1812 at a trading post on the Missouri. She was "the best woman in the fort," he noted, "aged ab[ou]t 25 years."

them into conflict with the formidable Blackfeet—two of whom were killed—while Clark led the others down the Yellowstone River to its juncture with the Missouri, where the parties reunited.

In September 1806, the explorers returned to St. Louis. Except for one man who fell sick and died early on, they had come through intact. Their remarkable journey unveiled vast new opportunities for trade and extended the nation's territorial ambitions to that fruitful country called Oregon. Yet their venture also revealed obstacles to American expansion, including natural barriers like the towering Rockies and defiant tribes that viewed Americans not as "fathers and friends" but as foes. Those opponents, limited initially to groups such as the Blackfeet at odds with American traders or trappers, would expand over time to include many western tribes alarmed by the intrusions of prospectors and settlers. ■

Mountaineers After a bleak trek through the Bitterroots in the fall of 1805—pictured here, with Sacagawea clad in a blanket—the explorers fared better on the way back by crossing the mountains in midsummer.

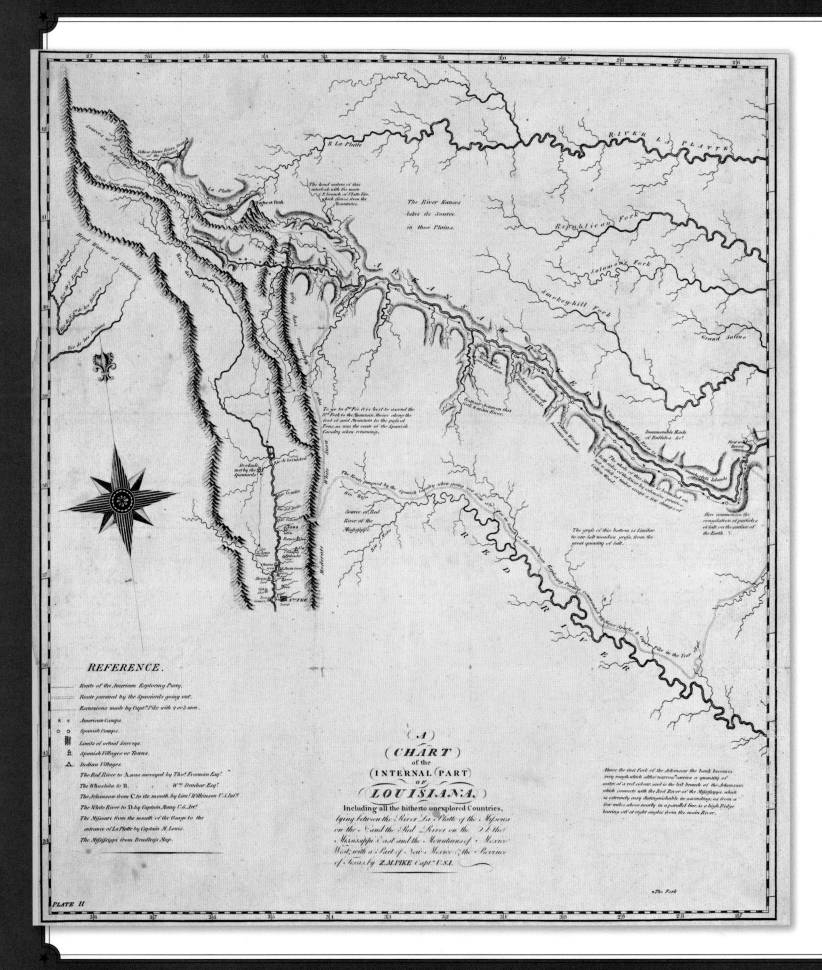

PIKE'S SOUTHWEST EXPEDITION
Across the Mexican Frontier

When Lt. Zebulon Pike left St. Louis in July 1806 with 23 men, he embarked on a risky mission that would take him far beyond his nation's limits. Promoted to captain in August, he was authorized by Brig. Gen. James Wilkinson to hold talks with several tribes on the Plains and advance to the headwaters of the Arkansas and Red Rivers, marking the boundary of Louisiana as claimed by the United States. Spain rejected that claim and considered much of the country Pike traversed its own. The risk of encountering Spanish forces increased as his party advanced up the Arkansas that fall and neared New Mexico. Pike's orders were to "move with great circumspection" to avoid inflaming the border dispute with Spain.

After a frigid winter's trek that carried his party past what was later dubbed Pikes Peak and up to the source of the Arkansas in the Rockies, he turned south and built a stockade in February 1807 along the Conejos, a tributary of the Rio Grande. He knew he was perilously close to New Mexico and offered no resistance when Spanish troops approached and hauled his ragged party off to the Palace of the Governors in Santa Fe. "You come to reconnoiter our country, do you?" asked Governor Joaquín del Real Alencaster, to which Pike replied firmly, "I marched to reconnoiter our own."

Whether the territory explored by Pike belonged rightfully to the U.S. or to Spain was an issue for higher authorities to resolve. The Americans were sent under guard to be interrogated by Alencaster's superior in Chihuahua. Along the way, Pike learned that New Mexicans paid steep prices for goods. His account of the expedition touted the prospects for trade in New Mexico and encouraged American merchants to inaugurate the Santa Fe Trail. Released from confinement in Chihuahua, Pike returned to the U.S. to find his commander, Wilkinson, tarnished by association with former vice president Aaron Burr, whose conspiracy to seize territory along the disputed Spanish-American border had been nipped in the bud. Suspicions that Pike was involved in foul play with Wilkinson faded when General Pike died a hero during the War of 1812. ∎

Zebulon Pike

PIKE'S PATH The 1810 map at left shows Pike's route up the Arkansas River into the Rockies, then south to the stockade where he was "met by the Spaniards" and hauled off to Santa Fe. The view at right, portraying country Pike traversed as he approached the Rockies, illustrated an 1819–1820 expedition by Maj. Stephen Long, who followed a similar path and labeled the Great Plains the "Great American Desert."

PIONEERING THE FUR TRADE
From St. Louis to Astoria

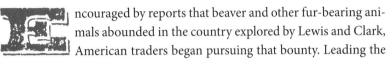

Encouraged by reports that beaver and other fur-bearing animals abounded in the country explored by Lewis and Clark, American traders began pursuing that bounty. Leading the way was Manuel Lisa of St. Louis, a merchant of Spanish heritage who in 1807 erected a trading post at the confluence of the Yellowstone and Bighorn Rivers. Men of his Missouri Fur Company, such as John Colter and George Drouillard of the Lewis and Clark expedition, invited tribes to the fort—and also hunted and trapped in tribal territory at great risk. Drouillard was killed in one clash, and Colter barely survived when Blackfeet warriors stripped him and had him run for his life.

Meanwhile, fur trader John Jacob Astor, a German immigrant based in New York, was planning to expand his operations to the Pacific by founding Astoria, an outpost at the mouth of the Columbia that would deal in beaver pelts brought downriver from the Rockies as well as sea otter pelts obtained from coastal tribes. In 1810, he sent one party around Cape Horn in his ship *Tonquin* to build Astoria and sent another party overland to that fort from St. Louis to locate good trapping and trading sites in the mountains. Led by merchant Wilson Price Hunt, who had no experience as an explorer, the overland party sought a shorter path to the Pacific than that traced by Lewis and Clark and struggled across the Dakota badlands and the Bighorn Mountains to the Snake River. They tried descending the treacherous Snake to the Columbia in canoes but gave up after a man drowned. The party then divided and suffered further losses. Only 45 of its 60 members reached Astoria, arriving there in 1812 after enduring what Hunt termed "all the hardships imaginable." Interpreter Pierre Dorion was among the casualties, but his Indian wife Marie—the only woman in the party—was rescued by the Walla Walla tribe.

Hunt and others who made it to the fort learned to their dismay that the *Tonquin,* after unloading its passengers there in 1811, had been lost along with most of its crew in a battle with Nootka Indians on Vancouver Island while seeking sea-otter pelts. Astoria was barely up and running when the War of 1812 began, and it was soon taken over by the British. Undeterred by such setbacks, Astor and other fur traders persisted and reaped profits in the West while extending American influence across the continent. ■

John Jacob Astor

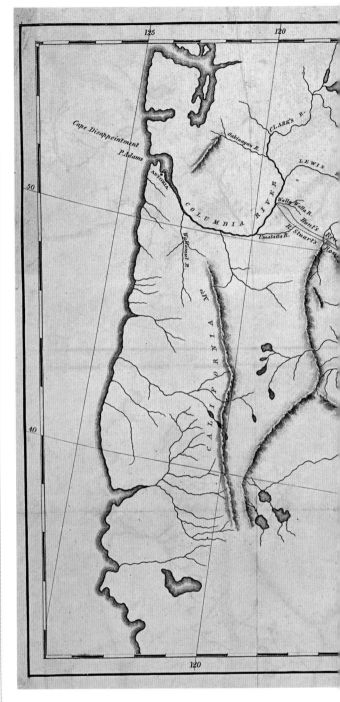

To Oregon and Back This map from Washington Irving's 1836 history of Astoria shows the paths taken by Wilson Hunt—who led an expedition from St. Louis to Astoria in 1810–12—and by Robert Stuart, who returned to St. Louis with six men in 1812–13 by way of South Pass, a vital corridor through the Rockies for the future Oregon Trail.

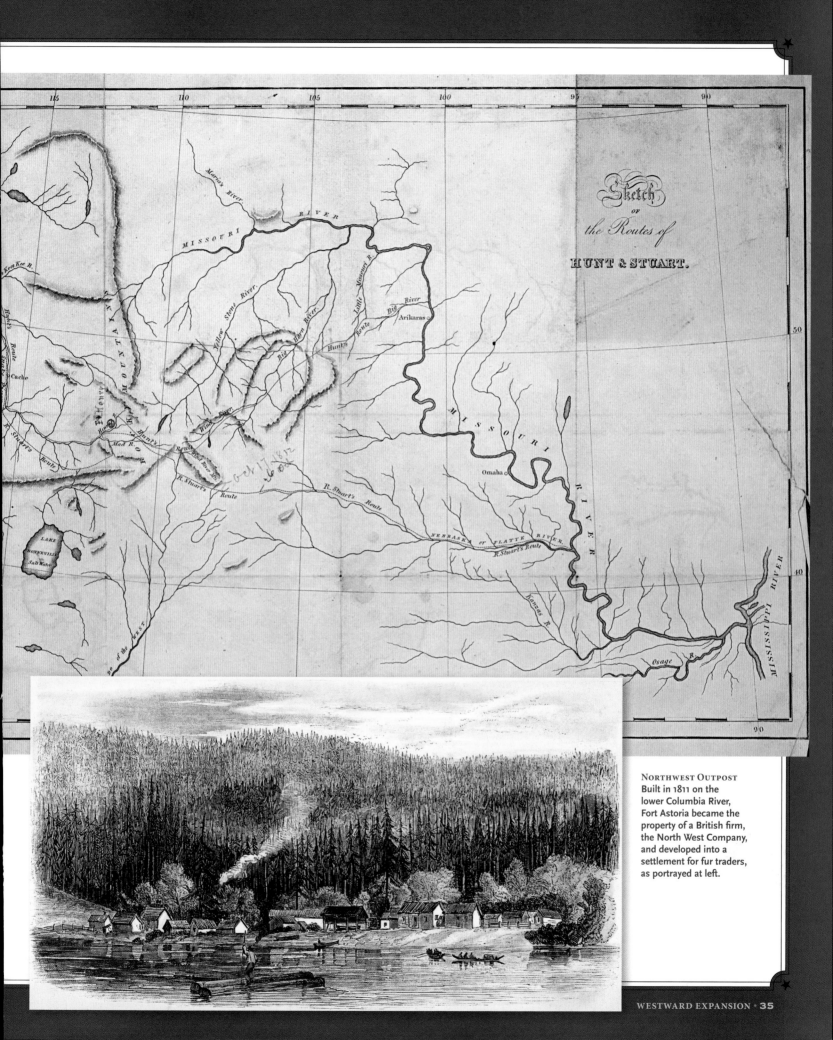

NORTHWEST OUTPOST
Built in 1811 on the lower Columbia River, Fort Astoria became the property of a British firm, the North West Company, and developed into a settlement for fur traders, as portrayed at left.

THE INDIAN WAR OF 1812

Harrison Versus Tecumseh

The War of 1812 was not just a conflict between the United States and Britain. It also pitted American forces against tribes fighting to protect their territory from settlers and treaty makers. Since the American Revolution, many such tribes below the Great Lakes had sided with the British. William Henry Harrison, governor of Indiana Territory, accused the British of arming and organizing "Indians within our limits for the purpose of assassination and murder." But tribal hostility was fueled less by British intrigue than by Harrison's purchases of Indian land from chiefs who often lacked authority to sell it. The Shawnee chief Tecumseh rallied tribes against such deals. "No tribe has a right to sell," he told Harrison. "Sell a country! Why not sell the air, the clouds, and the great sea, as well as the earth."

William Henry Harrison

Harrison respected Tecumseh but loathed his brother Tenskwatawa. Known as the Prophet, Tenskwatawa urged followers at Prophetstown, his village near the Tippecanoe River, to reject everything associated with the Americans, whom he called "children of the Evil Spirit." In 1811, while Tecumseh was away urging southern tribes to join his alliance, Harrison led troops against Prophetstown. Warriors there struck first, attacking Harrison's camp on November 7 and wreaking havoc before retreating under fire and abandoning their village. Harrison suffered heavy losses, but President James Madison called the Battle of Tippecanoe a "great defeat" for his foes.

When the U.S. and Britain went to war in July 1812, Tecumseh backed the British and besieged Harrison's forces at Fort Meigs in Ohio. Harrison withstood the siege

Tecumseh

and pursued his foes into Canada. On October 5, 1813, at the Battle of the Thames, British troops retreated under the American onslaught while Tecumseh stood fast and perished. Hopes for a tribal confederacy capable of halting American expansion died with him. ∎

BATTLE OF TIPPECANOE Urged on by Harrison (mounted at far left), American troops repulse warriors sent by Tecumseh's brother the Prophet. Harrison had not fortified his camp, and nearly a fifth of his 1,000 or so troops were killed or wounded.

ANDREW JACKSON'S WARPATH
From Horseshoe Bend to New Orleans

Andrew Jackson was not one to back down when challenged. During the War of 1812, he had two formidable challengers to contend with—British redcoats and Creek Indians known as Red Sticks for the painted war clubs they wielded. Both those foes aroused old grievances that Jackson had harbored since his youth. During the Revolutionary War, he lost two brothers who fought against the British. Jackson took up arms himself against the redcoats in his early teens and was captured and slashed on the head by a British officer for refusing to clean the man's boots. As an adult, Jackson joined settlers in Tennessee on campaigns against hostile Indians. Described in battle as "bold, dashing, fearless, and *mad upon his enemies,*" he believed that the only way to pacify the frontier was to crush defiant tribes. Peace talks and treaties, he wrote, "answer no other purpose than opening an easy door for the Indians to pass through to butcher our citizens."

In 1813, a bitter conflict in Alabama between Creek Indians allied with Americans and opposing Red Sticks inspired by Tecumseh's fiery rhetoric resulted in butchery by those warriors and led Jackson to retaliate. On August 30, Red Sticks overran Fort Mims—where American militiamen who had earlier attacked them were sheltered along with civilians—and massacred nearly 250 men, women, and children. Jackson, now serving as a general in the American volunteer army, swore vengeance and raised a force of 2,500 Tennesseans, supported by hundreds of Creek and Cherokee warriors at odds with the Red

Sticks. He was tough on his troops, who called him Old Hickory, but took good care of them.

In March 1814, Jackson's forces cornered the Red Sticks, who had barricaded themselves behind logs at Horseshoe Bend, with the Tallapoosa River at their backs. Jackson sent men swimming across the river to burn their huts and cut loose their canoes, leaving them stranded when his troops stormed their breastwork and broke through. More than 800 of the 1,000 or so Red Sticks engaged at Horseshoe Bend were killed. Creek chiefs who had sided with Jackson and expected to be rewarded were sorely disappointed. After the battle, he foisted a treaty on

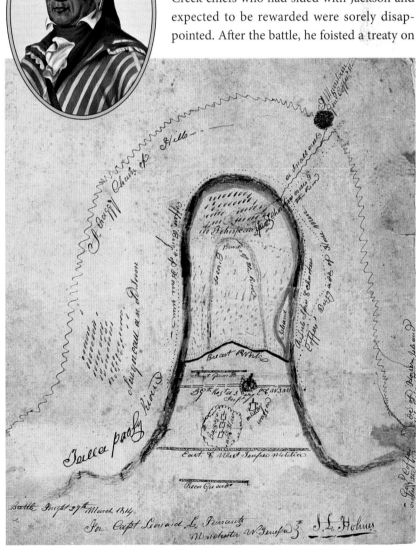

HERO ON HORSEBACK Portrayed opposite by artist Alonzo Chappel at New Orleans, where he defeated British forces in January 1815, Andrew Jackson also crushed an uprising by Creek Red Sticks inspired by Tecumseh. In March 1814, Jackson's troops overwhelmed Red Sticks trapped within Horseshoe Bend in Alabama (right). Chief Menawa (top) survived, but most of his warriors perished.

them that deprived their tribe of much of its territory—some 20 million acres in all—terms they submitted to after being warned that those who refused would "become enemies of the United States."

Jackson's harsh policies were not based on hatred for Indians as a race. After the fighting in 1813, he adopted an Indian boy named Lyncoya, found on the battlefield beside his dead mother. He raised the child at the Hermitage, his Tennessee estate, and said that he felt "an unusual sympathy for him." Jackson also befriended Indian chiefs of various tribes. But like the Creek leaders who backed him at Horseshoe Bend, they often found that his loyalty to his own kind trumped any obligations he had to them. Determined to make the South a safe and prosperous haven for American settlers, Old Hickory took ruthless measures against not only hostile bands like the Red Sticks but also peaceful tribes that declined to give up territory coveted by settlers.

BLASTING THE BRITISH

Victory over the Red Sticks at Horseshoe Bend elevated Jackson to the rank of major general in the United States Army and set him on the path to glory at New Orleans, where he arrived in December 1814 to defend that city against British forces arriving by sea. As battle loomed in early January 1815, neither side knew that the U.S. and Great Britain had just concluded a peace treaty in Europe, news of which would not reach America until February. Jackson placed most of his troops along the east bank of the Mississippi. They were well fortified and well armed. Volunteers from Tennessee and

DEFEATED CHIEF Jackson accepts the surrender of the Red Stick leader Red Eagle, also known as William Weatherford, the son of a Creek woman and a white trader. Not present when the battle erupted at Horseshoe Bend, he gave up afterward. "My people are all gone," he told Jackson.

Kentucky carried long hunting rifles that could hit targets more than 200 yards away, beyond the range of the muskets carried by their opponents.

"Stand to your guns," Jackson shouted as the enemy approached at dawn on January 8. "Don't waste your ammunition—see that every shot tells." Rank after rank of British troops marched into battle, including Scottish Highlanders advancing to the strains of bagpipes, and were scythed down before they reached Jackson's rampart. By the time the shooting stopped later that morning, more than 2,000 British soldiers had been killed, wounded, or captured. Among the dead lay their commanding general, Sir Edward Pakenham. The victory cost Jackson fewer than 100 casualties—a figure so small compared with the enemy's toll that he had to assure President Madison he was not exaggerating British losses or understating his own. ■

TECHNOLOGY

THE LETHAL LONG RIFLE

Frontier Americans had a powerful weapon that was often associated with Kentucky but originated in Pennsylvania. In the early 1700s, gunsmiths there developed a long rifle, whose grooved barrel imparted spin to the bullet and made it travel straighter than bullets fired from smoothbore muskets. The rifle's long barrel also provided more space for gas to expand when the gunpowder was ignited, increasing the bullet's velocity.

Long rifles were mainly hunting weapons, but some American soldiers used them in combat during the Revolutionary War and the War of 1812. Although they were more accurate and had a longer range than smoothbore muskets, they could be just as cumbersome to load and fire. During the Battle of New Orleans, Andrew Jackson compensated for the time it took his men to load their guns—some of which were long rifles and others muskets—by

forming three lines of troops. After the men in the first line fired, they stepped to the rear and reloaded while the men in the next line stepped forward and fired. The result was a "flashing and roaring hell" for troops on the receiving end. When the battle came to an end, the ground in front of the rampart was covered with dead and wounded British soldiers. They lay "in heaps," one observer wrote; "the field was completely red."

PEACE TREATY The War of 1812 was resolved on December 24, 1814, when the Treaty of Ghent was signed by John Quincy Adams, chief of the U.S. delegation, and other American and British negotiators.

BATTLE OF NEW ORLEANS Jackson directs fire on horseback against British troops charging his rampart along the east bank of the Mississippi on January 8, 1815. His staggering victory that day did not alter the outcome of the War of 1812, which had been decided two weeks earlier when the Treaty of Ghent was concluded. But the public learned of Jackson's triumph before word of that peace treaty arrived, and he became the nation's greatest military hero since George Washington.

MEXICAN INDEPENDENCE

Upheaval in the Borderlands

After the War of 1812, the United States pressured Spain to give up Florida and accept America's claims under the Louisiana Purchase. Spain was hard-pressed to resist those demands because its empire was crumbling. In 1808, Napoleon Bonaparte had invaded Spain. That weakened Spanish authority overseas and set the stage for the Mexican War of Independence, which began in 1810 when a dissident priest, Miguel Hidalgo y Costilla, vowed "Death to the Spaniards!"—a cry taken up by Indians, mestizos, and others at odds with Mexico's Spanish rulers.

SACRED CAUSE
Some who rebelled against Spain marched under this banner depicting the Virgin of Guadalupe, long revered by Mexicans.

Amid the upheaval, Spain was powerless to prevent Maj. Gen. Andrew Jackson from invading Florida in 1818. His stated purpose was to attack Seminole Indians, who were raiding settlements in Georgia and harboring escaped slaves from southern plantations as well as fugitive Red Sticks from Creek territory in Alabama. But Jackson also seized Spanish forts in Florida and strengthened the hand of Secretary of State John Quincy Adams, who was seeking major concessions from Spanish envoy Luis de Onís. Under the Adams-Onís Treaty, signed in 1819 and ratified in early 1821, Spain ceded Florida to the U.S. and accepted a boundary that gave America most of what it claimed under the Louisiana Purchase while leaving Texas, New Mexico, California, and adjacent territory under Spanish control. In September 1821, Mexico won independence from Spain and entered into prolonged negotiations with U.S. envoys, who tried to shift the border southward but eventually settled for the Adams-Onís line.

Mexico's long struggle for independence had convulsed the country and claimed more than a million lives. It emerged with an unstable government that struggled to meet its expenses and secure its northern frontier. Mexico lowered old Spanish barriers against foreign trade and immigration, admitting American merchants who paid duties on goods and granting land to settlers who became Mexican citizens. Some Americans skirted those requirements by trading or settling illegally in Mexico. One Mexican official urged restrictions on immigration and warned that American settlers were forerunners of conquest. "Where others send invading armies," he wrote, Americans "send their colonists." ∎

ACTA DE INDEPENDENCIA
DEL
IMPERIO MEXICANO
PRONUNCIADA POR SU JUNTA SOBERANA,
CONGREGADA EN LA CAPITAL DE ÉL EN 28 DE SETIEMBRE DE 1821

BIRTH OF A NATION Signed on September 28, 1821, this document proclaimed the Mexican Empire independent of Spain. The empire extended southward to Central America, most of which broke away from Mexico before it was reconstituted as a republic in 1824.

IGNITING THE REBELLION Father Hidalgo y Costilla wields a flaming torch, surrounded by Indians and other supporters, in a mural depicting the struggle for independence, which set Mexicans of different origins and loyalties against each other. Artist Juan O'Gorman portrayed rebels at right here and pro-Spanish officials and clergy who opposed them at left, near a Christ-like figure crucified for defying imperial Spain.

TRAVELING THE SANTA FE TRAIL

Caravans to New Mexico

Pioneered by merchant William Becknell, who in 1822 led a party of 21 men and 3 wagons from Missouri to New Mexico, the Santa Fe Trail introduced American traders to Mexican territory—and eventually brought American invaders there as well. Becknell seized the opportunity that arose when Mexico won independence from Spain and lowered trade barriers. He was the first American to bring goods in wagons to Santa Fe, which lay at the southern end of the Rocky Mountains and could be reached from Missouri by traders without encountering slopes too steep for their vehicles to ascend.

Although the terrain was manageable, the journey was taxing. Merchants who followed in Becknell's path had to ford the Arkansas River and other waterways that were treacherous when swollen. Their route took them through prime buffalo country, which provided them with meat as well as fuel in the form of buffalo chips but also exposed them to attack by warriors of various tribes that frequented those hunting grounds. Becknell told of two men in his party who ran afoul of Indians and were "stripped, barbarously whipped, and robbed of their horses, guns and clothes."

Traders bound for Santa Fe guarded against attack by gathering in May at a designated rendezvous—usually Council Grove, located near the edge

LONG HAUL Above, traders camp in Comanche country with their wagons arrayed in a defensive circle before continuing on to Santa Fe, portrayed at right after American forces marched down the Santa Fe Trail in 1846 and raised their flag over the town.

"THE ARRIVAL OF A CARAVAN AT SANTA FE
CHANGES THE ASPECT OF THE PLACE
AT ONCE . . . ONE NOW SEES EVERYWHERE
THE BUSTLE, NOISE AND ACTIVITY
OF A LIVELY MARKET TOWN."
—JOSIAH GREGG

JOURNEY'S END Traders approach Santa Fe, riding alongside their wagons, which were usually pulled by mules or oxen.

of the Plains in what is now Kansas. There they formed companies and elected captains, who posted guards every night of the journey near the wagons, parked in a circle with livestock in the center. Nervous guards new to that duty sometimes shot at anything that moved. Richens Lacy "Uncle Dick" Wootton, who went out on the trail to trap in Mexican territory at the age of 20, blazed away one night at an object that he took for an Indian but proved to be "Old Jack," a stray mule belonging to the company. "I felt sorry about it," Wootton remarked, "but the mule had disobeyed orders, you know, and I wasn't to blame for killing him."

LEGAL TENDER
Santa Fe traders returned with Mexican silver coins like this one, which were honored in Missouri.

The risk of attack increased after companies crossed the Arkansas and approached the Cimarron River in Comanche country. Comanches welcomed Mexican traders known as Comancheros but resented and harassed Americans who withheld their merchandise. Josiah Gregg, an astute participant and observer of commerce on the Santa Fe Trail, faulted his fellow merchants for avoiding trade "with the wild Indians." Tribes were "much less hostile to those with whom they trade," he noted. To avoid clashes with Comanche warriors along the Cimarron Route, some merchants followed the alternate Mountain Route to Santa Fe, which was longer and steeper, requiring a hard pull up Raton Pass at the present Colorado–New Mexico border.

Santa Fe traders dealt mainly in fabric and clothing as well as household implements—items that were scarce and expensive in New Mexico. Under Spanish rule, Mexico's economy had been based on extracting mineral wealth and other raw materials rather than on producing goods of the sort offered by American merchants. Those who could not sell all their wares in and around Santa Fe often ventured down the Camino Real (Royal Road) to Chihuahua, a larger and wealthier town. There in the marketplace called the Alameda, wrote Gregg, women shopped by candlelight after partaking "of their chocolate and their *cigarritos,*" and browsed in stores that were "literally filled from dusk till nine or ten o'clock."

By fall, merchants were homeward bound with satchels full of silver coins that helped fuel business on the Missouri frontier, where cash was scarce. "The circulating medium of Missouri now consists primarily of Mexican dollars," wrote one observer a decade after the Santa Fe trade began. Merchants also returned with mules purchased in Mexico. Mexicans were expert at handling mules that pulled wagons on the trail, and some also entered the trade as merchants.

In 1825, Congress commissioned a party to survey the trail. They piled up mounds of sod as markers, but the chief surveyor noted that the road was "already well enough marked by the wagons." Over the years to come, those heavy wagons would carve deep ruts, some of which remain visible to this day.

More significant than the survey were military escorts for Santa Fe traders that began in 1829. Designed to protect the merchants from Indian raids until they forded the Arkansas River and entered Mexican territory, those escorts foreshadowed a much larger commitment of U.S. forces, who would follow the trail all the way to Santa Fe when peaceful exchanges between Americans and Mexicans gave way to conflict. ∎

THE INDISPENSABLE MULE

Notoriously stubborn, mules have been goaded and cursed by humans down through the ages. If they were not essential to people engaged in arduous tasks like the Santa Fe trade, however, they would never have proliferated. Conceived when a donkey mates with a horse, mules are genetically incapable of reproducing. They became common through breeding, and people bred them because they were larger and stronger than donkeys and had greater endurance than horses.

The mules merchants brought back from New Mexico were not the first of their species in Missouri—which made the mule its state animal—but they were sturdy specimens, capable of hauling wagons for days on end. Mules also served well as pack animals (below) and as mounts for riders. Santa Fe trader James Webb swore by his mule Dolly and rode her when hunting buffalo. "I called Dolly to the gallop," he recalled, "and found she knew her business better than I did." Like most mules, she could be "tricky and headstrong," but he grew as attached to her as others on the trail did to their horses. "Dolly with all her naughtiness was an animal I loved," Webb declared.

TRAPPERS ON THE TRAIL
Expanding the Fur Trade

B y the early 1820s, Americans were once again feverishly pursuing "soft gold" in the form of beaver pelts, which were used to line men's hats and made up the bulk of the lucrative fur trade. Hindered by the War of 1812 and a financial panic in 1819, that trade was now rebounding and attracting many Anglo Americans as well as French Canadians. Several companies based in St. Louis joined in the quest for those pelts. None was more venturesome than a new outfit led by Missouri's lieutenant governor, William Ashley, and partner Andrew Henry, who had helped establish the Missouri Fur Company but now hoped to outdo that firm, which continued to bargain with tribes for furs. He and Ashley thought they could do better by sending out their own trappers. In March 1822, they advertised in St. Louis for "one hundred men to ascend the Missouri to the Rocky Mountains." Some of those trappers were crude and combative, but others were consummate mountain men—steady, shrewd, and observant like Jedediah Smith, who signed on with Ashley and Henry at the age of 23.

The revival of the fur trade came as a challenge for tribes like the Arikara, who welcomed traders to their villages along the Missouri but did not want them to deal with rivals such as the Lakota Sioux. Relations between those Sioux and the Arikara turned increasingly hostile as they vied for access to weapons and other trade goods. In the spring of 1823, two Arikaras died in a clash with employees of the Missouri Fur Company, who were trading with Sioux at an outpost called Cedar Fort. Soon afterward, trappers led by Ashley arrived at the Arikara villages, seeking horses, and came under attack by warriors who made no distinction between them and the despised traders at the fort. Fifteen of Ashley's men were killed. The toll might have been higher had not Jedediah Smith and other armed men on shore held the warriors off while wounded trappers found refuge on Ashley's keelboats. "Never in my opinion did men act with more bravery and coolness," Ashley said of those who held out on the beach. Smith was one of the last to retreat, his companions recalled, and later offered a prayer for a dying man that "moved us all greatly."

That summer, Lt. Col. Henry Leavenworth led a retaliatory campaign against the Arikara by several hundred U.S. troops, traders, and trappers, joined by scores of Sioux intent on scourging their tribal foes. Leavenworth

VOYAGEURS Paddle in hand, a French-Canadian fur trader descends the Missouri River with his son in an 1845 painting by George Caleb Bingham. The animal chained to the prow of the canoe may be a cat used to catch rodents that plagued frontier camps.

vowed to uphold the honor of "American arms," but the only clash of arms took place between Sioux and Arikara warriors, more than a dozen of whom were killed. Over the next few days, Leavenworth alternately negotiated with the Arikara and menaced them with cannon fire, which did little damage to the thick earthen walls around their settlements. Then overnight the Arikara fled. Leavenworth thought he had taught them a lesson and that tribes in the area would now "respect the American name and character." But the Sioux were not impressed with his campaign, and the Arikara were further embittered against Americans when their abandoned villages were torched by men of the Missouri Fur Company.

Ashley and Henry concluded that the Missouri

UNDER ATTACK Mountain men who responded to Ashley and Henry's notice (top) and ascended the Missouri risked attacks of the sort depicted above, carried out by Indians who did not want them dealing with rival bands or intruding on tribal hunting grounds.

BEAVER TRAP Castoreum, secreted by beavers, was used as bait to lure the animal to traps like this one.

was not a reliable avenue for the beaver trade and sent trappers out seeking alternate paths to the Rockies. In the fall of 1823, Smith led an exploratory party west across the Black Hills that included such notable mountain men as William Sublette, Thomas Fitzpatrick, and James Clyman, who told in his journal of a harrowing encounter with a grizzly that mauled Smith and nearly tore his scalp off, leaving one ear dangling. Smith implored Clyman to "sew up my wounds," and he did so with needle and thread, stitching "the lacerated parts together as nice as I could." Scarred but intact, Smith continued with his party to a village of Crow Indians near Wyoming's Wind River Range, aided by interpreter Edward Rose, who was of mixed African, Indian, and European ancestry and had lived among the Crow.

CROSSING THE DIVIDE

In early 1824, the trappers left the Crow village while the snow still lay deep and crossed the Continental

Divide at South Pass. Its gentle incline made the pass ideal for the wagons that would later follow the Oregon Trail, and Smith's venture encouraged fur traders to begin hauling goods to and from the Rockies by wagon. Come spring, he and his party were camped in prime beaver country along the upper Green River, where a year later Ashley would hold the first rendezvous for the firm's wide-ranging trappers and gather their pelts.

By 1826, Smith had formed his own company with Sublette and another partner. That fall, he set out from the vicinity of the Great Salt Lake and became the first American to lead a party overland to California. He was seeking not only beaver pelts but also a mythical river called the Buenaventura, which like the Columbia to the north was thought to originate in the Rockies and flow to the Pacific. He hoped to profit from this journey, but his overriding ambition was to explore "country on which the eyes of a white man had never gazed and to follow the course of rivers that run through a new land."

In November 1826, after crossing the Colorado River and the bleak Mojave Desert, Smith entered California's San Bernardino Valley with his trapping party and found horses and cattle grazing in green pastures. "Whether it was its own real beauty or the contrast with what we had seen," he wrote, "it certainly seemed to us enchantment." Padres at Mission San Gabriel took them in, but Governor José María de Echeandía soon learned of their arrival and summoned Smith for questioning. He had no license to trap in Mexico, and Echeandía suspected him of poaching—and perhaps spying on Mexico. Smith claimed that he was only seeking supplies and fresh horses. An American ship captain vouched for him, and the governor allowed him to purchase what he needed but insisted he then leave promptly by the same route he had entered California.

Instead, Smith went to trap in the San Joaquin Valley. Mexican authorities had little control there or in the Sacramento Valley to the north—the upper half of California's immense Central Valley. All the Mexican settlements lay near the coast, and only rarely did troops venture inland in pursuit of mission Indians who fled to the Central Valley or other Indians who lived there and raided coastal ranches. In years to come, hundreds of Americans would follow in Smith's path and trap or settle without permission in the interior, where they were at little risk of being apprehended. Unlike some American merchants who lived along the coast and married Mexican women, they would remain aliens in California and at odds with Mexican officials. Smith was the forerunner of those intruders, and Echeandía had reason to be wary of him. "As I see it," a Mexican officer who learned of Smith's evasive actions wrote the governor, "he mocks your excellency's high orders and even tramples on sacred national laws."

In May 1827, Smith left most of his party in the San Joaquin Valley and crossed the Sierra Nevada and the Great Basin with two companions. They nearly died of thirst before reaching the trappers' Rocky Mountain rendezvous, where Smith enlisted reinforcements and returned to California. Attacked while crossing the Colorado River by Mohave Indians who had recently clashed with

SCARRED FOR LIFE As shown in his portrait (top), Jedediah Smith wore his hair long to cover the scars of his bloody encounter with a grizzly in the Black Hills, portrayed above.

other trappers, he lost ten men. Then in July 1828, after rejoining his party and departing for Oregon, he held an Indian hostage with a rope around his neck to retrieve a stolen ax—and suffered devastating retribution. A few days later, his camp was overrun. Smith and two members of his party were away at the time, and they were among the few who survived.

Smith came through that ordeal, only to perish three years later when he ran afoul of Comanches along the Santa Fe Trail. His remarkable career served both to promote westward expansion and to demonstrate the daunting challenges and stiff resistance Americans would face as they defied boundaries and advanced across the continent. ∎

CUSTOMS OF THE MOUNTAIN MEN
Revelry, Courtship, and Conflict

othing did more to foster the popular impression of mountain men as boisterous and unruly than the annual rendezvous that brought them together at congenial sites in the mountains where Wyoming, Utah, and Idaho now meet. Fur traders collected pelts from mountain men at those gatherings and furnished them with supplies. The trappers spent part of their earnings on goods they needed to continue living in the mountains, where they operated for months on end in companies that were reorganized from year to year.

The rendezvous was also a festive occasion for mountain men and for Indians on good terms with them. Tribes had long gathered annually along the river they called the Siskadee (Green River) to trade and celebrate. The mountain men added a volatile new ingredient to that tradition—alcohol, which sometimes produced mayhem as well as merriment.

John Kirk Townsend, a naturalist who accompanied an overland expedition to Oregon in 1834, described the Green River rendezvous that summer. Indians of various tribes arrived there with furs and pelts "to trade for ammunition, trinkets, and 'fire water,'" he noted. Most of the trappers in attendance called themselves "white men," he added, but some of them were of mixed race and were "nearly as dark, and their manners nearly as wild, as the Indians with whom they constantly associate." The rendezvous was in fact one of the few places where people of color, including mountain men of African ancestry such as Edward Rose and James Beckwourth, stood on equal footing with whites. To Townsend, mountain men of whatever complexion were almost indistinguishable in behavior from the tribesmen in attendance. "These people," he said of the trappers, "with their obstreperous mirth, their whooping, and howling, and

GREEN RIVER RENDEZVOUS
Mountain men and Indians gather against the towering backdrop of the Rockies in a painting by Alfred Jacob Miller, who witnessed the Green River rendezvous in 1837. Miller's portrait of a characteristic mountain man (right) shows him wearing fringed buckskin and carrying a long rifle.

"THE ONLY AUTHORITY WHICH THE FREE TRAPPER ACKNOWLEDGED WAS THAT OF HIS INDIAN SPOUSE, WHO GENERALLY RULED IN THE LODGE, HOWEVER HER LORD BLUSTERED OUTSIDE."
—FRANCES FULLER VICTOR

TRAPPER'S BRIDE A mountain man takes his Indian bride in hand in another painting by Miller, who noted that the trapper purchased her from her family for $600, "paid for in the legal tender of the region: viz.: Guns $100 each, Blankets $40 each, Red Flannel $20 pr. yard, Alcohol $64 pr. Gal., Tobacco, Beads etc."

quarreling, added to the mounted Indians, who are constantly dashing into and through our camp, yelling like fiends, the barking and baying of savage wolf-dogs, and the incessant cracking of rifles and carbines, render our camp a perfect bedlam." Townsend blamed liquor for much of the uproar and told of one man who bought $20 worth of rum and $10 worth of sugar to regale two friends who were leaving.

What Townsend witnessed, however, was no more representative of the mountain man's daily life than the revelry of cowboys after long drives or sailors after months at sea. A few mountain men were teetotalers like Jedediah Smith, and many imbibed little or no liquor while on lengthy trapping expeditions. If they wanted a strong drink, they might settle for bitters consisting of buffalo gall (bile) mixed with water, a beverage thought to soothe the stomach. Lewis Garrard, who accompanied mountain men to Taos, New Mexico, on the Santa Fe Trail, described how they killed and consumed a buffalo on the spot: "The men ate the liver raw, with a slight dash of *gall* by way of zest . . . to hungry men, not at all squeamish, raw warm liver, with raw marrow, was quite palatable." Like Plains Indians, mountain men subsisted largely on game, supplemented by roots or berries, which when mixed with dried meat and fat formed a durable blend called pemmican.

AKIN TO INDIANS

Mountain men shared much with Indians besides their diet, including a fondness for buckskin clothing, which lasted longer in the wild than wool or cotton garments. Their closest connection with tribal culture came through marriage to Indian women, who were sometimes purchased as wives. Those unions might be temporary but were often lasting, producing children who might join their mother and father on his journeys.

For all the ties that bound them to Indians, trappers could also be merciless Indian fighters, who repaid the loss of one or two lives on the trail several times over when they tracked down warriors they held responsible. Conflict was sometimes averted, however, by diplomatic mountain men such as Thomas Fitzpatrick, known as Broken Hand for an injury he suffered while handling a defective gun. In later years, he served as an Indian agent and worked out peace treaties, but they seldom lasted long when

BEAD NECKLACE Ornaments such as this were traditionally made by Indians of shell beads, but glass beads prevailed after tribes came in contact with fur traders.

tribal territory was overrun by settlers or prospectors who, unlike mountain men, had no desire to rendezvous with Indians and wanted them out of the way.

By the time Townsend witnessed the frolics of the mountain men in 1834, their heyday was almost over. Intense competition between American trappers and British brigades sent out by the Hudson's Bay Company was depleting the beaver supply. Hatmakers were using silk in place of felt made from beaver pelts, and fur traders were shifting their efforts to collecting buffalo hides. As the beaver trade declined, adaptable mountain men like Fitzpatrick embarked on new ventures of far-reaching significance by guiding Americans to Oregon and California. ∎

EYEWITNESS

JOE MEEK'S SURVIVAL DIET

In 1832, mountain man Joe Meek, pictured here, joined a party of trappers led by William Sublette who nearly starved to death in the desert along the Humboldt River. Meek told his story to author Frances Fuller Victor, who incorporated his own words, including an Indian saying he picked up, in this passage from her book *The River of the West*:

It was the custom of a camp on the move to depend chiefly on the men employed as hunters to supply them with game, the sole support of the mountaineers. When this failed, the stock on hand was soon exhausted, and the men reduced to famine. This was what happened to Sublette's company . . . Owing to the arid and barren nature of these plains, the largest game to be found was the beaver, whose flesh proved to be poisonous, from the creature having eaten of the wild parsnip in the absence of its favorite food. The men were made ill by eating of beaver flesh, and the horses were greatly reduced from the scarcity of grass . . . The sufferings of the men now became terrible, both from hunger and thirst . . . everything was eaten that could be eaten, and many things at which the well-fed man would sicken with disgust. "I have," says Joe Meek, "held my hands in an ant-hill until they were covered with the ants, then greedily licked them off. I have taken the soles off my moccasins, crisped them in the fire, and eaten them. In our extremity, the large black crickets which are found in this country were considered game. We used to take a kettle of hot water, catch the crickets and throw them in, and when they stopped kicking, eat them. That was not what we called *cant tickup ko hanch*, (good meat, my friend), but it kept us alive."

ARTIST ON THE TRAIL
Alfred Jacob Miller's Rewarding Journey

Born in Baltimore in 1810, Alfred Jacob Miller studied painting in Europe as a young man. He had little success as an artist, however, until he went west in the spring of 1837 and met Capt. William Drummond Stewart, a wealthy Scottish soldier and adventurer who had traveled to the Rockies with fur traders and mountain men and was planning another trip. Stewart commissioned Miller to provide a pictorial record of their journey that summer with a caravan of the American Fur Company, which was destined for the Green River rendezvous. Miller took notes and made sketches along the way that he later transformed into paintings, including one showing Stewart on horseback at their camp (right) as they neared that annual gathering in the Rockies. "By the time the last vehicle has reached the ground, the Caravan has formed a circumference of 5 or 600 feet," Miller wrote of this picture; "the horses and mules are now unharnessed, and loosed to feed, leaving the vehicles at a distance of some 30 feet apart, forming a species of barricade; towards sundown the horses are driven in and picketed, and this scene forms the subject of our sketch."

Alfred Jacob Miller

Miller had ample time to observe the rendezvous and document the proceedings. "Here we rested over a month," he wrote, "under the shadow of the great spurs of the Wind River Mountains, encamping among 3,000 Snake [Shoshone] and other Indians." Trappers also attended, but the beaver trade was declining and the company's agents were seeking buffalo robes from Indians, who exchanged them "for blankets, guns, ammunition, tobacco, and a variety of smaller articles," noted Miller. "The first day is given up, by established custom, to a species of Saturnalia. Gambling, racing, boxing, and drinking are in the ascendant. On the second and succeeding days all this is changed. The American Fur Company's great tent is elevated, and trading goes briskly forward."

Like many artists of the Romantic era, Miller sometimes invented or embellished scenes to heighten their emotional impact. In one painting, he portrayed Pawnee Indians on a bluff, spying on the traders' caravan below, a dramatic view that owed more to his vivid imagination than his powers of observation. Miller's rewarding journey lasted only a matter of months but inspired scores of evocative paintings in the years to come that established him as one of America's pioneering Western artists. ∎

REST FOR THE WEARY Wagons form a broad circle amid tents and tepees in this painting by Miller entitled "Our Camp," showing the caravan at rest during the latter part of its journey to the rendezvous in the mountains.

REBELLION IN TEXAS
Origins of the Lone Star State

S tephen F. Austin would be remembered as the "father of Texas" for colonizing the future Lone Star State and helping Texas gain independence from Mexico in 1836. Yet that famous American, who was born in Virginia in 1793 and once declared that the main object of his labors was "to Americanize Texas," spent much of his adult life as a Mexican citizen. Austin pledged allegiance to Mexico in order to found a colony in East Texas, and Americans who joined him there as settlers in the 1820s took the oath as well.

Stephen F. Austin

Their loyalty to their adopted country was tested in the early 1830s by Mexican laws that restricted immigration from the United States, imposed tariffs on imported goods, and prohibited slaves from being introduced to Texas, as colonists from neighboring Louisiana and other southern states were doing. Some began agitating for independence, but Austin favored seeking recognition for Texas as a full-fledged Mexican state, with greater control over its own affairs. In 1833, he traveled to Mexico City to press for statehood but was jailed on suspicion of advocating insurrection. By the time he was freed in 1835, Mexico's authoritarian president, Antonio López de Santa Anna, had nullified his nation's original constitution and was tightening his grip on the country. Austin concluded that Texas should secede from Mexico and join the U.S., and he hoped more Americans would soon settle there to help bring that about. "A gentle breeze shakes off a ripe peach," he wrote. "Can it be supposed that the violent political convulsions of Mexico will not shake

Antonio López de Santa Anna

off Texas so soon as it is ripe enough to fall?" All that was needed was a "great immigration" of Americans, he concluded, and the peach would fall into their hands.

FIGHT TO THE FINISH Having fired his last shot, David Crockett meets death heroically by using his rifle as a club against oncoming Mexican troops in artist Robert Onderdonk's dramatic painting "The Fall of Alamo." Just how Crockett died at the Alamo remains unclear.

By 1835, there were already more than 30,000 people from the U.S. in Texas, including many illegal immigrants as well as those who had settled there officially under Austin and other *empresarios* (authorized colonizers). Anglo-Texans outnumbered Tejanos (Hispanic Texans) nearly ten to one and were weary of Mexican rule. Some Tejanos joined their rebellion but others held back, favoring neither Santa Anna nor his Anglo foes, who were too often disdainful of native-born Mexicans.

Although Austin helped launch the revolution in Texas in late 1835 and led troops against Mexican forces holding San Antonio, he soon relinquished his command for a task that suited him better—serving Texas as its envoy to the U.S.—and left the fighting to firebrands like Benjamin Milam from Kentucky. "Who will go with old Ben Milam into San Antonio?" he shouted. Three hundred men answered his call and seized the town in December in an attack that cost Milam his life.

Santa Anna set out to avenge that defeat. After brutally crushing an uprising in Zacatecas, he led several thousand troops northward into Texas and besieged the Alamo, an

> "I AM DETERMINED TO SUSTAIN MYSELF AS LONG AS POSSIBLE & DIE LIKE A SOLDIER WHO NEVER FORGETS WHAT IS DUE TO HIS OWN HONOR & THAT OF HIS COUNTRY— VICTORY OR DEATH."
>
> —WILLIAM TRAVIS

old Spanish mission in San Antonio serving now as a fort. Defending the Alamo were some 200 defiant rebels, led by 3 men born in the U.S. who made their last stand there—William Travis from South Carolina, who vowed to achieve victory or death; James Bowie from Louisiana, renowned for his proficiency with the lethal Bowie knife crafted by his brother Rezin; and David Crockett from Tennessee, who had recently lost his bid for reelection to Congress and said that if voters decided against him, "They might go to hell, and I would go to Texas." By early March, he and the others were trapped by Santa Anna's forces and under intermittent artillery fire. When the guns fell silent, Crockett cheered his comrades by playing his fiddle. He had little hope of surviving this struggle, however. "I think we had better march out and die in the open air," he told Susanna Dickinson, who remained in the Alamo with her husband and daughter. "I don't like to be hemmed up"

Before dawn on March 6, 1836, Santa Anna hurled his troops against the vastly outnumbered defenders, who expected no mercy and resisted to the bitter end. Travis, Bowie, and Crockett perished along with all the other fighting men in the Alamo, including Tejano José (Gregorio) Esparza, whose wife and children had remained there with him and were spared along with Susanna Dickinson and her child.

RETROSPECTIVE This late 19th-century view of the attack in 1836 shows the Alamo as it looked after it was remodeled in 1849.

REMEMBERING THE ALAMO

Founded in the early 1700s as Mission San Antonio de Valero, the Alamo was converted into a Spanish fort, manned by soldiers of the Alamo Company, who arrived in 1803 from the town of Alamo de Parras. Following the famous battle between Santa Anna's troops and the Alamo's doomed defenders, it became the property of the Texas Republic in late 1836, the United States in 1846, and the Confederate States in 1861 before reverting to control of the U.S. Army in 1865, which abandoned it in 1877.

By 1936, when President Franklin D. Roosevelt spoke at the centennial of the Battle of the Alamo, the monument had been thoroughly overhauled and bore little resemblance to the original fort. Its historical significance had evolved as well, and its defenders were now honored not just as Texans but as Americans. Roosevelt placed a wreath on what he called "this shrine where the blood of 182 Americans was shed." The actual toll of those who died defending the Alamo was slightly higher and included some Tejanos who were seeking independence and some Mexican citizens born in the United States. Hundreds of opposing Mexican troops also died fighting there to preserve Texas as part of their country. Remembering the Alamo fully means acknowledging all those from either side who fell there.

Vengeance at San Jacinto

It was a costly victory for Santa Anna. After losing nearly 600 men taking the Alamo, he divided his forces to mop up resistance in Texas, thinking that he had dealt a crushing blow to the rebellion. He got more resistance than he counted on from Texans and their commander in chief, Sam Houston, soon to become the first president of the Texas Republic. Incensed by the slaughter at the Alamo and a massacre in late March at Goliad, where scores of Texans were killed after surrendering, they caught Santa Anna off guard along the San Jacinto River on April 21 and charged his encampment with a shrill "Texan yell," recalled Creed Taylor of Houston's army. "Like a cyclone crashing through the forest, we went over the dirt and brush barricade without halting," he added. "A solid sheet of flame flashed from our rifles, and then, without waiting to reload,

HERO ON HORSEBACK Sam Houston, portrayed here, was a 43-year-old former aide to Andrew Jackson when he fought at San Jacinto in 1836.

we bore down and closed in upon the surprised and frightened enemy with clubbed guns, pistols, and hunting knives. It was a hand to hand struggle; and now came the blood-stirring cry, '*Remember the Alamo! Remember Goliad!*'"

Defeated and captured, Santa Anna agreed to recognize the independence of Texas in exchange for his freedom. But Texans who hoped their new republic would soon be part of the U.S. were disappointed. Stephen Austin died in late 1836, nine years before Texas was formally Americanized. One factor that delayed annexation was political opposition to admitting another slave state like Texas to the Union. Furthermore, Mexico renounced Santa Anna's deal with Texas and refused to acknowledge its independence. Not until leaders in Washington were prepared to defy Mexico would the U.S. grant Texas statehood. ∎

TEXANS TRIUMPHANT Holding his hat in one hand and his sword in the other to the right of a blue flag, Sam Houston urges his troops forward against Santa Anna's forces (right) in this 1895 painting of the Battle of San Jacinto by Henry McArdle, who drew on historical research and testimony from survivors.

CHEROKEE LEADER Elected principal chief of the Cherokee in 1827, John Ross was of Cherokee ancestry on his mother's side and deeply devoted to the tribe. After aiding Andrew Jackson against the Red Sticks during the War of 1812, he staunchly opposed Jackson's efforts to remove the Cherokee to Indian Territory.

INDIAN REMOVAL

From the Black Hawk War to the Trail of Tears

By 1830, many tribes had been forced west of the Mississippi to make way for American settlers, and others were under intense pressure to abandon their homelands. Among those who resisted removal were the Cherokee, who would ultimately be evicted and forced down the Trail of Tears. Another tribal group who clung to their ancestral ground and paid a steep price for doing so were the followers of the Sauk (Sac) chief Black Hawk. He and his band, including Sauk and allied Fox (Meskwaki) Indians, refused to comply with a treaty imposed by William Henry Harrison in 1804 that evicted them from their homelands along the east bank of the Mississippi, including the village of Saukenauk, situated where the town of Rock Island, Illinois, later emerged. Saukenauk was Black Hawk's birthplace and the burial place of his ancestors. "For this spot, I had a sacred reverence," he said, "and never could consent to leave it."

In 1831, however, Black Hawk and his people fled that village to avoid being attacked by U.S. troops. Threatened with starvation, they received food from the Army in exchange for Black Hawk's pledge to give up Saukenauk, remain west of the Mississippi, and recognize the compliant Chief Keokuk as leader of his tribe. Refusing to honor a promise extracted under duress, Black Hawk returned to Saukenauk in 1832 with more than 1,500 men, women, and children. Settlers in the vicinity feared attack by his warriors and formed militia companies that joined U.S. forces led by Brig. Gen. Henry Atkinson in pursuit of Black Hawk. A skilled commander who like Tecumseh had battled Americans during the War of 1812, he clashed with the pursuing soldiers and shielded his people until Atkinson

GREAT FATHER A political cartoon mocks Andrew Jackson's role as Great Father to American Indians at a time when he was pressing for removal of the Cherokee, Choctaw, and other tribes. Choctaws referred to 1829 as the year "the Devil became President."

TRAIL OF TEARS A modern portrayal of the forced Cherokee removal to Indian Territory that began in 1838 shows some members of the tribe hauling their belongings westward in wagons. Others were evicted from their homes by troops so abruptly that they were unable to take any possessions with them.

overtook them on August 1 where the Bad Axe River enters the Mississippi. Those who fled Atkinson's assault and crossed the Mississippi were targeted by their tribal foes the Dakota Sioux. Hundreds of Black Hawk's followers were massacred, and he surrendered soon afterward. The United States then stripped the Sauk and Fox of a 50-mile-wide tract west of the Mississippi.

MISSISSIPPI RIVER MASSACRE Fleeing American forces east of the Mississippi (right), Black Hawk's followers swim to the west bank of the river, where rival Dakota Sioux warriors await them on August 1, 1832.

OUSTING THE SOUTHERN TRIBES

One of Andrew Jackson's priorities as president was to remove from the South five tribes still residing there. Together, the Seminole, Creek, Cherokee, Choctaw, and Chickasaw had a population of well over 60,000, including some prosperous planters who owned black slaves. Trade and intermar-

riage with whites had exposed those tribes to American customs and standards. None had made greater progress by those standards than the Cherokee, who had their own constitution, council, and newspaper, published both in English and in a phonetic Cherokee script devised by Sequoyah.

After winning passage of the Indian Removal Act of 1830, Jackson pressured tribal leaders to exchange their land in the South for reservations in Indian Territory, which later became Oklahoma. Some who yielded received favors in return like Greenwood LeFlore, the son of a French-Canadian father and a Choctaw mother. The principal chief of the Choctaw, he signed a removal treaty and was granted land in Mississippi, where he developed a plantation worked by hundreds of slaves, while 15,000 other Choctaws set out on a grueling migration to Indian Territory that claimed more than 2,000 lives.

LeFlore's compliance stood in stark contrast to the defiance of John Ross, who was only one-eighth Cherokee but so committed to preserving the tribe's territory that he became its champion. Unable to sway Ross, Jackson persuaded Major Ridge—a Cherokee leader who had aided him in the past—and his son John that their tribe must remove to the West or lose everything to the state of Georgia, which planned to distribute Cherokee land to settlers. Jackson had no intention of halting Georgia's land grab, despite recent Supreme Court rulings that the Cherokee and other tribes were "domestic dependent nations," subject to the federal government but not to the states, which had no right to impose on them. In 1835, Major Ridge defied a Cherokee law making it a crime to dispose of tribal territory without tribal consent and endorsed a removal treaty. "I have signed my death warrant," he said. John Ridge also signed and left with him for Indian Territory, where they were later assassinated for approving the deal.

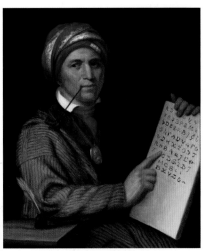

SEQUOYAH'S ALPHABET Portrayed here with symbols he devised to represent spoken Cherokee phonetically, Sequoyah enabled thousands of his people to become literate in their own language.

Jackson barely overcame opposition to that controversial removal treaty, which the Senate ratified by a margin of one vote. He then sent troops to evict the vast majority of Cherokees who opposed the treaty—over 16,000 people in all. Their forced migration to Indian Territory began when many were herded into stockades in May 1838 and lasted through the following winter. Some lost everything except their clothing. At least 4,000 died of exposure or disease—among them John Ross's wife, Quatie, who after offering "her only blanket for the protection of a sick child," one soldier wrote, "rode thinly clad though a blinding sleet and snowstorm, developed pneumonia, and died in the still hours of a bleak winter night."

Some Cherokees evaded removal, as did some members of the other four tribes, including Seminoles in Florida, who had long waged war against U.S. troops sent to evict them. After their traumatic removal, the exiles established impressive new settlements in Indian Territory and became known as the Five Civilized Tribes—a belated tribute from a society whose treatment of them had been less than civilized. ∎

SLAVES ON TRAILS OF TEARS

Not all those who suffered removal from the South to Indian Territory were Indians. Of the 5,000 or so people uprooted from the Chickasaw homeland in northern Mississippi, for example, about 1,000 were black slaves owned by Chickasaws. When Cherokees were evicted from their territory in and around Georgia and forced down the Trail of Tears, some 2,000 slaves went with them, hundreds of whom perished during that ordeal.

Unlike the other southern tribes, the Seminole harbored blacks who had escaped from bondage, including Abraham (right), who was born a slave in Georgia and found refuge in Florida. Some of them intermarried with Seminoles or were adopted by them, but most blacks lived in separate communities under Seminole authority and fought as allies of that tribe against U.S. forces during the Seminole War to avoid being re-enslaved. American officers induced some blacks in Florida to surrender by promising not to return them to their former owners and instead transport them to Indian Territory.

Only a few hundred Seminoles eluded capture and remained in the Everglades. Several thousand other Seminoles and allied blacks were removed to Indian Territory and placed under the authority of the Creek tribe, a number of whom were slave owners. That arrangement put those who were wholly or partly of African ancestry—known collectively as black Seminoles—at risk of being enslaved. Some later left Indian Territory and settled in Mexico.

BLACK SEMINOLE Allied with Seminoles fighting U.S. troops in Florida, Abraham was adopted into the tribe.

VIEWS OF NATIVE AMERICA
George Catlin's Indian Portraits

Artist George Catlin was in New York exhibiting his Indian Gallery, which included many vivid portraits of tribal chiefs, when he learned in late 1837 that the great Seminole war leader Osceola had been seized while meeting with U.S. officers under a white flag. Shocked at the deceptive manner in which Osceola had been captured and eager to portray the chief, Catlin traveled to Fort Moultrie at Charleston, South Carolina, where Osceola was imprisoned. Although suffering from a severe throat infection that would soon end his life, Osceola posed for Catlin's memorable portrait of him (opposite) and greatly impressed the artist. As Catlin wrote, "This gallant fellow is grieving with a broken spirit, and ready to die, cursing the white man, no doubt to the end of his breath."

Catlin owed his success not just to his artistry but to his deep appreciation for his subjects, which encouraged even those like Osceola who had reason to curse white men to trust and cooperate with him. Some Indians feared that Catlin

George Catlin

by picturing them would capture their spirit and do them harm. During a trip he took up the Missouri River in 1832, a Mandan medicine man said that those in his village who posed for Catlin were "fools and would soon die." Catlin overcame such fears by demonstrating that his purpose as an artist was to honor and preserve the spirit of his subjects on canvas.

Catlin later ventured onto the Plains and portrayed tribes with fierce reputations, including the Comanche and Sioux. When he exhibited his Indian Gallery—billed in one newspaper as representing the country's "wildest tribes"—he assured audiences that the Indians he visited were hospitable to people who dealt fairly with them and were seldom as cruel as the white men who imposed on them. "It is astonishing," he declared, "that under all the invasions, the frauds and deceptions, as well as force, that have been practiced upon the American Indians to push them from their lands . . . these abused people have exercised so little cruelty as they have." ■

ROVING ARTIST Portrayed above by fellow painter William Fisk in 1849, when he was in his early 50s, George Catlin based much of his work on wide-ranging field trips he made among Indians in the 1830s. He completed "Sioux Indians Hunting Buffalo" (left) in 1835 after observing men of that tribe pursuing bison on the Plains and the portrait of Osceola (opposite) after the Seminole war leader was captured in 1837. "The Sioux are a bold and desperate set of horsemen," he wrote, "and great hunters."

PIONEERING THE OREGON TRAIL
A Wagon Road to the Pacific

In May 1843, nearly a thousand people gathered at Independence, Missouri, to launch what was known as the Great Migration. They hoped to become the first party of settlers to reach Oregon in wagons, which were essential for families traveling with their belongings. Under a treaty of joint occupation, the United States and Great Britain were competing for control of Oregon, which then embraced the present states of Oregon, Washington, and Idaho. Americans could now travel there on the Oregon Trail, but that wagon road was rough and those who set out on it in 1843 were inexperienced. When editor Horace Greeley learned of their venture, he declared, "The emigration of more than a thousand persons in one body to Oregon wears the aspect of insanity."

One man who thought otherwise and aided the emigrants was Marcus Whitman, who had left his medical practice in New York in 1835 to become a Presbyterian missionary to Indians in Oregon. At that time, wagons followed the Oregon Trail only as far as the Rockies and were being used to haul goods to and from the trappers' rendezvous. Whitman joined one such caravan that summer to investigate prospects for a mission and ended up using

CROSSING OREGON Emigrants (left) pass Mount Hood on the Barlow Road, a branch of the Oregon Trail that allowed settlers to reach the Willamette Valley without traveling down the Columbia River, as pioneers did in 1843. That Great Migration was the first of many treks to Oregon by families who packed their belongings in wagons (above).

his surgical skills to extract an arrowhead from the back of mountain man Jim Bridger. Whitman expressed surprise that Bridger's old battle wound was not infected, to which he replied, "In the mountains, Doctor, meat don't spoil." Before returning east, Whitman met with Nez Perce Indians who seemed receptive to Christianity. In 1836, he again went west by wagon, this time with his bride, Narcissa, the Reverend Henry Spalding, and Spalding's wife, Eliza. Eliza and Narcissa were the first American women to travel overland to Oregon, which they reached with their husbands on horseback after abandoning their wagon. The Spaldings founded a mission among the Nez Perce, and the Whitmans established one among the Cayuse.

After journeying east in 1842 to urge his superiors not to close those struggling missions, Whitman

ANTAGONISTS Missionaries Narcissa and Marcus Whitman (below) ran afoul of Chief Tomahas (above) and other Cayuse leaders.

joined the Great Migration and proved of great help to its members. He told them that they could reach Oregon in wagons on an extension of the trail that mountain men had pioneered from their rendezvous in 1840. He also warned that they would have to send work parties ahead to make rough stretches passable for their Oregon Emigrant Company, two-thirds of whom were women or children.

RISKS OF THE ROAD

The trail the emigrants followed took them up to the Platte River (known to Indians as the Nebraska) and westward along its banks for some 200 miles. Broad and level, the Platte River Valley offered a fine corridor for wagons, but its hazards included swarms of insects that could cause fevers and cloudy water

WHITMAN MISSION A covered wagon approaches the Whitman mission, located in eastern Washington's Walla Walla Valley. Founded in 1836, the mission later expanded to include several log buildings where children were housed and instructed as well as a corral and a gristmill. Marcus Whitman's efforts to encourage Americans who arrived by way of the Oregon Trail to settle in the area alarmed and antagonized some Cayuse Indians.

PIONEER Born in Ohio in 1830, Ezra Meeker went west on the Oregon Trail as a young man and later helped mark and preserve the historic road.

the company reach the Columbia, where many abandoned their wagons and traveled downriver in rafts to settle in the Willamette Valley.

Whitman's contribution to the Great Migration of 1843 would be overshadowed by his violent death four years later during a Cayuse uprising that also claimed the lives of his wife and others at their mission. He proved less successful at spreading his faith than at expanding his nation. Determined that Oregon become American territory "rather than an English colony," he wrote, "I was happy to have been the means of landing so large an emigration on the shores of the Columbia." ■

that could cause diarrhea or dysentery. Those who fell ill could ride in the wagons, but the pace was slow—10 or 15 miles a day—and many people walked, often at some distance from the vehicles to avoid the clouds of dust raised by their wheels and the plodding animals. When buffalo were sighted along the trail, men raced in pursuit with guns blazing, risking injury to themselves and others.

Turning up the North Platte River, the emigrants passed Chimney Rock and other lofty monuments before reaching Fort Laramie, a trading post later taken over by the Army. Supplies purchased there helped sustain families as they traversed rough terrain in what is now Wyoming and ascended the Sweetwater River to Independence Rock, on which one emigrant left this inscription: "The Oregon Co. arrived July 26, 1843." By summer's end, they had crossed South Pass and reached Fort Hall on the upper Snake River where travelers in parties bound for California left the Oregon Trail. The company's guide departed to lead a small party to California, and Whitman took his place. Thereafter, progress was slow as he oversaw efforts to improve the trail. Not until late that year did

DEMISE OF THE WHITMANS

Marcus Whitman served as a preacher and doctor to Cayuse Indians at a mission he and his wife, Narcissa, founded near the Columbia River in what later became Washington Territory. They made it clear to the Cayuse that accepting Christianity meant rejecting cherished tribal traditions—a sacrifice many refused to make. Tribal opposition increased as Americans settled in the area and the Whitmans began boarding and teaching white children. "The poor Indians are amazed at the overwhelming numbers of Americans coming into the country," Narcissa wrote in early 1847.

Later that year, measles spread from the mission school to Cayuse villages. Marcus tried to help all those who fell ill, but the mortality rate was much higher among his Indian patients. Accused of using bad medicine to kill them, he died that November at the mission along with Narcissa and several others in an attack led by Tomahas and another chief who had lost a child to measles. They and three other accused assailants were convicted and executed in 1850. Five years later, the Cayuse were pressured into ceding most of their land and ended up on a reservation in what is now Oregon.

FATAL ASSAULT A Cayuse warrior menaces an unwary Marcus Whitman and his horrified wife in this fanciful depiction of the attack.

EXPLORATION AND INSURRECTION

John Frémont and Kit Carson in California

L t. John C. Frémont of the U.S. Corps of Topographical Engineers was traveling up the Missouri River by steamboat in May 1842 to launch his first western expedition when he met a fellow passenger whose name and fame would long be linked to his—Christopher "Kit" Carson. At 32, Carson was three years older than Frémont and had spent half his life scouring the West since taking to the Santa Fe Trail in 1826 to escape his dreary apprenticeship to a saddler in Missouri, who offered a paltry reward of one penny "to any person who will bring back the said boy." Carson was "quiet and unassuming," recalled Frémont, with a "clear steady blue eye and frank speech and address." Hired as a guide for $100 a month, he proved invaluable not just to Frémont but to the nation their explorations helped expand.

John C. Frémont

That summer, Frémont surveyed the Oregon Trail as far as South Pass with Carson as his guide and climbed one of the highest mountains in the Rockies—known subsequently as Frémont Peak—atop which he planted an American flag. In 1843, he recruited Carson and other experienced mountain men for his second expedition, which took them to the Columbia River then down along the western rim of the Great Basin into Mexican territory that winter. Frémont had no orders to cross the border, but he often went his own way, much to the annoyance of his superiors. In early 1844, having reached Pyramid Lake just east of the Sierra Nevada, he decided to cross those mountains and enter California with his party. His stated reasons for doing so were to obtain fresh horses there and search for the Buenaventura River that supposedly cut through the mountains to the Pacific—a legendary waterway that Jedediah Smith and others who explored California prior to Frémont had concluded did not exist.

Kit Carson

Another likely motive for Frémont's venture was a desire to further his nation's territorial ambitions, which now included California. Several hundred Americans had arrived there overland in recent years, mainly

AT HIS PEAK On his first expedition in 1842, Frémont raises an American flag atop the peak later named for him. Kit Carson served as a guide on this venture to the Rockies and Frémont's next two expeditions, when he entered Mexican California.

that outpost, Swiss-born John Sutter, had sworn allegiance to Mexico but welcomed Americans, hoping that they would become faithful members of his colony. Instead, they would soon raise their own flag in California, with Frémont's blessing.

Frémont risked disaster by crossing the snowbound Sierra in midwinter, but his party persevered with the help of Carson and other men accustomed to hardship. "We were nearly out of provisions," Carson recalled, "but we had to cross the mountains, let the consequences be what they may." After butchering many of their horses and mules to avert starvation, they reached Sutter's Fort in March and purchased replacements. Not until they departed did Sutter notify Mexican officials of their arrival, allowing them to proceed unhindered. The only Mexicans they met as they left California were traders who had been attacked by Indians in the Mojave Desert. Carson and a companion then tracked down the culprits, reclaimed horses stolen by them—and brought back two bloody Indian scalps. "To me such butchery is disgusting," wrote the expedition's German-born cartographer, Charles Preuss, "but Frémont is in high spirits. I believe he would exchange all observations for a scalp taken by his own hand." What most impressed Frémont, though, was that Carson had risked his own hide to avenge wrongs done to strangers.

Frémont's lively account of his second expedition—edited and enhanced by his gifted young wife, Jessie Benton Frémont, daughter of Missouri senator Thomas Hart Benton—extolled Kit Carson and drew attention to California at a time when President James Polk was intent on acquiring it. Frémont returned to California with his third expedition in 1845, knowing that the United States would soon annex Texas, making war with Mexico likely. His well-armed party of 60,

MAPPING THE FRONTIER Frémont used the telescope at top while surveying the West and produced this detailed map of the region with the help of cartographer Charles Preuss. Not an explorer by nature, Preuss became lost in California in March 1844 and subsisted on wild onions, nuts, and insects before summoning his "last ounce of strength" and finding his way to Frémont's camp.

by following the Humboldt River across the Great Basin to the Sierra Nevada. Most who overcame that steep barrier then skirted another obstacle—a law that only those who became Mexican citizens could obtain land—by settling in the Sacramento Valley near Sutter's Fort. The owner of

SHASTA CAMP Frémont stopped here below Mount Shasta on his way to Oregon in 1846 shortly before he learned that war with Mexico was imminent, reversed course, and took charge of the Bear Flag Revolt.

including Carson and other marksmen, "constituted a formidable nucleus for frontier warfare," wrote Frémont. In March 1846, after Mexican authorities in Monterey, California's capital, ordered him to withdraw, he defied them by building a fort atop nearby Gavilan Peak. "If we are hemmed in and assaulted," Frémont vowed in writing, "we will die every man of us, under the Flag of our country." Warned that hostilities might endanger American residents in California, he backed down and headed toward Oregon, only to reverse course in May when a messenger told him that war with Mexico was imminent. Frémont now had a grand opportunity to make "the Pacific Ocean the western boundary of the United States."

Emboldened by his return, Americans who had settled illegally in California and feared being evicted rebelled against Mexico and raised their own Bear Flag. "Some were good men," one American in California said of those Bear Flag rebels, "and some about as rough specimens of humanity as it would be possible to find anywhere." Frémont joined their cause and took charge of captives they were holding, including Mariano Vallejo, former commandant of Mexican California, who was sympathetic to Americans but was imprisoned at Sutter's Fort. Frémont's men later seized and killed three Mexican messengers in apparent retaliation for the death of two Bear Flag rebels, whose bodies had reportedly been mutilated. By one account, Carson took part in the execution of those Mexican captives after being told by Frémont that he had "no room for prisoners."

Whether or not they were responsible for those deaths, Frémont and Carson furthered a rebellion that alienated Californios—the territory's Mexican residents—and set them at odds with U.S. forces who later occupied their country. Critics questioned whether Frémont had authority to join the Bear Flag Revolt and acted properly. Many Americans admired him for seizing the initiative in California, however, and esteemed Kit Carson for helping him reach that promised land and lay claim to it. ∎

RAISING THE BEAR FLAG

In June 1846, after seizing Sonoma, a Mexican frontier garrison above San Francisco Bay, William Todd—a nephew of Mary Todd Lincoln—and other Americans fashioned a Bear Flag for their fledgling Republic of California, as described in this firsthand account by George "Babe" Williams:

Captain Frémont had told us, if we succeeded in taking the fort, to lower the Mexican flag and raise some sort of flag of our own; but not to use the American emblem. As I have stated, there was intense excitement and everything done that day was done hurriedly . . . I held the cloth while William Todd, with a piece of red chalk, drew a star on the upper left hand corner. While this was being done, some one, probably Henry Ford, suggested that we add to the design a grizzly bear, which was promptly done by Mr. Todd,—the bear shown standing on his hind feet in a threatening position . . . Then a red woolen shirt, somewhat faded, was torn into strips, and a wide border sewn . . . This flag, so hurriedly made, was promptly placed on the staff from which we had taken the Mexican banner . . . I have no doubt that within the next ten days there were a dozen Bear Flags made and floated.

FLAG-RAISING California rebels raise a Bear Flag similar to the one above, adorned with a lone star like the Texas flag. Although pictured here in uniforms, the rebels were a motley, unkempt bunch that their captive Mariano Vallejo likened to "white Indians."

ANNEXING TEXAS
Tyler, Polk, and the Road to War

The Mexican War originated in a bitter border dispute between Texas and Mexico. Texans were expansive by nature, and after winning independence in 1836 they sought to enlarge their country by setting aside its historical southern boundary since Spanish times—the Nueces River—in favor of the Rio Grande, which originates in the Rockies and enters the Gulf of Mexico 100 miles below the Nueces. Mexico would not yield everything north and east of the Rio Grande without a fight. That would mean surrendering Santa Fe and other towns in New Mexico as well as Mexican settlements such as Laredo on the north bank of the lower Rio Grande. Fighting erupted along the disputed border after Texas president Mirabeau Lamar sent an ill-fated expedition in 1841 to New Mexico, where several Texans were executed as spies or died in captivity.

LONE STAR **The Texas state flag bears the lone star of the old Texas Republic.**

In 1844, President John Tyler of Virginia—a lame duck derided as "His Accidency" after succeeding the deceased William Henry Harrison—secured an annexation treaty with Texas. Although the Senate rejected it, the issue dominated that year's presidential campaign. The Whig nominee, Senator Henry Clay of Kentucky, warned that annexing Texas would lead to war with Mexico. His opponent, Democrat James Polk of Tennessee, favored annexation—a popular stand in the South, where admitting Texas as a slave state was seen as balancing the anticipated admission of free states such as Wisconsin and Iowa. Many in the North and West also wanted to admit Texas because expanding the nation mattered more to them than limiting slavery.

In 1845, Polk became president and annexed Texas. Mexico threatened war, and negotiations proved fruitless. In January 1846, Polk enforced the boundary claimed by Texas by ordering U.S. troops led by Brig. Gen. Zachary Taylor to cross the Nueces River and advance to the Rio Grande. In late April, they clashed with Mexican troops asserting their nation's historical claim to land between the Nueces and Rio Grande. On May 11, Polk asked Congress to declare war, using strong words that loyal Mexicans and even some patriotic Americans would dispute: "Mexico has passed the boundary of the United States, has invaded our territory and shed American blood upon the American soil." ∎

WAR MAP **Published in New York in 1847, this map of the United States of Mexico (los Estados Unidos de Méjico) shows the Rio Grande as the international boundary claimed by the United States of America. Also delineated here are invasion routes followed by American commanders in 1846, including Zachary Taylor's path from the Nueces River to the Rio Grande, which he crossed soon after the U.S. declared war on Mexico in May.**

COMMANDER IN CHIEF An ardent American expansionist, President James Polk entered the Mexican War to secure the Rio Grande boundary with Mexico, as claimed by Texas, and went on to annex a broad swath of Mexican territory extending westward to California.

CHAPTER TWO
1846–1861
THE MEXICAN
WAR
★ AND THE ★
GOLD RUSH

GOLD DIGGINGS A woman holding a picnic basket stands with three prospectors at work during the California gold rush, one of the greatest mass migrations in American history.

THE MEXICAN WAR AND THE GOLD RUSH

orn in Andover, Massachusetts, in 1818, Isaac Stevens was a seventh-generation New Englander of Puritan ancestry. He had no inkling when he left Andover and entered the U.S. Military Academy that his future lay in the West. Upon graduating first in his class as an Army engineer, he hoped to be assigned to construct fortifications in Boston Harbor. "I wish to be near home," he wrote. Yet powerful historical forces would propel him and other ambitious Easterners westward, beginning with the outbreak of the Mexican War in 1846. That conflict drew military officers like Stevens into sprawling campaigns beyond the Rio Grande and brought the

nation vast new territories in the Southwest to add to its recent acquisition of Oregon.

After the war, Stevens surveyed a promising route for a transcontinental railroad to the Pacific Northwest—two decades before tracks would be laid across the northern

Plains—and then served as the first governor of Washington Territory, carved out of Oregon. An uncompromising man who antagonized various Indian tribes to which he assigned reservations as well as a number of white settlers in Washington, he was better suited for military command than civilian

Battle of Buena Vista

Isaac Stevens

1846 The Mexican War begins, and U.S. troops occupy New Mexico, California, and other Mexican territory.

1853 Washington Territory organized with Isaac Stevens as its first governor. Gadsden Purchase finalizes the border between the U.S. and Mexico.

1848 Gold is discovered at Sutter's Mill in California. The Mexican War ends with the Treaty of Guadalupe Hidalgo, which transfers California and much of northern Mexico to the United States.

1850 California enters the Union as a free state under the Compromise of 1850, which allows settlers in other territories acquired from Mexico to decide whether to permit or prohibit slavery.

1854 Congress passes the Kansas-Nebraska Act, which leads to conflict over whether to allow slavery in Kansas Territory.

rule. In 1861, an irrepressible conflict between North and South over whether to allow slavery in the nation's western territories thrust him back into uniform. General Stevens died in battle a year later, leading Union troops with an American flag in hand that he retrieved from a color-bearer shot down by opposing Confederates. For him and others whose careers spanned the tumultuous years between the Mexican War and the Civil War, the great issue to be decided was whether a country that expanded westward so suddenly and dramatically could hold together under the Stars and Stripes and remain one nation indivisible.

Some saw that crisis coming when the first battles were fought between American and Mexican troops along the disputed Texas border in May 1846. Three months later, Pennsylvania representative David Wilmot introduced legislation in Congress prohibiting slavery in any territory acquired from Mexico as a result of the war. By then, U.S. forces had occupied New Mexico and California. Among those who voted in favor of the Wilmot Proviso, which did not become law, was Congressman Abraham Lincoln of Illinois, an outspoken critic of the war. Lincoln accused President James Polk of instigating the conflict by sending U.S. troops into an area above the Rio Grande that belonged rightfully to Mexico. "I more than suspect that he is deeply

> "WE GO WESTWARD
> AS INTO THE
> FUTURE,
> WITH A SPIRIT
> OF ENTERPRISE
> AND ADVENTURE."
> —HENRY DAVID THOREAU

conscious of being in the wrong," Lincoln said of Polk, "that he feels the blood of this war, like the blood of Abel, is crying to Heaven against him." Lincoln's stance was unpopular back home. Many people there and in the country at large were glad to see their nation expand at Mexico's expense and hailed the peace treaty in 1848, which confirmed America's territorial gains, later supplemented by the Gadsden Purchase in 1853.

GOING FOR GOLD

It was often said that to the victors go the spoils. Never was that truer than in California, where gold was discovered in January 1848, shortly before Mexico acknowledged defeat and ceded that area to the United States. The ensuing gold rush swelled the population of California more than tenfold within two years and made it the first American territory in the Far West to achieve statehood. By the early 1850s, more than $100 million in gold had been extracted there, and merchants across the country had reaped handsome profits by supplying tens of thousands of prospectors who journeyed overland to California or transporting many others to San Francisco by sea.

That craze eventually subsided, but traffic on western trails remained brisk as Mormons flocked to their promised land in Utah and settlers headed for Oregon and Washington. In the late 1850s, new gold and silver rushes helped populate

Telegraph, 1860

1857 President James Buchanan sends U.S. troops to occupy Utah Territory and remove Mormon leader Brigham Young as governor there.

1859 Prospectors rush to Colorado and Nevada in search of gold and silver, leading to the organization of those two territories in 1861.

1861 Completion of the transcontinental telegraph renders the Pony Express obsolete and links the North to the loyal western states of California and Oregon as the Civil War unfolds.

1858 The Overland Mail Company launches stagecoach service between Missouri and California. Texas Rangers clash with Comanches along the border of Texas and Indian Territory.

Overland Mail Company coach

1860 Paiutes clash with prospectors and other settlers near Pyramid Lake in Nevada, disrupting service on the newly formed Pony Express.

Colorado and Nevada, which were soon organized as territories. Faster means of transportation and communication bridged the gap between far-flung settlements. Hundreds of steamboats plied the Mississippi and Missouri Rivers, and stagecoaches began carrying passengers and mail across the West in a matter of weeks on routes that lumbering wagons took months to traverse. In 1860, the fledgling Pony Express carried dispatches between Missouri and California in just ten days—only to suspend operations a year later when the transcontinental telegraph was completed and flashed messages across the country instantaneously.

Along with those dramatic advances came new hazards, including conflicts with Indians that erupted as prospectors, settlers, and soldiers intruded on tribal territory. A larger struggle loomed when fighting erupted between proslavery and antislavery forces in Kansas in the mid-1850s. By 1860, when Lincoln was elected president promising to preserve the West as "Free Soil," unspoiled by slavery, that issue had become the wedge that split the Union. The first message sent by wire across the continent in 1861 was addressed to Lincoln several months after the Civil War began. Speaking on behalf of the people of California, the state's chief justice, Stephen Field, expressed "their loyalty to the Union and their determination to stand by its government in this its hour of crisis." ∎

ABANDONED SHIP A print portraying San Francisco in 1850 shows the Niantic Hotel, built atop the remains of the ship *Niantic*. The ship was abandoned after it arrived from Panama with forty-niners aboard and its officers and crew left to join the gold rush.

THE WEST IN 1861 This map shows western states and territories when the Civil War began and the border with Mexico that resulted from the treaty ending the Mexican War (1848) and the Gadsden Purchase (1853). With the exception of ocean or river ports or railroad terminuses such as St. Joseph, Missouri, the settlements indicated here were reached by trails. The Oregon, Mormon, and Pony Express Trails converged in Nebraska Territory along a path later followed by the Union Pacific Railroad.

Seattle

Columbia River

45°

OREGON

40°

Sacramento River

Pyramid Lake

Rich Bar
Gold Hill
Virginia City
Carson City
Sutter's Mill

San Francisco

Sacramento

NEVADA TERR.

35°

CALIFORNIA

Los Angeles

San Diego

PACIFIC OCEAN

30°

— California Trail   — Oregon Trail
— Gila River route   — Pony Express
— Mormon Trail   — Santa Fe Trail
● Battle   ○ City
1861 borders shown

0   200 Miles

25°

120°

115°

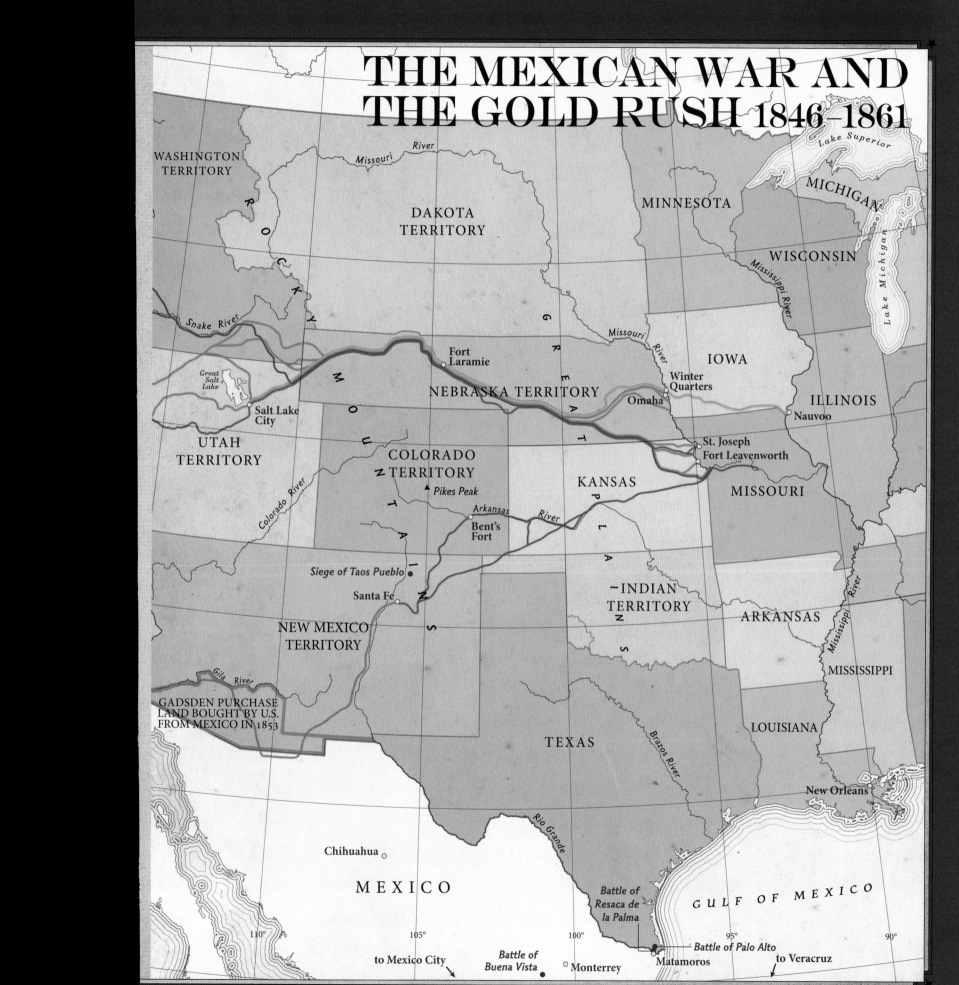

THE MEXICAN WAR AND THE GOLD RUSH 1846–1861

WASHINGTON
TERRITORY

Lake Superior

MICHIGAN

Missouri River

DAKOTA
TERRITORY

MINNESOTA

WISCONSIN

Mississippi River

Lake Michigan

ROCKY

Snake River

G R E A T

Missouri River

IOWA

Fort
Laramie

*Great
Salt
Lake*

M
O
U
N
T
A
I
N
S

NEBRASKA TERRITORY

Winter
Quarters

Omaha

ILLINOIS

Nauvoo

Salt Lake
City

UTAH
TERRITORY

COLORADO
TERRITORY

▲ *Pikes Peak*

St. Joseph
Fort Leavenworth

KANSAS

P L A I N S

MISSOURI

Colorado River

Arkansas   *River*

Bent's
Fort

Siege of Taos Pueblo •

Santa Fe

NEW MEXICO
TERRITORY

–INDIAN
TERRITORY

ARKANSAS

Mississippi River

MISSISSIPPI

Gila River

GADSDEN PURCHASE
LAND BOUGHT BY U.S.
FROM MEXICO IN 1853

LOUISIANA

TEXAS

Brazos River

New Orleans

Rio Grande

Chihuahua ○

MEXICO

Battle of
Resaca de
la Palma

GULF OF MEXICO

110°

105°

to Mexico City

Battle of
Buena Vista

100°

○ Monterrey

Matamoros

95°

Battle of Palo Alto

to Veracruz

90°

BUENA VISTA Advancing in the foreground at left under their flag, American troops march into battle at Buena Vista on February 23, 1847. Their commander, Maj. Gen. Zachary Taylor (top), known as Old Rough and Ready, burnished his reputation by repelling numerically superior Mexican forces at Buena Vista and succeeded James Polk as president in 1849.

THE INVASION OF MEXICO

Waging War for Western Territory

he Mexican War originated along the Texas border, but President James Polk was looking far beyond the Lone Star State. He intended to annex New Mexico, California, and other Mexican territory. That could not be achieved simply by occupying the disputed zone between the Nueces River and the Rio Grande where the fighting began. On May 18, 1846, after winning two battles against Mexican forces north of the Rio Grande at Palo Alto and Resaca de la Palma, Zachary Taylor led U.S. troops across that river and occupied Matamoros. An invasion was under way that would culminate at Mexico City and force authorities there to cede a large portion of their country to the United States.

The U.S. Army had fewer than 6,000 regular troops when the war began. Most of the soldiers who invaded Mexico were volunteers. More than 10,000 raw recruits poured into Taylor's camp below the Rio Grande within a few months. Many of them disdained Mexicans, and some assaulted civilians in and around Matamoros. Lt. George Meade, who would later command Union troops at the Battle of Gettysburg, stated in a letter he sent home that volunteers had "killed five or six innocent people walking in the streets, for no other object than their own amusement." Unruly recruits were stealing "the cattle and corn of the poor farmers," he added, "and in fact act more like a body of hostile Indians than civilized whites." Some Mexicans responded to the invasion by waging guerrilla warfare against the American soldiers and met with fierce reprisals by Texas Rangers, organized in 1835 when Texas rebelled against Mexico. They were among Taylor's toughest troops and became known to Mexicans as *"los diablos Tejanos"* (Texas devils).

Moving inland from Matamoros, Taylor seized Monterrey in September 1846 and went on to wage a hard-fought battle with some 15,000 Mexican soldiers led by Santa Anna at Buena Vista the following February. Although outnumbered more than three to one, the Americans held their ground and forced Santa Anna to withdraw, thanks in part to heroic efforts by the Mississippi Rifles, a regiment led by Col. Jefferson Davis, the future Confederate president. By the time Taylor won the Battle of Buena Vista, Polk had already assigned another commander, Maj. Gen. Winfield Scott, to take charge of the war by landing an army at Veracruz on the Gulf of Mexico and advancing on Mexico City. Meanwhile, other American forces were pursuing the objective that mattered most to the president by bringing New Mexico and California under the Stars and Stripes. ■

SEIZING THE SOUTHWEST
The Occupation of New Mexico

ew American officers who served in the Mexican War were asked to do more with less than 51-year-old Brig. Gen. Stephen Watts Kearny. In May 1846, he took charge of what was grandly called the Army of the West but consisted of only about 1,650 men, most of them volunteers without military experience. After drilling those recruits for a few weeks at Fort Leavenworth on Missouri's western frontier, Kearny was expected to march them down the Santa Fe Trail, take possession of New Mexico, establish a new government there, and then continue across the desert to support U.S. naval forces occupying California—an arduous odyssey of some 2,000 miles.

That was a tall task for Kearny's small army, but President Polk and others in high places did not expect much resistance to the American occupation of New Mexico and California. Both those territories had come close to breaking away from Mexico around the same time that Texas won independence. And both had commercial ties to the United States, forged by Santa Fe traders in New Mexico and by coastal merchants in California who purchased cattle hides from Mexican ranchers and shipped them east to be processed into leather. Senator Benton of Missouri expressed the hope of many in Washington that Mexicans in American-occupied territory "would remain quiet and continue trading with us as usual, upon which condition they shall be protected in all their rights and be treated as friends." His words were reminiscent of Thomas Jefferson's statement that Americans would respect the rights of Indians who

OCCUPYING SANTA FE Standing below an American flag with a sword at his side, General Kearny takes possession of Santa Fe on August 18, 1846. A vivid portrait of him done around 1900 (opposite) was based on earlier paintings of Kearny, who died in 1848.

submitted to U.S. authority and be their "fathers and friends."

Kearny's campaign that summer seemingly fulfilled American hopes for a friendly takeover of the Southwest. Rather than confronting Mexican foes, Kearny's troops battled thirst, hunger, disease, and other natural hazards as they marched down the Santa Fe Trail. "It was by no means, an unusual occurrence for us," a volunteer wrote, "to kill in the morning, within a quarter mile of camp, twenty rattlesnakes . . . One Major awoke one morning with one of these reptiles coiled up against his leg, it having nestled there for warmth. He dared not stir until a servant came and removed the intruder." That major's "servant" was probably a slave. Some officers from Missouri and other slave-holding states brought such servants with them during the Mexican War, but common soldiers had to fend for themselves.

In late July, the Army of the West reached Bent's Fort on the Arkansas River, which then formed the boundary between the U.S. and Mexico east of the Rockies. Traders Charles and William Bent placed their fort at Kearny's disposal and told him what to expect when his forces entered New Mexico, where Charles resided. Other Santa Fe traders were awaiting Kearny at Bent's Fort with their wagons and goods and would follow his army into New Mexico, where they hoped to do business as usual. Among them was Samuel Magoffin of Missouri, accompanied by his bride, Susan, who on the night of July 30, her 19th birthday, suffered a miscarriage at the fort. "In a few short months I should have been a happy mother and made the heart of a

COLONEL DONIPHAN Before taking charge of the First Missouri Mounted Volunteers under Kearny, Alexander Doniphan proved his mettle as a militia commander in 1838 when he refused a reckless order to execute Joseph Smith and other Mormon leaders.

father glad," she wrote in her diary. A week later, she and her husband forded the shallow Arkansas River and crossed into Mexico with the traders' caravan. She found it hard to leave her "dear native land," but soon the foreign territory she was entering would belong to her country.

BEYOND SANTA FE Doniphan's Missourians ride past San Felipe Pueblo after departing Santa Fe for Chihuahua, where they planned to join Brig. Gen. John Wool's forces.

A BLOODLESS TAKEOVER

In Santa Fe, Governor Manuel Armijo had few regular troops to resist Kearny's army. Most were ill-equipped militiamen, including Pueblo Indians, many of whom had supported a rebellion in 1837 that Armijo suppressed. He concluded that his forces were no match for the American invaders and withdrew to Chihuahua in mid-August. That left the path to Santa Fe open for Kearny, who now faced a task that would

prove harder than occupying New Mexico—winning over its inhabitants. Instead of placing the occupied territory under military rule, he had orders to establish a civil government that would include Mexican officials who pledged allegiance to the United States. New Mexico would not officially be part of the U.S. until Mexico ceded it by treaty in 1848. Yet Kearny told the populace that "I absolve you from all allegiance to the Mexican government," and sought to legitimize American rule in this Catholic country by having a priest stand by while officials swore an oath to the U.S. "in the name of the Father, Son, and Holy Ghost." An American soldier who watched that ceremony thought those officials took that pledge "for fear of giving offense to our army."

Kearny remained in Santa Fe long enough to establish a

HISTORIC SHOT A rare Mexican War photo shows General Wool and his staff on horseback. By the time Doniphan's regiment reached Chihuahua, Wool had moved on.

Fe and continued west with 100 men and Carson as their guide. Not until they approached the Colorado River in late November did they learn that since Carson and his men left Los Angeles, Mexican insurgents there had attacked American troops. "I suppose we may expect a small chunk of hell when we get over there," wrote John Griffin, an Army surgeon with Kearny. In fact, there would be hell to pay in both California and New Mexico before those occupied territories were brought firmly under American control. ■

new law code spelling out the rights of New Mexicans. Like his superiors in Washington, he was confident that they would welcome or at least tolerate American rule and thought that a reduced force would be sufficient to secure New Mexico after he left for California with 300 U.S. dragoons (mounted infantry). A newly arrived regiment from Missouri commanded by Col. Sterling Price would remain in Santa Fe, but the volunteers who made up most of Kearny's army would depart in December under Col. Alexander Doniphan, a shrewd Missouri lawyer and former militia commander. Doniphan would lead those forces southward along the Rio Grande to Chihuahua, with the Magoffins and other American traders following safely behind. Along the way, his soldiers would win two battles against determined but poorly armed Mexican foes, whose heavy casualties proved sobering for American volunteers new to combat and its grim aftermath. The carnage "was such that no man could help but feel that war was an evil of the worst kind," wrote George Gibson of Missouri, "and one which should be avoided if possible."

Kearny departed Santa Fe on September 25, after appointing Charles Bent civil governor of New Mexico. On October 6, Kearny's men were startled by a small band of mountain men who approached yelling like Indians. They were led by Kit Carson, who was carrying military dispatches from California and informed Kearny that U.S. forces had taken possession there over the summer and had matters in hand. Anticipating no trouble, Kearny sent most of his dragoons back to Santa

BENT'S FORT

Faithfully reconstructed as a national historic site on the north bank of the Arkansas River in 1976, Bent's Fort was established in 1833 by traders Charles and William Bent and their partner, Ceran St. Vrain. Their outpost on the Santa Fe Trail hosted U.S. troops who invaded New Mexico in 1846. Its greatest impact, however, was on tribes that traded there, particularly the Cheyenne and Arapaho. Those two groups divided into northern and southern branches during this period, in part because Bent's Fort lured Southern Cheyennes and Arapahos and altered their way of life. William Bent's Cheyenne wife, Owl Woman, was a reassuring presence for those who visited the fort and traded buffalo hides for various goods, itemized by one witness as "red cloth, beads, tobacco, brass wire for bracelets, hoop iron for arrow points, butcher knives, small axes or tomahawks, vermilion, powder and bullets."

Such trade benefited Indians materially but also made them more dependent on white merchants and brought them into competition with white hunters. One Cheyenne chief who visited the fort complained that "whites have been amongst us, and destroyed our buffalo, antelope, and deer." George Bent, born at Bent's Fort to Owl Woman and her husband in 1843, later joined Cheyenne warriors in battle against Americans.

TRADING POST Consisting of two stories around a plaza, Bent's Fort hosted trader Samuel Magoffin and his wife, Susan, who noted in 1846 that it had "quite a number of boarders."

"The enemy continued to retreat for about a half mile when they rallied and came at us like devils with their lances."
—U.S. Army surgeon John Griffin, at San Pasqual

Battle of San Pasqual Mexican horsemen armed with lances clash with General Kearny's blue-coated dragoons at San Pasqual on December 6, 1846. Kearny claimed victory because his foes withdrew, but it was a costly battle for the Americans against Californios renowned for their equestrian skills. Observers likened them to centaurs because they seemed at one with their mounts.

TAOS PUEBLO This ancient village was the site of a fiery battle on February 4, 1847, between American troops and Pueblo warriors who rose up against Governor Charles Bent (inset), assassinated in Taos a few weeks earlier. Although Bent had a Mexican wife, many Mexicans and Pueblos in Taos resented him and the American forces who installed him as governor.

RESISTING THE OCCUPIERS

Clashes in California and New Mexico

Like New Mexico, California was occupied by American forces who initially encountered no resistance. Aided by Capt. John Frémont, who formed a battalion that included former Bear Flag rebels, Commodore John Stockton of the U.S. Navy took control of northern California in July 1846 and advanced down the coast. After occupying Los Angeles, he entrusted that town to Lt. Archibald Gillespie and men from Frémont's battalion. Residents disdained those unruly soldiers and resented Gillespie for serving as their judge and ruling arbitrarily. In September, they took up arms and forced the Americans out. By November, Mexican insurgents controlled most of southern California except for San Diego, which remained in Stockton's hands

When Brig. Gen. Stephen Watts Kearny arrived in California from New Mexico, he found the road to San Diego blocked by defiant Californios on horseback at San Pasqual. At dawn on December 6, Kearny's dragoons attacked those insurgents and were chasing after them when they turned on their pursuers with lances. Kearny lost 35 of his 100 men killed or wounded before driving off his foes, whom he judged "among the best horsemen in the world." After reaching San Diego, he

drilled marines from Stockton's fleet to fight as infantry and shatter cavalry attacks. "Let the enemy do the charging," he advised, "and your rifles will do the rest." On January 8, 1847, Stockton and Kearny's forces crossed the shallow San Gabriel River under fire and went on to rout opposing horsemen and retake Los Angeles, ending armed opposition to American rule in California.

In New Mexico, meanwhile, resistance was mounting to the American governor, Charles Bent. After foiling a plot in Santa Fe, Bent traveled to his hometown of Taos without a military escort and refused demands to release men from Taos Pueblo held in jail there. On January 19, 1847, Pueblos and Mexicans ran rampant, freeing the prisoners, killing the American sheriff and other officials, and attacking Bent at home as his family looked on. He "fell dead at our feet," his daughter recalled. Elsewhere, other Americans were slain before troops led by Col. Sterling Price advanced from Santa Fe, scattered Mexican insurgents, and stormed the church at Taos Pueblo, where defiant warriors were holed up. That attack on February 4 crushed the uprising but cost Price over 50 casualties and killed 150 men of Taos Pueblo, devastating one of the oldest communities in the West. ■

THE FRUITS OF VICTORY

Redrawing the Mexican-American Border

The decisive campaign of the Mexican War began in March 1847 when troops led by Maj. Gen. Winfield Scott seized Veracruz on the Gulf Coast and prepared to advance on Mexico City. President Polk sent diplomat Nicholas Trist to join Scott and press Mexican officials to accept a peace treaty confirming the Rio Grande as the southern boundary of Texas and ceding New Mexico and California to the United States, in exchange for which Trist could offer up to $20 million.

In September 1847, Scott's forces entered Mexico City in triumph and raised their flag over the capital. Trist conducted polite negotiations with Mexican authorities, and Polk concluded that he was too soft on them and recalled him. Worried that Polk might seek harsher terms and prolong the war, Trist ignored the order recalling him and secured the terms Polk originally requested, while lowering the U.S. offer to $15 million to make the deal more palatable for the president.

On February 2, 1848, at Guadalupe Hidalgo

on the outskirts of Mexico City, Trist joined Mexican officials in signing the treaty. "This must be a proud moment for you," one of them said to him, "no less proud for you than it is humiliating for us." Trist, who felt no pride in gaining territory through conquest, replied, "We are making *peace*, let that be our only thought." Polk was furious with Trist for disobeying his order but accepted the treaty, which was ratified by the Senate in March. Mexicans living in areas ceded to the U.S. in 1848—including the future states of New Mexico, Arizona, Utah, Nevada, and California—were granted U.S. citizenship if they so desired.

The Mexican-American boundary was finalized with the Gadsden Purchase in 1853 when the U.S. acquired nearly 30,000 square miles of territory between the Rio Grande and the lower Colorado River for $10 million. That sum combined with the amount paid to Mexico in 1848 was a small price for territories that turned out to be rich in minerals. The California gold rush alone repaid U.S. treaty expenditures several times over. ■

TRIUMPHAL ENTRY On September 14, 1847, Maj. Gen. Winfield Scott enters the grand plaza of Mexico City, over which an American flag waves in the distance. At lower left, a bystander picks up a cobblestone as if to hurl it at the Americans. Eager to avoid a prolonged occupation that would expose U.S. troops to attack, Scott backed the peace treaty that Nicholas Trist signed with Mexican officials at Guadalupe Hidalgo (top).

NEW FRONTIER The Gadsden Purchase in 1853 created the modern U.S.-Mexico border south of the 1848 border, shown here by a line running due west from the Rio Grande in southern New Mexico and then along the winding Gila River in present-day Arizona to the Colorado River. The Gadsden Purchase gave the United States possession of the fertile Mesilla Valley in southern New Mexico and level terrain for a railroad from Texas to southern California, which was not completed until the early 1880s.

GOLD COUNTRY Word that gold had been discovered at Sutter's Mill, shown below in the foreground, lured prospectors to the area and gave rise to the town of Coloma, pictured in the background. James Marshall drew the rough sketch at left, showing men completing work on the mill when he made the find in January 1848.

STRIKING GOLD

The Discovery at Sutter's Mill

J ohn Sutter was not seeking gold. His was hoping to profit by sawing timber in the foothills of the Sierra Nevada, west of his fort in California's Sacramento Valley. In 1847, he formed a partnership with James Marshall, a carpenter who had settled near Sutter's Fort a few years earlier and joined the Bear Flag Revolt. Marshall oversaw construction of a sawmill on the South Fork of the American River and employed Mormons who had come to California as soldiers during the Mexican War and completed their terms of service. On January 24, 1848, Marshall examined the newly dug tailrace that would carry water from the sawmill back to the river. "My eye was caught by something shining in the bottom of the ditch," he recalled. "I reached my hand down and picked it up; it made my heart thump, for I was sure it was gold."

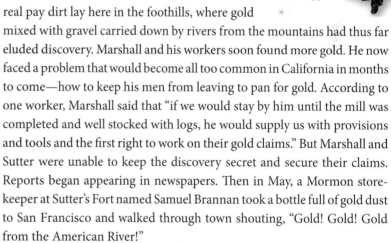

Gold nugget

Small amounts of gold had been found earlier near Mexican settlements on the coast, but the real pay dirt lay here in the foothills, where gold mixed with gravel carried down by rivers from the mountains had thus far eluded discovery. Marshall and his workers soon found more gold. He now faced a problem that would become all too common in California in months to come—how to keep his men from leaving to pan for gold. According to one worker, Marshall said that "if we would stay by him until the mill was completed and well stocked with logs, he would supply us with provisions and tools and the first right to work on their gold claims." But Marshall and Sutter were unable to keep the discovery secret and secure their claims. Reports began appearing in newspapers. Then in May, a Mormon storekeeper at Sutter's Fort named Samuel Brannan took a bottle full of gold dust to San Francisco and walked through town shouting, "Gold! Gold! Gold from the American River!"

The rush was on, and few could resist joining in. Many American troops in California deserted to look for gold, noted Lt. William T. Sherman, the future Civil War commander who was then serving as chief of staff to Col. Richard Mason, California's military governor. "Our servants also left us," Sherman wrote, "and nothing less than three hundred dollars a month would hire a man in California." Sutter's claim to land where the sawmill was located, based on a deal made with a local Indian tribe, was denied by Mason. Besieged by prospectors and abandoned by his workers, Sutter was ruined by gold fever, which would soon draw fortune hunters to California from around the world. ∎

THE INDEPENDENT GOLD HUNTER ON HIS WAY TO CALIFORNIA.

I NEITHER BORROW NOR LEND

MAD RUSH TO CALIFORNIA

Invasion by Land and by Sea

ithin two years of the discovery at Sutter's Mill, the gold rush brought nearly 100,000 prospectors to California. Among them were numerous foreigners, including Mexicans, Chileans, Peruvians, and others from South America as well as Europeans and Asians. A few hundred emigrants from China reached San Francisco in 1848, and within four years California's Chinese population would swell to more than 20,000. Some went seeking gold, but like other foreigners they faced stiff competition from American prospectors, so many of whom arrived by land and by sea in 1849 that they became known collectively as forty-niners.

Newspapers back East printed tantalizing stories in 1848 of the fortunes to be made in California, but many people remained skeptical until President James Polk delivered a message to Congress that December. Accounts of the "abundance of gold in California," he declared, "would scarcely command belief were they not corroborated by authentic reports of officers in the public service." Among them was Col. Richard Mason, who toured the diggings and sent 230 ounces of gold to Polk, assuring him that there was more gold in California "than will pay the cost of the war with Mexico a hundred times over."

Spurred by Polk's message, thousands of forty-niners on the East Coast set out for California by sea. Far from being rugged individualists who sought only their own success, many who made that voyage formed companies and shared with their fellow members both the expenses of the venture and any profits they made

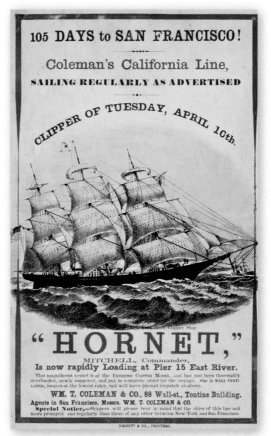

RAPID TRANSIT Before the swift clipper *Hornet*, above, appeared in 1851, most ships took from four to six months to reach California from the East Coast. Overland journeys there could take just as long and, like the ocean voyages, were often made by men who banded together rather than by the "independent gold seeker" satirized opposite.

in the goldfields. One such company organized in New York consisted of 76 members of the Methodist Episcopal Church, who purchased their own ship after each man invested $300, receiving in return "an equal interest in the ship, mining implements and eighteen months' provisions."

They embarked for California in June 1849, with 50 Bibles and no alcohol on board. Before the year ended, some 750 ships left ports on the Atlantic or Gulf Coast for California, most of them packed with prospectors. Other ships carried fortune hunters to Panama, where they journeyed across the isthmus to the Pacific and embarked for California. That journey might take only a few months, compared with several months for the voyage around Cape Horn, but it exposed travelers to deadly tropical diseases.

Most of the forty-niners who lived west of the Appalachians traveled overland to California. Some went out on the Santa Fe Trail and continued along the Gila River route that American troops had followed to California in 1846. But the majority took the Oregon Trail to Fort Hall and then followed the California Trail along the Humboldt River to one of several passes through the Sierra Nevada. Whichever path they followed, few parties reached California overland in 1849 without loss of life. Cholera, which spread quickly in camps with poor sanitation, took a steep toll among travelers on the trails that summer. Some parties were accompanied by physicians, but they could do little to combat the disease and often succumbed themselves. "Our company doctor has got the cholera very bad," wrote one forty-niner. "He is out of his head this evening and will probably die before morning."

ADOLPH SUTRO'S LEGACY
1830–1898

When Adolph Sutro arrived in San Francisco by ship in 1850, it was a ramshackle, crime-ridden boomtown of some 30,000 people, many of them transients. When he died there in 1898, it was the nation's ninth largest city, with more than 300,000 inhabitants, and a much nicer place to live, thanks in part to civic improvements he made as a landowner and builder and the city's mayor.

Sutro was one of a number of German Jews who came to San Francisco during the gold rush and flourished there, including merchants Levi Strauss—who won fame and fortune by marketing blue jeans—and August Helbing, who hired young Sutro to guard his store at night. Slashed on the cheek by a thief, he covered the scar with fashionable muttonchop whiskers. Sutro went on to make San Francisco a more attractive locale for respectable citizens than for robbers, using profits he reaped by excavating a deep tunnel in Virginia City, Nevada, that provided drainage and ventilation for miners extracting silver there. He built the monumental Sutro Baths in San Francisco, reconstructed the Cliff House nearby, and created a public park overlooking the Pacific. After winning election as mayor in 1894, he graced the city by planting tens of thousands of trees. San Francisco's phenomenal growth led him to predict that the West Coast would one day be "capable of supporting 30,000,000 people and support them well."

MASTER BUILDER Adolph Sutro had so many talents, interests, and accomplishments that Mark Twain said part of him was "sufficient equipment for an average man."

Many gold seekers overloaded their carts and wagons, and the trails were littered with discarded equipment and the bloated bodies of oxen and other draft animals that collapsed of exhaustion, hunger, or thirst. Despite such travails, more than 40,000 American prospectors reached California overland by late 1849.

COOPERATION AND CONFLICT

Partners fared better than loners in the goldfields. Even those who arrived on their own rather than in companies often formed partnerships with one or more other prospectors. Most individuals had basic equipment such as picks, shovels, and pans for separating gold from gravel, but partners could better afford more elaborate and efficient devices for extracting gold. Some of it lay near the surface along rivers, but men often had to dig deep in dry streambeds or gulches to find ore and formed teams for that purpose. Men also banded together to build dams and expose riverbeds for mining, divert water into sluice boxes that trapped gold, or construct flumes to provide those at dry diggings with the water they needed to process their pay dirt. In the early 1850s, prospector Edward Matteson pioneered hydraulic mining in California by fitting a nozzle to a hose designed by one of his partners and washing away hillsides to expose ore. (Hydraulic mining was later banned in California because it clogged rivers with sediment and caused flooding.)

Partnerships between miners were not just more productive but more secure than individual efforts, which left men susceptible to robbers and claim jumpers, who could take possession if a miner was away from the spot he claimed for any length of time.

Cooperation among forty-niners did not lessen conflict between them and foreigners. Among the Mexican prospectors in California were many veteran miners who were envied and resented by less-skilled American fortune hunters. In 1850, California imposed a tax of $20 a month on foreign miners. Some left because they could not afford that tax. Others departed because they were scorned and harassed. Some of the harshest treatment was directed at people who were not foreigners but natives of the country—California Indians, often relegated to scrounging for gold in tailings that forty-niners had already sifted through. Some prospectors considered all Indians hostile and attacked them. "When you are in a country where you know he is your enemy," one forty-niner said of the wild Indian of his nightmares, "why not cut him down as he most surely will you?" ■

NEWS AND VIEWS Below, an Easterner reads of the gold rush near a poster offering passage to San Francisco in an 1850 painting by William Sidney Mount entitled "California News." The frenzy to reach California inspired the cartoon at right, featuring real or fanciful vessels, including airships like the one in the upper left, which were being developed then but could not carry passengers across the continent.

THE WAY THEY GO TO CALIFORNIA.

LIFE IN THE MINING CAMPS
The Pleasures and Perils of Prospecting

Mining camps in the early days of the gold rush often consisted of nothing more than a few tents or shacks located near a river or gulch where prospectors staked their claims. At goldfields rich enough to attract scores of fortune hunters, mining towns emerged, offering men such conveniences as stores, saloons, hotels, and boardinghouses for those who were weary of camping out. Hastily constructed, those settlements seldom lasted long once the gold was exhausted. Louise Clappe, who arrived in California with her physician husband in 1849 and wrote under the pseudonym "Dame Shirley," described the town of Rich Bar, located on a fork of the Feather River, as consisting of a single street "thickly planted with about forty tenements." The residences varied in elegance from the "palatial splendor" of the Empire Hotel to a miner's hut "formed of pine boughs and covered with old calico shirts."

Most prospectors worked from dawn to dusk except on Sundays, which was often a day of rest or recreation for those not inclined to worship. Leonard Kip, a lawyer from Albany, New York, who tried his hand at mining but was more of an observer of the gold rush than a participant, pictured the scene at mining camps when the workday came to an end and men laid down their tools: "Leaving their picks in the holes, they carefully bring back the pans, for the wash bowl is a valuable article, serving more uses than one . . . It is no uncommon thing to see the same pan used for washing gold, washing clothes, mixing flour cakes, and feeding the mule. The camp fires are lighted, supper prepared, and then a long evening is ahead." Few miners read books by candlelight, he added, for candles were "a dollar apiece" and used sparingly, but many prospectors gathered around fires and sang songs, which often harked back nostalgically to "the home which all have left behind them."

Evenings were also times for revelry in mining towns, where liquor flowed freely, gambling was rampant, and fights

GLITTERING PROSPECTS Miners use various techniques—including panning for gold and funneling water through a sluice box called a Long Tom to separate gold from gravel—in this illustration showing an emerging mining town in the background. For many men, joining the gold rush was the adventure of a lifetime. Like a soldier posing with weapons in hand, the young miner pictured opposite holds the tools of his trade.

Mining equipment

MINER AT HOME Portrayed in 1853, William Peck sits beside a mining pan in his cabin at Rough and Ready, a short-lived gold rush hamlet near the long-lasting town of Nevada City, pictured below in 1852. Mining pans could be used for domestic tasks, but shovels and pickaxes were strictly for digging.

were frequent. There were no police, but serious offenses seldom went unpunished. In one case Kip described, a thief who was spotted entering a miner's tent was chased down, hauled before a hastily assembled jury, and condemned to receive a "hundred lashes, have his head shaved, and his ears cut off, and be drummed out of the mines; a sentence which was carried out on the spot."

Forty-niners were at far less risk of being robbed or shot than of being injured at work or felled by cholera or other diseases. The perils of prospecting were often greater than its rewards and led some disillusioned fortune hunters to return home. Others remained in California and took up occupations that were less hazardous and brought a steady income that might allow them to raise a family—if they were fortunate enough to find a wife in a land where females were few and far between.

WOMEN IN A MAN'S WORLD

According to the census of 1850, men outnumbered women in California more than ten to one. But the ratio of men to women was far higher in the mining districts. Many of the women counted in that census (which excluded Indians) were Mexican Americans and had little contact with the forty-niners. Life in this ultramasculine society could be disorienting and annoying for women, but it also presented them with opportunities. Some arrived with their husbands and served as their business partners, minding stores or working alongside them in the goldfields. Other women pursued their own trades by providing services such as cooking or laundering that were more expensive and profitable in California than back East. Prostitution was common enough in mining towns, but it was a far less rewarding occupation for women than running a laundry or operating a boarding house, where rents ranged from five to ten dollars a day. Single women in such positions often received marriage proposals from lonely miners but could afford to be choosy when seeking a mate.

Few men or women lived easy lives in gold rush California, no matter how much they profited from their efforts. When Dame Shirley arrived in the mining town of Rich Bar and checked in at the Empire Hotel, she found the wife of the proprietor "cooking supper for some half a dozen people" while her two-week-old baby kicked and screamed in a cradle beside her. Another woman in town had assisted her during childbirth, but soon after the baby arrived that helper "was taken seriously ill, and was obliged to return to her own cabin, leaving the poor exhausted mother entirely alone! Her husband lay seriously sick himself at the time, and of course could offer her no assistance. A miner, who lived in the house . . . carried her some bread and tea in the morning and evening, and that was all the care she had." A short time after she returned to work at the hotel, Dame Shirley related, the woman "died of peritonitis (a common disease in this place), after an illness of four days only." ■

EYEWITNESS

DAME SHIRLEY IN GOLD COUNTRY

In this passage from her firsthand account of life in the California mining town of Rich Bar, Dame Shirley describes her visit with a successful "mangler"—a laundress operating a mangle to wring out wet clothing:

To-day I called at the residence of Mrs. R. It is a canvas house containing a suite of three "apartments" . . . There is a barroom blushing all over with red calico, a dining-room, kitchen, and a small bed-closet. The little sixty-eight-pounder woman is queen of the establishment. By the way, a man who walked home with us was enthusiastic in her praise. "Magnificent woman, that, sir," he said, addressing my husband; "a wife of the right sort, *she* is. Why," he added, absolutely rising into eloquence as he spoke, "she earnt her *old man*" (said individual twenty-one years of age, perhaps) "nine hundred dollars in nine weeks, clear of all expenses, by washing! Such women ain't common, I tell *you*. If they were, a man might marry, and make money by the operation." . . . He looked at *me* as if to say, that, though by no means gloriously arrayed, I was a mere cumberer of the ground, inasmuch as I toiled not, neither did I wash. Alas! I hung my diminished head . . . But a lucky thought came into my mind. As all men cannot be Napoleon Bonapartes, so all women cannot be *manglers*. The majority of the sex must be satisfied with simply being *mangled*.

SLAVERY ON THE FRONTIER

The Uneasy Compromise of 1850

The Mexican War and the California gold rush brought the divisive issue of slavery in the West to the fore. In 1848, the nation was evenly divided, with 15 free states and 15 slave states. The annexation of Mexican territory at war's end raised the question of whether that balance could and should be maintained. The Missouri Compromise of 1820 had admitted Missouri as a slave state but prohibited slavery in all other territory north of latitude 36° 30', the line formed by Missouri's southern border. That line ran through the middle of California, providing no basis for either allowing or prohibiting slavery there. Southerners joined the gold rush, and some brought slaves with them, but most forty-niners regarded slave labor in the goldfields as a dire threat to free labor. In late 1849, California applied for admission to the Union under a constitution declaring that "neither slavery, nor involuntary servitude, unless for the punishment of crimes, shall ever be tolerated in this state."

In 1850, Congress debated whether to admit California as a free state and allow slavery in other areas ceded to the United States by Mexico. Many Northerners backed the Wilmot Proviso introduced in 1846, which proposed prohibiting slavery in all territory acquired during the Mexican War. Many Southerners agreed with Senator John Calhoun of South Carolina, who warned that excluding slaveholders from that territory would destroy "the equilibrium between the two sections" and lead the South to secede from the Union.

After heated arguments, Congress adopted a compromise backed by Senators Henry Clay of Kentucky, Daniel Webster of New Hampshire, and Stephen Douglas of Illinois. In return for admitting California as a free state and banning the slave trade in the District of Columbia, the Compromise of 1850 bowed to southern demands for a tough new fugitive slave law, which required officials in free states to pursue escaped slaves and return them to their owners. It also organized two new territories in the West—Utah and New Mexico—and left the decision whether to allow or prohibit slavery there to settlers and their representatives. That concept, known as popular sovereignty, satisfied neither abolitionists nor defenders of slavery. When Stephen Douglas applied popular sovereignty to an act organizing the territories of Kansas and Nebraska in 1854, his compromise produced a bloody conflict in Kansas that foreshadowed the Civil War. ∎

GREAT COMPROMISER Henry Clay addresses the Senate in 1850 during debate over slavery in the West. The compromise he crafted—his last achievement before he died in 1852—perpetuated the Union as what Lincoln called a "house divided . . . half slave and half free."

THE MORMON EXODUS

Seeking a New Zion in the Desert

or Mormon leader Brigham Young, word that President Millard Fillmore had appointed him governor of the newly created Utah Territory in 1850 came as a mixed blessing. Young was pleased to govern Utah's Mormons but was painfully aware that territorial status placed them under federal supervision. He would have to put up with judges and officials sent by Washington—men he later described as "blackhearted, sycophantic demagogues." People in other western territories would come to share his distrust of the federal government, but Mormons had more reason than most to fear outside interference, for they had immigrated to Utah to escape persecution.

The Mormon exodus began in 1846 after they were driven from Nauvoo, Illinois, where they had settled with their founder, Joseph Smith, who was killed by an angry mob in 1844. Those who opposed him and his followers considered the Book of Mormon that Smith revealed and the Church of Jesus Christ of Latter-day Saints that he established heretical. They were also jealous of the worldly success of the industrious Mormons and appalled by reports that

Brigham Young

WINTER QUARTERS At left, Mormons gather at Winter Quarters, established along the Missouri River in 1846 to shelter the faithful until they set out for their new home in the Great Basin. Cabins at this camp resembled the one above in Utah, housing a polygamous Mormon family.

Smith, Young, and other leading Mormons took multiple wives.

Mormons made their way across Iowa in 1846 and camped at Winter Quarters, near present-day Omaha, Nebraska. In April 1847, Young led a pioneer company in search of a new home for his people in the Great Basin. They crossed Nebraska along the north bank of the Platte River to avoid emigrants following the Oregon Trail on the south side. When they reached the Rockies, Young and others came down with fever and remained behind. By the time he recovered and reached the site chosen by the pioneers, on the east shore of the Great Salt Lake, they had already dammed a creek and planted seeds there. "This is the right place," he declared.

Young then returned east to organize the Mormon migration. Between 1847 and 1860, some 45,000 people followed the Mormon Trail pioneered by Young and his company to settle in Utah. Most traveled by wagon, but several thousand made the journey on foot, hauling their belongings in handcarts. In 1856, two companies with handcarts set out belatedly and were caught in fall snowstorms. Nearly 200 people perished, and others were in pitiful condition when rescue parties from Utah reached them. One Mormon who aided them, George Grant, told of hundreds of men and women "worn down by drawing handcarts through snow and mud; fainting by the way side; falling, chilled by the cold; children crying . . . their feet bleeding, and some of them bare to snow and frost." The sight was "almost too much for the stoutest of us," Grant stated.

THE BEEHIVE TERRITORY

Using irrigation, Mormons sustained their fast-growing population and founded dozens of settlements far from Salt Lake City. Before Utah Territory was organized, they called their homeland Deseret, meaning "honeybee." The beehive,

CROWDED CAPITAL By the 1860s, when this photograph was taken, the conflict between Mormons and the federal government had been resolved and Salt Lake City was bustling, with a population approaching 20,000.

later represented on the Utah state flag, was a fitting emblem for their hardworking, highly cooperative society. Although they tried to avoid conflict with Indians and sought to convert them, Mormons clashed with the powerful Ute tribe, for which Utah was named. Utes raided settlements that infringed on their tribal hunting and fishing grounds and resisted Mormon efforts to stop them from seizing captives from other tribes and selling them as slaves.

That conflict was resolved in 1854 through negotiations between Young and the Ute chief Wakara, but Young soon found himself at odds with the American government. In 1852, Mormon apostle Orson Pratt had caused an uproar by announcing that polygamy was an accepted church practice. Among those who differed with Pratt on that issue was his first wife, Sarah, who had to share him with several other wives and called polygamy the "direst curse with which a people or nation could be afflicted." John Frémont, the presidential candidate of the newly formed Republican Party in 1856, termed polygamy one of the "twin relics of barbarism" along with slavery, and Senator Stephen Douglas labeled Mormons "alien enemies and outlaws." Young's frequent disputes with officials from Washington led to charges that he held the United States in contempt.

In 1857, President James Buchanan decided to oust Young as governor and sent 2,500 troops to uphold federal authority in Utah. Young received no official word as to their intentions. He assumed they were sent to achieve "our overthrow and destruction" and sought Indians as allies against them. Amid the crisis, some anxious settlers joined Indians in targeting emigrants from Arkansas and Missouri

who were heading west through southern Utah and taunted Mormons. After being promised safe passage, nearly 120 of those emigrants were massacred at Mountain Meadows in September. Many Mormons took part, but only one was later tried, convicted, and executed.

Except for that massacre, little blood was shed during the so-called Utah War. Raiders led by Lot Smith and Orrin Porter Rockwell, the reputed "destroying angel of Mormondom," burned wagon trains supplying U.S. troops but spared the teamsters. Mormons abandoned much of northern Utah to avoid the oncoming soldiers before a settlement was reached in 1858. Young stepped down as governor but remained the territory's dominant figure until his death in 1877. Not until 1896, after Mormon leaders renounced polygamy, was Utah admitted as a state. ∎

NATURAL HISTORY

PLAGUES OF LOCUSTS

In 1848, Mormon settlers in Utah were plagued by insects described variously as crickets or grasshoppers that ate up their crops until seagulls from the Great Salt Lake began devouring the pests. "The sea gulls have come in large flocks from the lake and sweep the crickets as they go," one Mormon wrote. "It seems the hand of the Lord is in our favor." Those seemingly heaven-sent gulls were later honored with a statue in Salt Lake City. Many similar plagues were reported in Utah in decades to come. The culprits were usually grasshoppers—or more specifically Rocky Mountain locusts, which feasted on crops and sometimes devoured anything resembling vegetation, including green clothing. One settler remarked that "it would not take them long to eat up a fellow's pantaloons when the color suited them."

Locusts were common in the Salt Lake Valley and other parts of the Great Basin before Mormons arrived there. Indians sometimes harvested them as food. But fields that settlers irrigated and cultivated lured great swarms of grasshoppers, which in turn lured seagulls and other birds that preyed on the insects. Mormons also noticed that browsing sheep trampled many locusts before they matured and took flight. The introduction of livestock may be one factor behind the disappearance of Rocky Mountain locusts, which by the early 1900s no longer darkened the skies over Utah.

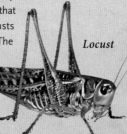

Locust

WOMEN ON THE WAGON TRAILS
Intrepid Pioneers

Many of those who went west in wagons during the 1850s did so as families, including wives, mothers, and single women, who often found husbands during or soon after the journey. While most men set out eagerly in search of new homes, some women became pioneers reluctantly. One wife recalled that when her husband proposed immigrating to California, she pleaded, *"O let us not go."* Leaving friends and kin for an uncertain future in a strange land was wrenching, but most women responded as Margaret Hereford Wilson, the grandmother of Gen. George Patton, did when her husband set his sights on California: "I am going with him," she wrote, "as there is no other alternative."

Young, unattached women were more likely to savor the journey than those with husbands and children. Nineteen-year-old Harriet Buckingham of Ohio, who set out for Oregon in 1852 with her aunt and uncle, marveled at prairie flowers whose "fragrance surpassed any garden flowers," and greeted an approaching antelope not with pot shots, as a man might have, but with pleasure. "It was a beautiful little creature," she wrote. "It gazed at us for a moment & then bounded away to the Bluffs." Most wives and mothers, however, had little time to rest or reflect when there were meals to cook, clothes to wash, sick children to nurse, healthy ones to keep from straying or falling under wagon wheels—and oxen to drive when men fell ill. "I am all used up," wrote one woman after taking on that task for her ailing spouse.

When Amelia Stewart Knight embarked on the Oregon Trail in 1853 with her husband, she had seven children to look after and another on the way. One week into their journey, they were drenched by an April rainstorm. "Bed clothes nearly spoiled," she wrote in her diary. "Cold and cloudy this morning, and every body out of humour ... Almira says she wished she was home, and I say ditto." But there was no turning back, and she successfully gave birth to her eighth child as they neared their destination in the new territory of Washington—her home until she died in 1898 at the age of 81. ∎

ON ROUTE At right, three women with their arms crossed form the backbone of this Mormon family heading west in wagons. Many women documented their journeys in letters or diaries like the one above, kept by emigrant Sarah Davis in 1850.

ROUGH PASSAGES

Travel by Steamboat and Stagecoach

————◄•◆•►————

n April 9, 1852, the steamboat *Saluda* left Lexington, Missouri, with more than 170 passengers on board. At least half were Mormons, heading upriver to Council Bluffs, Iowa, to join a wagon train bound for Utah. They had been delayed for several days in Jefferson after the *Saluda* suffered damage attempting to round a treacherous point above town. As the repaired vessel headed out, Capt. Francis Belt was heard to say, "I will round the point this morning or blow this boat to hell." He signaled full speed ahead, and moments later the *Saluda*'s red-hot boilers exploded, tearing the boat apart. Bodies and debris were flung high and wide. One witness in Lexington came upon the remains of Captain Belt and reported that "every thread of clothing had been blown off his body." Estimates of the number of people killed in the disaster ranged from 75 to 100.

Between 1811—when the first steam-powered vessel began operating west of the Appalachians—and 1848, more than 700 steamboats exploded, burned, hit snags and sank, or met with other calamities in western waters. Not all those accidents caused fatalities, but passengers had reason to be

FULL STEAM AHEAD At left, two steamboats on the moonlit Mississippi River engage in a race—a contest that could turn deadly if boilers overheated and burst. Throughout much of the 19th century, levees in New Orleans (above) and other western river ports were jammed with steamboats carrying passengers and freight.

wary. Nonetheless, millions of Americans rode steamboats during the 1850s. All forms of travel then could be dangerous, and those vessels were far more comfortable than wagons or stagecoaches. Many offered passengers such diversions as gambling halls and steam-powered calliopes, which "blowed 'Yankee Doodle' sky high," one traveler wrote, "and tore '[Oh!] Susanna' wide open!"

Steamboats crowded the Ohio and Mississippi Rivers in the Midwest and plied the Sacramento and Columbia Rivers in the Far West. Most rivers in between were too shallow or turbulent for steamboats, with the notable exception of the Missouri. In 1860, the steamboats *Chippewa* and *Key West* traveled far up that river from St. Louis to Fort Benton in what would soon be designated Montana Territory—a journey of more than 3,000 miles that set a record for steam-powered navigation within the continent.

RIDING COACH Passengers sit in front and on top of a crowded Concord stagecoach on a rough western road in this 1860s engraving.

OREGON LINE A poster for the California and Oregon Coast Overland Mail Company, established in 1860, touts that stagecoach line as safer for passengers than ocean travel.

CROSS-COUNTRY COACHES

On September 16, 1858, Waterman Ormsby, a correspondent for the *New York Herald,* set out from Missouri for San Francisco on the first westbound stagecoach of the Overland Mail Company. He was accompanied by John Butterfield, the company's president, and six other passengers, but only Ormsby went all the way to California—a bone-jarring, 23-day journey of 2,800 miles through Arkansas, Indian Territory, Texas, and New Mexico, with frequent station stops to change horses, drivers, or wagons and grab a bite. Ormsby nearly came to grief one night during a harrowing dash down a rocky road in Arkansas. "Our driver's ambition to make good time overcame his caution," he wrote, "and away we went, bounding over the stones at a fearful rate . . . to feel oneself bouncing—now on the hard seat, now against the roof, and now against the side of the wagon—was no joke."

Stagecoaches were notorious for rocking and swaying on rough western roads, which is just what they were designed to do. In the early 1800s, the Abbot-Downing Company in Concord, New Hampshire, mastered the technique of cradling its coaches on leather thoroughbraces that cushioned passengers and prevented vehicles from tipping over on bad roads by allowing them to rock and sway like boats on rough seas. Mark Twain, who went west in a stagecoach carrying passengers and mail in 1861, paid tribute to the thoroughbrace when he wrote that his Concord coach was "an imposing cradle on wheels." ■

EXPRESS SERVICE
Stagecoaches (above) similar to the handsome Concord (left) wait outside the express office of Wells, Fargo and Company in Virginia City, Nevada. Founded in 1852, the company combined express deliveries of gold, silver, cash, and other consignments with regular mail and passenger service. After taking over John Butterfield's pioneering Overland Mail Company in 1860, Wells, Fargo dominated the stagecoach business in the West.

BATTLES ON THE PLAINS
Warriors Versus Soldiers and Rangers

Not until Americans began settling on the Plains or crossing the region in large numbers in the mid-1800s did conflict between U.S. forces and Indians begin there in earnest. Starting around 1850, the Army established forts on the western frontier of settlement as well as outposts along the Oregon Trail, Santa Fe Trail, and other pathways to protect travelers. In 1851, leaders of tribes on the northern Plains were summoned to a peace council at Fort Laramie on the Oregon Trail. That September, Sioux, Cheyenne, Shoshone, Crow, Assiniboine, Gros Ventre, Mandan, and Arikara chiefs arrived there with numerous followers. Thousands of Indians camped around the fort as the talks got under way. Mountain man Thomas Fitzpatrick served as principal negotiator for the United States and distributed $50,000 in presents to the assembled tribes, a first installment in annual payments promised to those who came to terms. The agreement reached at Fort Laramie called for the tribes to keep peace with each other and avoid harming Americans "passing through their respective territories," which were loosely defined in the treaty—the first step toward establishing reservations for Plains Indians. In return, the U.S. promised to protect the tribes against any depredations by Americans.

Neither side was capable of living up to that treaty or a similar agreement with tribes along the Santa Fe Trail negotiated at Fort Atkinson in 1854. Some older chiefs who had seen their tribes ravaged by cholera and other diseases favored peace, but they could not make young warriors refrain from battle, which brought them respect within tribal circles. Few U.S. officers, for their part, were willing or able to stop Americans from intruding on tribal territory and causing trouble. Instead, some officers sided forcefully with travelers or settlers even in minor disputes with Indians. In 1854, Lt. John Grattan barged into a Lakota Sioux camp to punish a young Indian there for killing an emigrant's cow. After Grattan opened fire, warriors annihilated him and his company. A year later, Col. William Harney retaliated for that massacre and other incidents by attacking a Lakota camp near Ash Hollow in Nebraska and killing or capturing more than 150 men, women, and children. The words Harney uttered when he launched that expedition could serve as a motto for the relentless war for the Plains that followed: "By God, I'm for battle—no peace."

MEETING PLACE Indians camp outside Fort Laramie in a painting from the late 1850s by Alfred Jacob Miller, who witnessed the fort in 1837 when it was a trading post. Rebuilt in 1841 and taken over by the U.S. Army in 1849, it attracted thousands of Indians in the days leading up to the Treaty of Fort Laramie in 1851.

RANGERS IN PURSUIT Texas Rangers chase Comanches by moonlight (above) in an engraving based on accounts of raids led by renowned officers such as Jack Hays (near right) and Rip Ford (far right). Texas Rangers were often aided by warriors from tribes at odds with Comanches, including Lipan Apaches and Tonkawas.

Turmoil in Texas

Nowhere else on the Plains did the tide of white settlement advance farther west in the mid-1800s than in Texas—and nowhere did settlers pay a steeper price for infringing on tribal territory. As early as the 1830s, pioneers had begun venturing out from the woodlands of East Texas into Comanche country on the prairie. Like the Sioux, the Comanche consisted of several bands or divisions. The southernmost division, known as Penateka (Honey Eaters), lay directly in the path of advancing Texans and sought to stem the tide by attacking their settlements, killing men, and abducting women and children. An attempt by Texans to resolve the conflict in 1840 ended disastrously when they invited Penateka chiefs to the Council House in San Antonio and told

ASH HOLLOW Mounted officers direct Col. William Harney's troops against Lakota Sioux at Ash Hollow on September 3, 1855. Harney blamed those Sioux for the massacre of Lieutenant Grattan's company a year earlier.

them they would be held hostage until all the captives were released. Fighting erupted and spilled out into the streets, leaving several Texans and dozens of Penatekas dead. Chief Buffalo Hump of the Penateka retaliated by sacking towns as far east as the Gulf Coast.

In years to come, Texas Rangers went on the offensive, targeting Penatekas, Kotsotekas (Buffalo Eaters), and other defiant Comanches. Capt. John Cotton "Jack" Hays readied Rangers for those campaigns by equipping them with Colt revolvers that could be fired from horseback and training them to fight like Comanches, often traveling by moonlight to surprise their foes at dawn. In 1858, an officer who had served under Hays, Capt. John "Rip" Ford, was authorized by Texas to follow "any and all trails" of hostile bands and "chastise them." Guided by Tonkawa Indians who had long been foes of Comanches and knew their country well, Ford's Rangers crossed into Indian Territory and thrashed Kotsotekas led by Chief Iron Jacket, who wore an old Spanish coat of mail that failed to stop the bullet that ended his life. In Ford's words, his victory at Antelope Hills demonstrated that Comanches could be "followed, overtaken, and beaten."

Not to be outdone by Ford, Maj. Earl Van Dorn of the U.S. Army went after Buffalo Hump, who survived attacks on his camp but lost many of his followers. Comanches were losing ground, but some of their toughest foes, including Ford and Van Dorn, would soon turn to fighting against the Union as Confederates. Not until after the Civil War ended and the nation reunited would the U.S. have the capacity to win the war for the Plains. ■

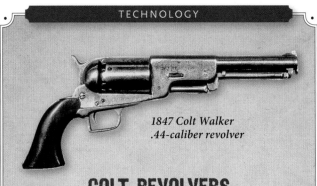

1847 Colt Walker .44-caliber revolver

COLT REVOLVERS

In the late 1830s, arms maker Samuel Colt began producing an innovative revolver that could fire five shots without being reloaded. Cocking the gun automatically rotated the cylinder and positioned another bullet for firing. That was a significant breakthrough, but there was little demand for the weapon until Texans got hold of it. Pistols were accurate only in close combat and were sometimes issued to sailors for that purpose. In 1839, the small Texas Navy ordered 180 of Colt's revolvers. Capt. Jack Hays later acquired Colts for his Texas Rangers, who learned to shoot effectively from horseback in close fights with Indians. The revolvers also came in handy when Rangers dismounted or had horses shot from under them.

After using the revolvers to defeat Comanches in battle, Lt. Samuel Walker of Hays's company wrote Colt that "those daring Indians had always supposed themselves superior to us, man to man, on horse . . . The result of this engagement was such as to intimidate them." Walker later met with Colt and helped him design a larger, more powerful revolver with six chambers.

The six-shooter soon became the weapon of choice in the West, and Colt's models were hugely popular. "There are probably in Texas about as many revolvers as male adults," journalist Frederick Law Olmsted wrote in 1857 after touring the South, "and I doubt if there are one hundred in the state of any other make."

OREGON'S OFFSPRING
The Painful Birth of Washington Territory

When Washington was separated from Oregon in 1853, Isaac Stevens became governor of the new territory and superintendent of Indian affairs. A hard-driving Army engineer, he hammered out stringent treaties confining tribes in Washington to reservations. The danger of defying Americans had been demonstrated when Cayuse Indians were seized and hanged for attacking the Whitman mission in eastern Washington in 1847. Some tribal leaders concluded that resistance was futile and stood by their deals with Stevens. Chief Seattle, speaking for the Duwamish and Suquamish tribes on Puget Sound, said that in signing a treaty with the governor in January 1855 they "put away all bad feelings" and became "friends of the Americans." A year later, however, a war party of treaty opponents attacked settlers in Seattle, named for that friendly chief, and caused panic before retreating under fire from a warship in Puget Sound, the U.S.S. *Decatur*.

The brief Battle of Seattle was a mere flare-up compared with the firestorm that erupted when treaty foes in eastern Washington were further antagonized by prospectors seeking gold along the Colville and Fraser Rivers on either side of the Canadian border. Chief Kamiakin of the Yakima warned intruders that their trails would be "marked with blood." His warriors killed several Americans and routed a company of U.S. troops. The Yakima were then joined by other tribes and held out against the Army until Col. George Wright brought infantry, cavalry, and artillery to bear and crushed them at the Battle of Spokane Plains on September 5, 1858.

Stevens was a brave officer who would later give his life for the Union. But he lacked the diplomatic finesse to address the legitimate grievances of tribal leaders such as Chief Leschi of the Nisqually, who took up arms to oppose the dismal reservation his tribe received near Puget Sound and was later arrested at Stevens' insistence, tried, and executed. George Gibbs, who served as a negotiator for the governor, wrote that his talks with coastal tribes "were too much hurried, and the reservations allowed them were insufficient." Stevens' biggest mistake, Gibbs reckoned, was bringing together the Yakima and other proud tribes in eastern Washington "and cramming a treaty down their throats." ■

BATTLE OF SEATTLE In a painting by Emily Inez Denny, one of the first American children born in Seattle, settlers there seek refuge in a blockhouse from attacking Indians. Denny was two when the attack occurred on January 26, 1856, and she reached safety with her parents, who had arrived from Illinois on the Oregon Trail. The ship in the background may represent the sloop of war *Decatur*, which bombarded the attacking warriors and was credited with saving Seattle.

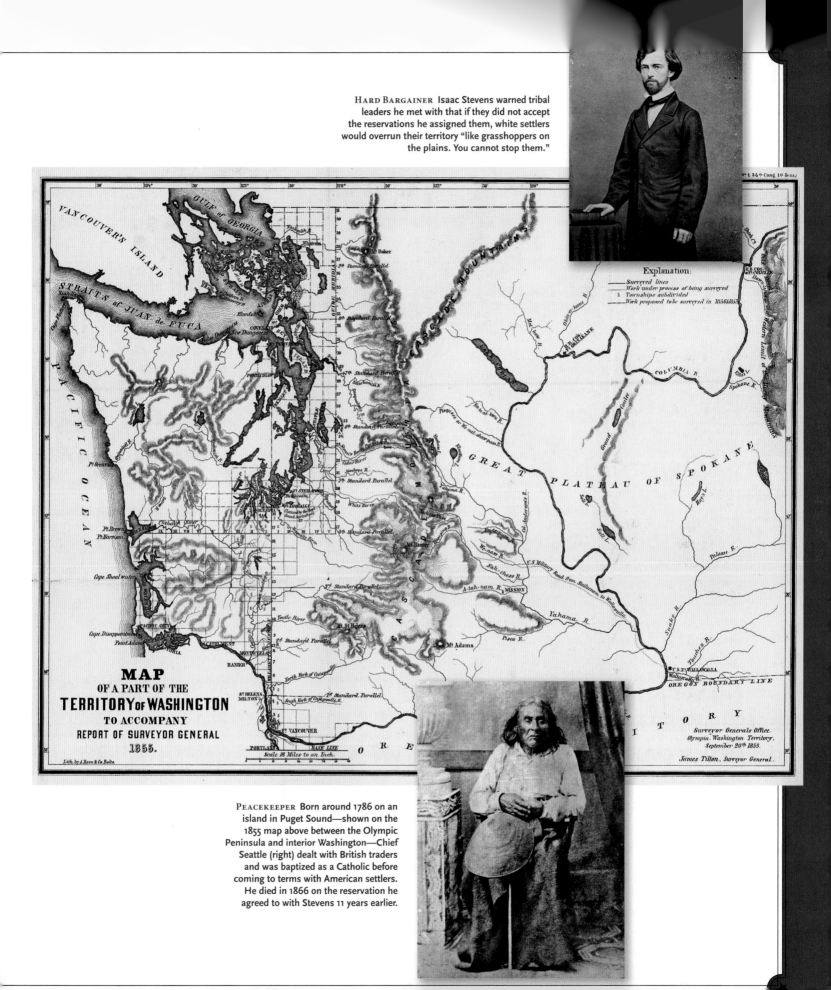

HARD BARGAINER Isaac Stevens warned tribal leaders he met with that if they did not accept the reservations he assigned them, white settlers would overrun their territory "like grasshoppers on the plains. You cannot stop them."

MAP
OF A PART OF THE
TERRITORY OF WASHINGTON
TO ACCOMPANY
REPORT OF SURVEYOR GENERAL
1855.

Scale 18 Miles to an Inch.

Lith. by A. Hoen & Co. Balto.

Explanation:
— Surveyed lines
— Work under process of being surveyed
S Townships subdivided
— Work proposed to be surveyed in 1856 1857

Surveyor Generals Office.
Olympia. Washington Territory,
September 20th 1855.

James Tilton, Surveyor General.

PEACEKEEPER Born around 1786 on an island in Puget Sound—shown on the 1855 map above between the Olympic Peninsula and interior Washington—Chief Seattle (right) dealt with British traders and was baptized as a Catholic before coming to terms with American settlers. He died in 1866 on the reservation he agreed to with Stevens 11 years earlier.

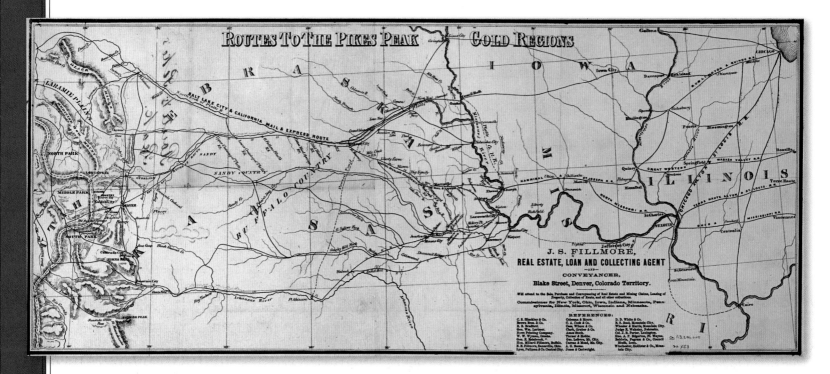

PROSPECTING ACROSS THE WEST

Gold and Silver Rushes Galore

The California gold rush was the first of many such upheavals that drew fortune hunters westward in droves and spawned new territories in the process. Miners who failed to strike it rich in California looked elsewhere and sometimes found redemption. Granville Stuart of Virginia, for example, headed home from California in 1857, made a detour around Salt Lake City to avoid the confrontation there between Mormons and federal troops, and ended up hitting pay dirt along Gold Creek in the future Montana Territory.

The gold craze in Montana was slow to develop compared with the frantic rush to the Front Range of the Rockies after gold was discovered near Pikes Peak in 1858. One pioneering party there led by William Greeneberry "Green" Russell came away with only about $500 worth of gold, but a Missourian who saw them at work thought they were onto something big and spread the word back home. Newspapers played up such tantalizing reports, knowing that a gold rush would profit local businesses that supplied miners heading west. In 1859, more than 100,000 prospectors set out for Colorado. "Pikes Peak or Bust" was their slogan. Many who reached their goal came up empty and went home busted. Unlike California,

Colorado did not harbor vast placer deposits—gravel from which gold could be sifted out. Much of its mineral wealth was contained in rocks laced with veins of ore. Some who laid claim to those lodes became fabulously wealthy, but many of those who remained in Colorado ended up extracting the ore or refining it for modest wages in industrial mining towns such as Central City.

Another rush in 1859 lured tens of thousands of prospectors to the boomtowns of Virginia City and Gold Hill at the western edge of the future Nevada Territory (organized in 1861 like Colorado Territory). Placer mining in Nevada yielded little compared with the wealth extracted in silver and gold from the legendary Comstock Lode, named for the hapless Henry Comstock, who talked the men who discovered that lode into giving him a share. Comstock then sold his share for about $10,000, forfeiting millions in future profits, and later committed suicide in Montana. His career exemplified the boom-and-bust nature of the mining business, which ultimately reduced Virginia City and Gold Hill to ghost towns. The places that endured and grew into modern cities were towns such as Sacramento, Reno, and Denver that supplied miners and became transportation hubs. ■

BOOMTOWN Soon after Green Russell's gold strike near Pikes Peak drew attention to Colorado in 1858, miners rushed there on numerous routes (opposite). Thousands staked claims along Clear Creek, west of Denver, where Central City developed. By 1864, when the picture below was taken, the placer deposits were exhausted and Central City thrived on hard-rock mining amid hillsides stripped bare for lumber and fuel.

William Greeneberry
"Green" Russell

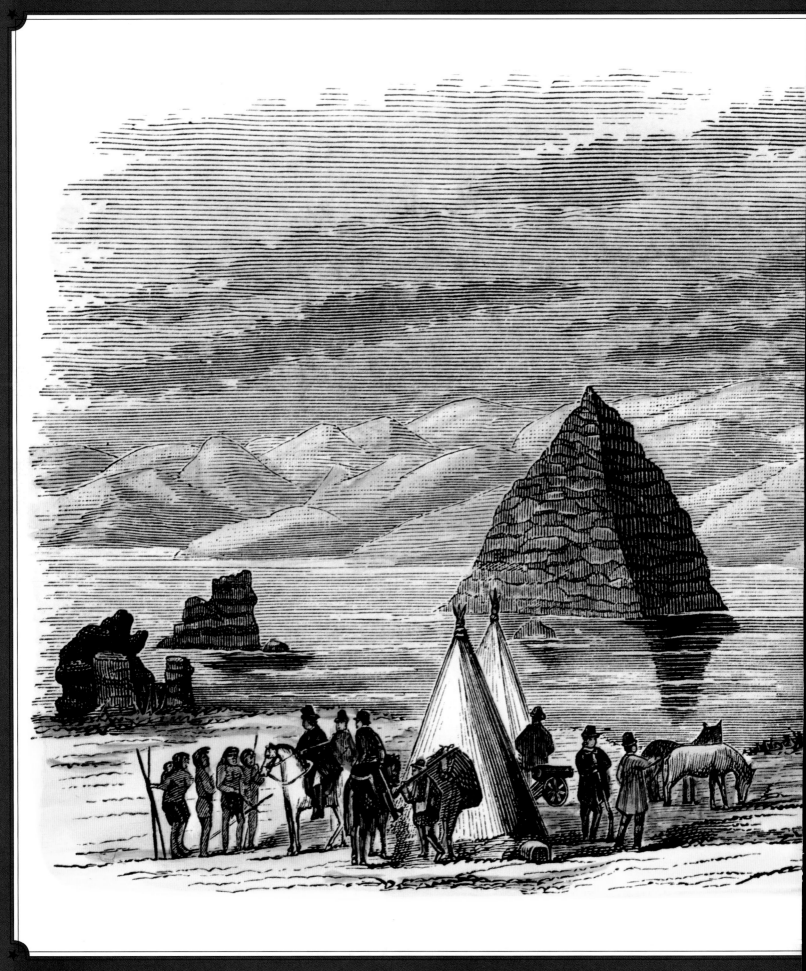

SHOWDOWN IN NEVADA
Miners, Paiutes, and the Pyramid Lake War

T he rush to Nevada's mines in 1859 produced a few big winners and many losers. Thousands of prospectors went bust, but the biggest losers were people with prior claims to the region's bounty—Northern Paiutes whose ancestors had lived near Pyramid Lake for ages. Sometimes called "Diggers" because they gathered roots and seeds, they also subsisted by hunting and fishing on the lakes and rivers of western Nevada. Miners who overran their territory began diverting streams and fouling them with debris. A more imminent threat was the tendency of the newcomers to disdain and abuse Indians, who were often blamed for crimes committed by unknown culprits. Some reckless intruders went so far as to raid Paiute camps and abduct women or girls.

The sudden influx of white men strained the ties that a prominent Paiute called Captain Truckee had forged with Americans. In 1844, he helped emigrants reach California by guiding them up the Truckee River to the pass that later bore the name of the ill-fated Donner Party, stranded there in the snow in late 1846. He also accompanied John Frémont to California on

PYRAMID LAKE In 1844, when John Frémont reached this shimmering lake named for the rocky pyramid in its midst (left), Paiutes were the area's only inhabitants. By the early 1860s, Paiutes were under siege by white prospectors and settlers, who established Virginia City (above) and other towns in the mineral-rich Washoe Valley south of the lake.

WAR LEADER Around 30 years old when he led Paiutes in battle against soldiers and settlers, Numaga was described by a journalist as having a "quiet dignity and self-possession of manner which marked him as a superior man."

his third expedition, according to Truckee's granddaughter, Sarah Winnemucca. Her father, Chief Winnemucca, was Truckee's son-in-law and the leader of a Paiute band. In the late 1850s, Sarah and her younger sister Elma were entrusted to Maj. William Ormsby, a former militia officer who came to Nevada as a stagecoach agent. He and his wife took the girls into their home as companions for their daughter and helped raise them.

Those family ties did not prevent Ormsby from coming to blows with Paiutes. In the spring of 1860, they gathered at Pyramid Lake to fish and began talking of waging war on the troublesome whites. As was customary among many tribes, they called on a war leader rather than a peacetime chief like Winnemucca. Their chosen leader, Numaga, was a gifted warrior, but he foresaw dire consequences if they challenged the numerous and well-armed Americans. "You will be forced among the barren rocks of the north," he warned, "you will see the women and old men starve, and listen to the cries of your children for food. I love my people; let them live." Yet Numaga was soon compelled to fight when Paiutes rescued

FRIEND AND FOE Maj. William Ormsby had close ties to Sarah Winnemucca and her family but died fighting Numaga's Paiute warriors on May 12, 1860.

two girls who had been abducted and held at Williams Station—a stop for stagecoaches and the newly organized Pony Express—and then killed several men there and left the station in flames. The war was on, and Numaga's foe would be one of the few settlers with military experience, Major Ormsby.

Numaga anticipated that Ormsby's raw recruits would be overeager and laid a trap for them below Pyramid Lake. On May 12, they rode right into it, chasing after a small group of warriors until hundreds more emerged from behind trees and brush and hemmed them in. Some of them escaped, but Ormsby and more than 60 of his men were slaughtered. As often happened in such conflicts, the tribe's initial victory exposed them to overwhelming retaliation. In early June, 200 U.S. troops and 500 volunteers led by a former Texas Ranger, Col. Jack Hays, defeated Numaga's warriors. Paiutes fled north into the Black Rock Desert, where they went hungry as he had warned. Numaga later arranged a truce that spared the lives of Paiute refugees, but they had to wait years before receiving a reservation along Pyramid Lake that offered them refuge from hostile settlers. ∎

SARAH WINNEMUCCA
CIRCA 1844–1891

Her Paiute name was Thocmetony (Shell Flower), but she grew up as Americans were infiltrating her homeland and became known as Sarah. "I was a very small child when the first white people came into our country," she recalled in her autobiography. "They came like a lion, yes, like a roaring lion, and have continued so ever since." Her maternal grandfather, Captain Truckee, called white men his "brothers" and befriended Maj. William Ormsby, at whose home Sarah lived while in her teens. Her father, Chief Winnemucca, grew alarmed when prospectors flooded Paiute country in 1859. He said that "we could no longer be happy as of old," Sarah recalled, "as the white people we called our brothers had brought a great trouble and sorrow among us." In 1860, before the war began that claimed Ormsby's life, Sarah and her sister left his home and briefly attended a Catholic academy in California until white parents complained about "Indians being in school with their children." Fluent in English, she appeared on stage in the 1860s and was billed as a "princess."

Like her grandfather, Sarah often cooperated with American authorities, including Army officers. But like her father, she lamented the wrongs done to her people. As a lecturer and author in her later years, she denounced federal Indian policies. "You dare to cry out Liberty," she protested, "when you hold us in places against our will, driving us from place to place as if we were beasts."

BLOODY KANSAS
Prelude to the Civil War

JOHN C. FREMONT.

The war that split the Union in 1861 was between North and South, but it had its origins in the West. For decades, northern and southern politicians had papered over their differences, but the issue of whether to allow slavery in western territories defied all efforts at compromise. The latest effort, the Kansas-Nebraska Act of 1854, only heightened the controversy by leaving the decision to settlers in those new territories and their legislators. Nebraska was settled largely by people from neighboring Iowa and other northern states and would prohibit slavery. But fierce competition developed in Kansas between proslavery settlers from neighboring Missouri and other southern or Border States and antislavery settlers from as far away as New England.

By 1856, Kansas was a battleground. Debate over the issue grew so heated that blows were struck in Congress. In May, Representative Preston Brooks attacked Senator Charles Sumner of Massachusetts with a cane for a speech in which he blasted Senator Andrew Butler of South Carolina, a relative of Brooks, for backing the Kansas-Nebraska Act and

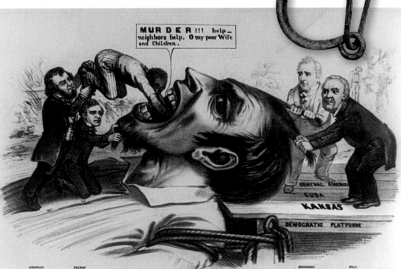

MURDER!!! help— neighbors help, O my poor Wife and Children.

FORCING SLAVERY DOWN THE THROAT OF A FREESOILER

HARD TO TAKE Above, a political cartoon portrays Democrats who backed the Kansas-Nebraska Act forcing a Free-Soiler to swallow slavery. In 1856, the Free-Soil movement spawned the Republican Party, which nominated Frémont for president and sponsored this map (right), showing free states in red, slave states in black, and territories in green except for disputed Kansas, shown in white.

pandering for that "harlot, slavery." The attack on Sumner shocked many Northerners, including 56-year-old abolitionist John Brown, who had settled in Kansas with several of his adult sons in 1855 to agitate against slavery there. When Brown and his cohorts learned that Sumner had been beaten senseless, his son Jason recalled, they "went crazy—*crazy*. It seemed to be the decisive, finishing touch."

On the night of May 24, 1856, Brown led four of his sons and three other followers in attacks that killed five pro-slavery men living along Pottawatomie Creek. Brown was subsequently indicted for murder, but like many on both sides who wreaked havoc in "Bloody Kansas" he escaped punishment in court. Eventually, foes of slavery in Kansas prevailed

Dred Scott

there, but few were true abolitionists like Brown. Many wanted their territory to be for whites only. After antislavery settlers formed their own government in Topeka in opposition to a rival proslavery government, they voted to bar free blacks from Kansas—a provision nullified before Kansas entered the Union as a free state in 1861.

Another dispute that arose in the West and brought the nation a step closer to civil war was a lengthy court battle involving Dred Scott, a slave who sued for his freedom in Missouri in 1847 on the grounds that his master had taken him from Missouri for an extended period to the free state of Illinois. The case eventually reached the U.S. Supreme Court, which ruled against Scott in 1857. Chief Justice Roger Taney, a former slave owner from Maryland, wrote in his opinion that neither "slaves, nor their descendants" were recognized as U.S. citizens by the framers of the Constitution and that therefore neither Scott nor anyone of the "negro race" had the right to sue in court. Furthermore, he argued that owners could take their slaves to any American territory because the federal government had no right to interfere with the property rights of citizens there. Taney's logic undermined all congressional efforts to limit slavery in western territories going back to the Missouri Compromise of 1820.

The Dred Scott ruling encouraged militant southern defenders of slavery called fire-eaters to reject any compromise with Northerners on that issue, including the Kansas-Nebraska Act. Its chief sponsor, presidential hopeful Stephen Douglas of Illinois, lost support from his fellow Democrats in the South, who went on to form their own party, leaving Douglas vulnerable to a challenge from antislavery Republicans and their nominee, Abraham Lincoln. Radical abolitionists like John Brown, for their part, concluded that slavery was too deeply embedded in the U.S. Constitution and the American legal system to be eliminated without a fight.

In October 1859, Brown and 21 followers, including 5 black men, raided the federal arsenal at Harpers Ferry, hoping to seize weapons and ignite a slave rebellion in the South. They were soon crushed by U.S. forces led by Lt. Col. Robert E. Lee of Virginia. Convicted of treason, Brown went to the gallows on December 2, 1859, warning that the "crimes of this guilty land will never be purged away but with blood." Soon the nation would fracture, causing carnage that would make Bloody Kansas seem tame by comparison. ■

SOCIAL HISTORY

BLACK SEMINOLES IN EXILE

Slavery remained legal in Indian Territory until it was abolished nationwide in 1865. Black slaves were owned there by members of four tribes removed from the South—the Cherokee, Creek, Choctaw, and Chickasaw. Blacks among the Seminole were sometimes called slaves because they were subject to Seminole Indians, to whom they paid tribute in the form of crops they raised or other goods. But few were actually held in bondage. Black Seminoles—some of whom were partly of Indian ancestry—had their own villages and property. They had been allowed to carry weapons until their tribe was placed under Creek authority in Indian Territory, which left them vulnerable to slave catchers there.

In 1849, many black Seminoles fled Indian Territory under the leadership of John Horse (inset) and settled below the Rio Grande in the Mexican state of Coahuila. They were joined there by Seminole Indians led by Chief Wild Cat, who sympathized with them and resented living under Creek authority. In exchange for receiving refuge in Mexico, where slavery was illegal, the Seminole exiles helped defend Coahuila against Comanches and other raiders from Texas. Known to Mexicans as Juan Caballo, John Horse and a number of his followers were tough veterans of the Seminole War. They served Mexico well until the 1870s, when most black Seminoles returned to Indian Territory, where their tribe now had its own reservation. No longer at risk of being enslaved, some enlisted as scouts in the U.S. Army.

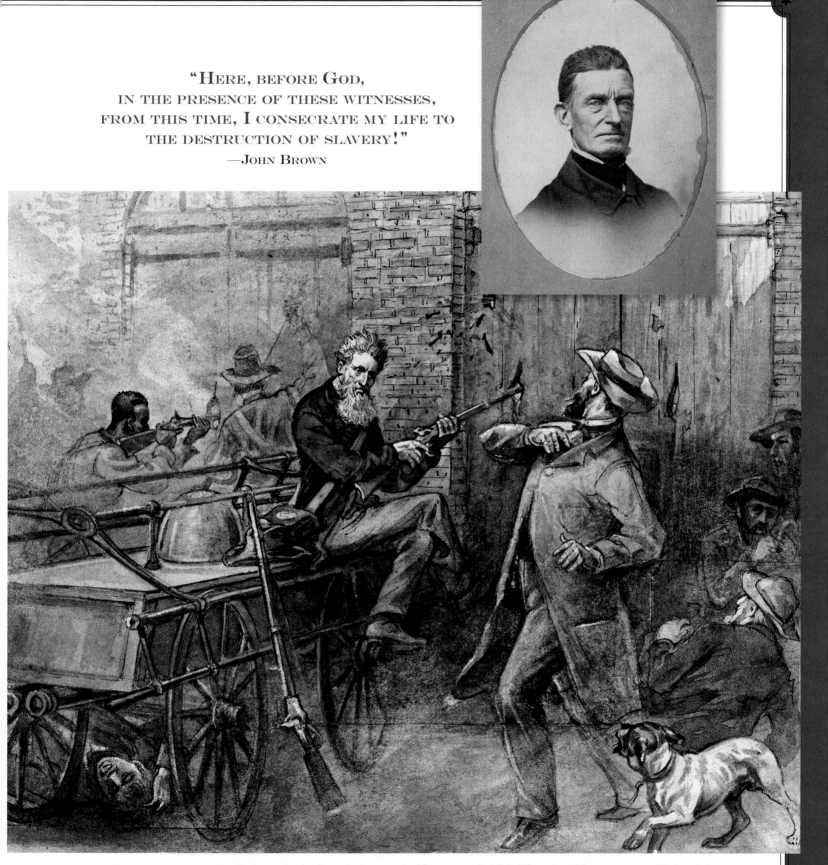

"HERE, BEFORE GOD, IN THE PRESENCE OF THESE WITNESSES, FROM THIS TIME, I CONSECRATE MY LIFE TO THE DESTRUCTION OF SLAVERY!"
—JOHN BROWN

RADICAL ABOLITIONIST Born in Connecticut in 1800, John Brown evolved from a stern, dark-haired figure in middle age (top) to a white-bearded patriarch of 59 when he raided the federal arsenal at Harpers Ferry (above). His execution made him a martyr to his fellow abolitionists, who sang his praises in an anthem declaring that his body was "mouldering in the grave," but his "soul is marching on!"

THE PONY EXPRESS

A 2,000-Mile Relay Race

Few ventures undertaken in the West were more impressive or improbable than the Pony Express. In early 1860, William Russell overcame objections from his business partners, Alexander Majors and William Waddell, and announced a new service that would carry urgent mail across the West in just ten days, compared with three weeks for the rival Overland Mail Company. Russell planned to accomplish that by using swift express riders on horseback rather than stagecoaches for deliveries and by following a fairly straight route from St. Joseph, Missouri, to San Francisco that was some 800 miles shorter than the circuitous, 2,800-mile-long Overland Mail route through Texas. That meant operating the Pony Express in country with severe winter weather and establishing 190 stations along the way so that horses would not travel more than a dozen miles or so at a stretch and lose speed.

Only a businessman like Russell with promotional flair and a gambler's instincts would have risked such an investment when his company was in financial trouble. Formed in 1854 to supply Army posts in the West by wagon train, Russell, Majors, and Waddell prospered in the freight business until the late 1850s, when the partners suffered losses supplying U.S. forces in Utah against Mormon opposition. Russell figured that the costly Pony Express would bring his struggling company priceless publicity and help it land a big government contract to deliver mail in bulk by stagecoach along the shorter central route.

On April 3, 1860, the first Pony Express rider left St. Joseph, the westernmost rail depot at that time. Strapped over his saddle was a leather pouch called a *mochila,* filled with letters and dispatches, often written on tissue

CLOSE CALL At left, a Pony Express rider eludes pursuing Indians on the Plains. As shown on the poster above, the company handled letters as well as telegrams, which riders relayed across a gap in the nation's telegraph network that was closed 18 months after the Pony Express debuted.

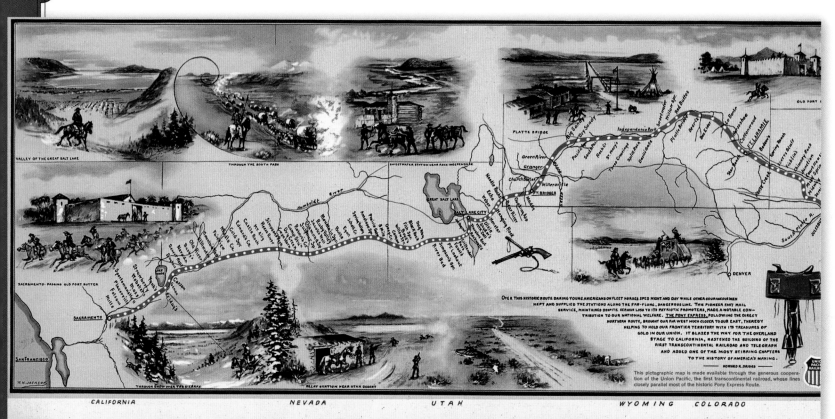

CALIFORNIA   NEVADA   UTAH   WYOMING   COLORADO

STORIED ROUTE A commemorative map (above) shows the Pony Express line and stations. Expressmen like Billy Johnson (far left) were careful with mail, but one rider vanished during the Paiute uprising in Nevada. This letter (near left) was found when his mail pouch was recovered two years later.

paper to reduce their weight. Deliveries cost up to five dollars an ounce, a steep rate that customers would pay only for vital business news and other urgent messages. Many such notices were already being by sent by telegram, but in 1860 there was no telegraph connection between central Nebraska and western Nevada. The Pony Express filled that gap.

Soon after the first Pony Expressman departed St. Joseph, another headed east from Sacramento, California, with a pouch delivered from San Francisco by steamboat. Typically, a rider changed horses several times during his run and covered up to 75 miles before passing the pouch to the next man in the relay. They followed paths that were well established by 1860—including the Oregon Trail across Nebraska and Wyoming—and were often seen hurrying past slow-moving wagons. One of the earliest eyewitness accounts of the Pony

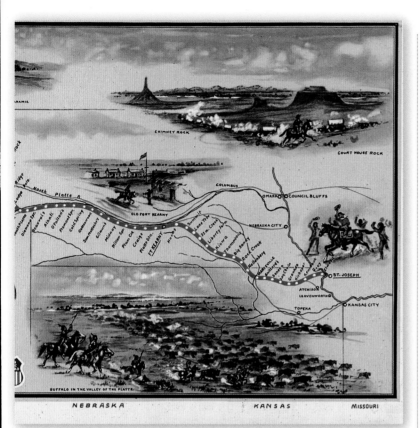

NEBRASKA   KANSAS   MISSOURI

Snow could fall along higher elevations of the route as early as September. When riding at night through blizzards, one expressman recalled, "I just had to trust to the instincts of the horses." In November 1860, riders defied the elements by relaying word that Lincoln had been elected president between the telegraph terminals in Nebraska and Nevada in just six days.

A year later, such messages would streak across the country like lightning on the newly completed transcontinental telegraph line, which rendered the Pony Express obsolete. By then, the partners who launched the business had lost control of it due to heavy losses and a financial scandal involving Russell. Their firm would soon fold, but the time-honored partnership between horse and rider that made the Pony Express possible would long endure in the West. ∎

Express in action came from Adolph Sutro, who was returning to San Francisco from his mining operations in Virginia City, Nevada, in April when he encountered an expressman riding east through the high Sierra in a snowstorm. "On the very summit we met a lonely rider dashing along at a tremendous rate," Sutro noted. "We wondered what could possibly induce him to go on through that gale, and thought it must be some very important business."

Although Pony Expressmen were often portrayed riding at full gallop, they usually cantered at 10 to 15 miles an hour, about the quickest pace a horse could sustain from one station to the next. Only when necessary, such as when they were being pursued, did riders spur their horses to top speed. Chasing expressmen was something of a sport for Indians, but the race could be deadly serious when tribes were actively hostile to intruders. During the Pyramid Lake War in 1860, Paiutes attacked stations and riders in Nevada. A daring expressman named Robert "Pony Bob" Haslam kept the mail going when others were unable or unwilling to ride by covering more than 360 miles in 36 hours. Overall, Indian attacks caused less trouble and delay for the Pony Express than harsh winter weather.

TECHNOLOGY

TRANSCONTINENTAL TELEGRAPH

Between 1844—when Samuel Morse successfully demonstrated his electromagnetic telegraph—and 1860, nearly 50,000 miles of telegraph wire were strung in the United States. But a gap of more than 1,000 miles yawned in the West. Companies such as Western Union possessed the technology to span the continent, including relays to amplify weak signals and glass insulators to stop electricity in the wires from conducting into the poles. The big challenge was hauling equipment to distant construction sites, including vast areas with no timber for poles.

In June 1860, Congress passed the Pacific Telegraph Act, which helped fund the project and gave government messages priority when it was completed. Work began westward from Omaha, Nebraska, and eastward from Carson City, Nevada, in the spring of 1861, spurred by the outbreak of the Civil War and the need for federal authorities to communicate rapidly with the loyal states of California and Oregon. The telegraph lines often paralleled the Pony Express route, and riders could witness construction that would soon bring their service to an end (inset). On October 19, 1861, the lines were joined in Salt Lake City. Looking back long afterward, James Gamble, who oversaw construction at the western end, wrote that completion of the transcontinental telegraph linked California "in electrical bonds to the great national family union." Not until 1865, however, would that bitterly divided national family be reunited.

CHAPTER THREE
1861–1869

PRESERVING THE
UNION
★★★ AND ★★★
SPANNING
THE CONTINENT

LINKING UP Construction crews of the Central Pacific and Union Pacific Railroads meet at Promontory Summit in Utah, where their tracks joined on May 10, 1869. Completion of the transcontinental railroad here helped bind the nation together after the Civil War.

1861–1869

PRESERVING THE UNION AND SPANNING THE CONTINENT

U riah Oblinger of the Eighth Indiana Cavalry Regiment was preparing to take part in the Union invasion of Georgia in May 1864 when he wrote for the first time to his hometown acquaintance and future wife, Martha "Mattie" Thomas. "I should love to have the pleasure of your correspondence," he told her, adding that it would relieve "a good many lonesome hours of my camp life." Later that year, after his regiment helped Maj. Gen. William Tecumseh Sherman seize Atlanta, he completed his three-year enlistment and returned home hoping to wed Mattie, but her father would not consent. Since turning 19, he had been serving in uniform rather

than making a living and could not easily support a family. Many young Civil War veterans in his position sought work in the West. Some helped build the Union Pacific Railroad from Nebraska to its junction with the Central Pacific in Utah. Others went looking for gold in Montana or became cowboys in Texas. Oblinger farmed in Illinois and Minnesota until he and Mattie were finally able to marry in 1869, after which they settled on land he claimed in Nebraska under the Homestead Act, passed in 1862. They lived in a sod house on the open prairie, but they were glad to be

Chief Little Crow

Flag of the Sixth Kansas Cavalry

1862 Union troops in New Mexico defeat Confederates advancing from Texas. Dakota Sioux warriors led by Chief Little Crow attack soldiers and settlers in Minnesota.

1863 Arizona Territory organized by the Union. Confederate guerrillas from Missouri attack Lawrence, Kansas.

1861 The Civil War begins. Most of the West remains under Union control with the exception of Missouri and Indian Territory, which are contested by Unionists and secessionists, and the Confederate states of Louisiana, Arkansas, and Texas.

Gen. Banks's slouch hat

1864 Confederates repulse Union forces led by Maj. Gen. Nathaniel Banks, advancing up the Red River in Louisiana to invade Texas. Union troops led by Kit Carson evict Navajos from their homeland.

self-sufficient homesteaders rather than tenants as before. "What a pleasure it is to work on one's own farm," Mattie wrote. "I would rather live as we do than to have to rent and have some one bossing us."

Not all those in states convulsed by the Civil War waited until the conflict was over to seek land or other opportunities in the West. Remote territories far beyond the Mississippi were little affected by the struggle between North and South and offered refuge for men who preferred not to risk death fighting their fellow Americans. Young Samuel Clemens, whose home state of Missouri was bitterly divided between Unionists and secessionists, served briefly as a Confederate militiaman in 1861 before heading for Union-controlled Nevada Territory and taking the pen name Mark Twain in Virginia City, whose phenomenal output of silver and gold helped the wartime North remain solvent. Except for a short-lived invasion of New Mexico by Confederates from Texas, who hoped to bring much of the American Southwest under their flag but were repulsed at Glorieta Pass in 1862, the Far West and its mineral wealth remained firmly in Union hands for the duration.

Although there were no massive Civil War battles in the West to compare with the carnage at Shiloh in 1862 or at Gettysburg in 1863, the conflict proved disastrous for Missouri

> "THE LAST RAIL IS LAID, THE LAST SPIKE IS DRIVEN. THE PACIFIC RAILROAD IS FINISHED."
> —TELEGRAM TO PRESIDENT ULYSSES S. GRANT, MAY 10, 1869

and its neighbors as brutal guerrilla warfare spilled over into Unionist Kansas and Confederate Arkansas. In Indian Territory, the Cherokee and other tribes with divided loyalties were torn apart by the war. Elsewhere in the West, the Dakota Sioux and other tribes that had been pressed onto inadequate reservations by inequitable treaties lashed out at settlers and soldiers. Some tribes or bands like the Navajo were forced onto reservations at gunpoint or attacked by troops on their reservations, like the followers of the Cheyenne peace chief Black Kettle who were massacred in 1864 at Sand Creek in Colorado. In the late 1860s, when General Sherman turned from battling heavily armed Southerners to overseeing campaigns against lightly armed Indians, he did not ease up on his foes. "War is cruelty," he once declared. "The crueler it is, the sooner it will be over." Yet as the decade drew to a close, the wars he waged against Indians were not ending but intensifying.

REUNITING THE NATION

During the postwar era known as Reconstruction, the former Confederate states were restored to the Union. The federal government ultimately failed in its efforts to secure the rights of those in the South who had been freed from slavery and granted citizenship. But it succeeded in binding

Transcontinental railroad

1866 Work on the first transcontinental railroad accelerates as the Union Pacific advances westward from Omaha, Nebraska, and the Central Pacific pushes eastward from Sacramento, California.

1868 Fort Laramie Treaty with tribal leaders fails to bring lasting peace to the northern Plains while the Medicine Lodge Treaty of 1867 unravels on the southern Plains.

1869 Transcontinental railroad is completed as the Union Pacific and Central Pacific link up at Promontory Summit in Utah.

1865 The Civil War ends. Stand Watie of the Cherokee is the last Confederate general to surrender.

1867 Long cattle drives begin in earnest from Texas to rail depots in Kansas, where Abilene and other towns situated at trail's end cater to cowboys.

Cattle drive

the West more securely to the Union and drawing settlers there into the democratic process by organizing a half dozen new territories during the 1860s and admitting Kansas, Nebraska, and Nevada as states. Feuds sometimes developed between territorial governors—appointed by presidents who were staunch Unionists such as Ulysses S. Grant—and territorial legislators elected by voters with ties to the South. Yet wartime fears that Westerners might join Southerners in seceding soon dissipated.

Nothing did more to link the West to the nation as a whole than the construction of railroads, several of which began advancing across the Plains as the Union and Central Pacific neared completion. The fabled West of hard-riding cowboys and hair-raising Indians that became embedded in American popular culture was partly a product of those railroads. Long cattle drives from Texas to rail depots in Kansas in the late 1860s helped make cowboys legendary and encouraged ranchers to begin raising herds elsewhere in the West. They counted on railroads to deliver their goods to market, as did homesteaders or farmers who settled on land granted to railroads by the government. For Plains Indians, the "Iron Horse" and the vast expansion of grazing and settlement it made possible constituted the ultimate challenge to their proud horse culture—and a powerful symbol of everything they were fighting against. ∎

WAR AND PEACE This map shows Civil War battle sites in the West, including contests between Union and Confederate forces at Wilson's Creek in Missouri and Glorieta Pass in New Mexico, and clashes between American troops or settlers and Indians at New Ulm, Minnesota, and Sand Creek in Colorado. After the war, work accelerated on the Union Pacific and Central Pacific Railroads, which met at Promontory Summit in Utah, and cattle were driven north from Texas to depots on the Kansas Pacific Railway and other destinations.

STEAMING AHEAD In a Currier and Ives print entitled "The Route to California," a train follows tracks laid by Central Pacific Railroad crews in the late 1860s along the Truckee River, on the eastern flank of the Sierra Nevada.

PRESERVING THE UNION AND SPANNING THE CONTINENT 1861–1869

MONTANA TERRITORY

Missouri River

DAKOTA TERRITORY

MINNESOTA

Lake Superior

WISCONSIN

MICHIGAN

IDAHO TERRITORY

Snake River

R O C K Y

Belle Fourche River

WYOMING TERRITORY

Cheyenne River

Fort Laramie

G R E A T

Dakota Sioux Uprising

Mississippi River

Lake Michigan

Promontory Summit

Great Salt Lake

UNION PACIFIC RAILROAD

Ogallala

Missouri River

NEBRASKA

Omaha

Council Bluffs

IOWA

ILLINOIS

INDIANA

Cheyenne

UTAH TERRITORY

M O U N T A I N S

Denver

COLORADO TERRITORY

KANSAS PACIFIC RAILWAY

Sand Creek

Ellsworth

Topeka

Abilene

Lawrence

Kansas City

Sedalia

MISSOURI

KY.

Wilson's Creek

Colorado River

Arkansas River

Fort Lyon

GOODNIGHT-LOVING TRAIL

KANSAS

P L A I N S

Baxter Springs

Pea Ridge

Tahlequah

TENNESSEE

Grand Canyon

Canyon de Chelly

Santa Fe

Glorieta Pass

WESTERN TRAIL

INDIAN TERRITORY

ARKANSAS

ALA.

ARIZONA TERRITORY

NEW MEXICO TERRITORY

Valverde

Fort Sumner

Bosque Redondo

Red River

Mississippi River

MISSISSIPPI

SEDALIA AND BAXTER SPRINGS TRAIL

Shreveport

Gila River

Mesilla

TRAIL

TEXAS

San Angelo

CHISHOLM TRAIL

Brazos River

Sabine Crossroads

LOUISIANA

New Orleans

Rio Grande

Bandera

San Antonio

Nueces River

MEXICO

GULF OF MEXICO

Legend

— Transcontinental railroad
— Other railroad
— Cattle trail
• Site
○ City

1869 borders shown

110° 105° 100° 95° 90°

WAR ON THE FRONTIER

North Against South in the West

When the Civil War began in April 1861, there were four slave-holding states west of the Mississippi River. Unlike Louisiana, Arkansas, and Texas, Missouri was prevented from seceding by Union forces. Maj. Gen. John C. Frémont, the famed explorer and former presidential candidate, took command in St. Louis and vowed that he would "neither lose the state nor permit the enemy a foot of advantage." On August 30, after Union troops were defeated by Confederates at Wilson's Creek in south-west Missouri, Frémont imposed martial law and announced that the slaves of all rebellious Missourians "are hereby declared free." Lincoln feared that proclamation would drive Missouri and two other slave-holding Border States, Kentucky and Maryland, into the Confederate camp. He overruled Frémont and removed him. Lincoln would

Henry Hopkins Sibley

later issue his own Emancipation Proclamation, which exempted the Border States but declared all slaves in Confederate areas "forever free."

Slavery was not the only cause for conflict in the West. Fighting extended to remote areas with no slaves but much mineral wealth that would help finance war efforts. In October 1861, more than 3,000 Texans commanded by Brig. Gen. Henry Hopkins Sibley left San Antonio on horseback to seize control of New Mexico Territory—the first objective in a campaign that Confederates hoped would bring Colorado, Nevada, and California under their flag as well. Sibley's forces were preceded by a Texas battalion led by Lt. Col. John Baylor, who entered southern New Mexico virtually unopposed and claimed everything there below the 34th parallel (the lower half of today's New Mexico and Arizona) as the Confederate territory of Arizona. In January 1862, Sibley linked up with Baylor at Mesilla, the capital of Confederate Arizona. Nearly 4,000 Union troops commanded by Brig.

Edward Canby

Gen. Edward Canby stood between Mesilla in the south and Santa Fe in the north, the capital of Union-controlled New Mexico.

WESTERN SHOWDOWN Texas Confederates in the foreground target Union troops at Pigeon's Ranch in New Mexico during the Battle of Glorieta Pass on March 28, 1862. The Confederate snare drum at left was recovered after the Texans withdrew.

UNION ARMADA Gunboats of David Porter's fleet steam past Alexandria, Louisiana, during the Red River Campaign, commanded by Union general Nathaniel Banks, who was repulsed after leaving the protection of the gunboats in April 1864 and proceeding inland with his troops.

In February, Texans advanced up the Rio Grande and repulsed Canby's troops at Valverde. Sibley was unwell during that battle and relinquished command temporarily to a subordinate. Some of his soldiers thought he was not ill but drunk. His "love for liquor exceeded that for home, country or God," one Confederate charged. Doubts about Sibley's sobriety and fitness to command would later return to haunt him. But for now, the pressure was on Canby, who withdrew all the way to Fort Union in northeastern New Mexico, leaving Albuquerque and Santa Fe undefended. After occupying New Mexico's capital on March 10, Sibley prepared to seize Fort Union and invade Colorado. Union volunteers from Denver and nearby mining camps responded to that threat by marching several hundred miles to bolster Canby's forces at Fort Union.

As Texans advanced from Santa Fe on March 26, Coloradans led by Maj. John Chivington met them at Apache Canyon and prevailed there. Two days later, however, the Confederates renewed their offensive and were pressing their foes back through Glorieta Pass toward Fort Union when Chivington's men slipped around their flank on a mountain trail and destroyed the wagon train carrying their food, ammunition, and other essentials. "We have been crippled," lamented Sibley, who had remained back in Albuquerque during the battle and withdrew now under pressure from Canby. Hungry, thirsty, and demoralized, hundreds of Texans were captured or died under the glaring sun during that ignominious retreat to San Antonio. Sibley's reputation as a resourceful Army officer in the West and inventor of the Sibley tent was badly tarnished. Never again did Confederate forces threaten the Union's hold on the Far West, where a new Arizona Territory loyal to the United States, carved out of western New Mexico, was organized in 1863.

RED RIVER CAMPAIGN

In July 1863, Maj. Gen. Ulysses S. Grant captured Vicksburg and the Union took full control of the Mississippi River. Placed in command of the entire Union Army in early 1864, Grant was reluctant to commit troops to campaigns in the West now that Confederates there were isolated. Yet Lincoln and others in Washington prevailed on him to authorize an invasion of Texas, aimed at seizing its cotton fields, stemming the flow of weapons into that state from Mexico, and discouraging Napoleon III of France, who had intervened in Mexico, from backing the Confederacy. The coastal approach to Texas from Union-occupied New Orleans, seized by Adm. David Farragut in 1862, was closely guarded by Confederates. So the invasion plan called for 30,000 troops led by Maj. Gen. Nathaniel Banks to ascend the Red River in steamboats to Shreveport, Louisiana, before crossing into Texas.

A former governor of Massachusetts and speaker of the U.S. House of Representatives, Banks had more political clout than military acumen. Much like Sibley, he came close to achieving his goal, only to falter under pressure. Setting out in March with a fleet that consisted of transports carrying his troops, shielded by gunboats commanded by Rear Adm. David Porter, Banks made slow progress up the Red River, which was running low. In early

POLITICAL GENERAL **Although the failure of the Red River Campaign ended his military career, Nathaniel Banks returned to Congress after the Civil War and served as chairman of the House Foreign Affairs Committee.**

April, he decided to disembark with his troops and march to Shreveport. No longer under the protection of gunboats, they were attacked on April 8 at Sabine Crossroads by Confederates led by Maj. Gen. Richard Taylor, son of former president Zachary Taylor. Banks fell back to Pleasant Hill, regrouped there, and repulsed a second attack by Taylor the next day. "Had Banks followed up his success vigorously he would have met but feeble opposition," Taylor wrote afterward. But Banks withdrew and rejoined his fleet, which risked being stranded in low water. Only quick work by Union engineers, who constructed dams on the Red River and then allowed water to rush through chutes, enabled the fleet to retreat safely to the Gulf of Mexico.

Following the collapse of the Red River Campaign, Grant concentrated on crushing the Confederacy in the East. Yet fighting continued in the West until the bitter end. Not until June 1865, two months after Gen. Robert E. Lee surrendered to Grant at Appomattox, Virginia, did the last Confederate forces west of the Mississippi accept defeat and lay down their weapons. ∎

TECHNOLOGY

SIBLEY TENT

While serving as a U.S. Army officer in the West before the Civil War, Henry Hopkins Sibley admired the portable tepees of Plains Indians and designed a tent that was similar in shape but had just one pole at the center (right), supported at its base by a tripod. Sibley also invented a stove whose smoke vented through a pipe atop the tent. More than 40,000 Sibley tents were produced for use by the Union Army during the Civil War. Each one could accommodate a dozen men, sleeping in a circle with their feet toward the center. The main drawback was lack of ventilation when the flaps were closed. As one recruit from Massachusetts remarked, "In cold or rainy weather, when every opening is closed, they are most unwholesome tenements, and to enter one of them of a rainy morning from the outer air, and encounter the night's accumulation of nauseating exhalations from the bodies of twelve men (differing widely in their habits of personal cleanliness) was an experience which no old soldier has ever been known to recall with any great enthusiasm."

Sibley patented his tent in 1856. It would have earned him a fortune had he remained loyal to the United States. But when his home state of Louisiana seceded and he joined the Confederate Army, General Sibley was denied royalties for the tents purchased by the Union Army. He died impoverished in 1886 at the age of 70.

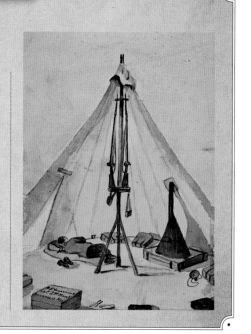

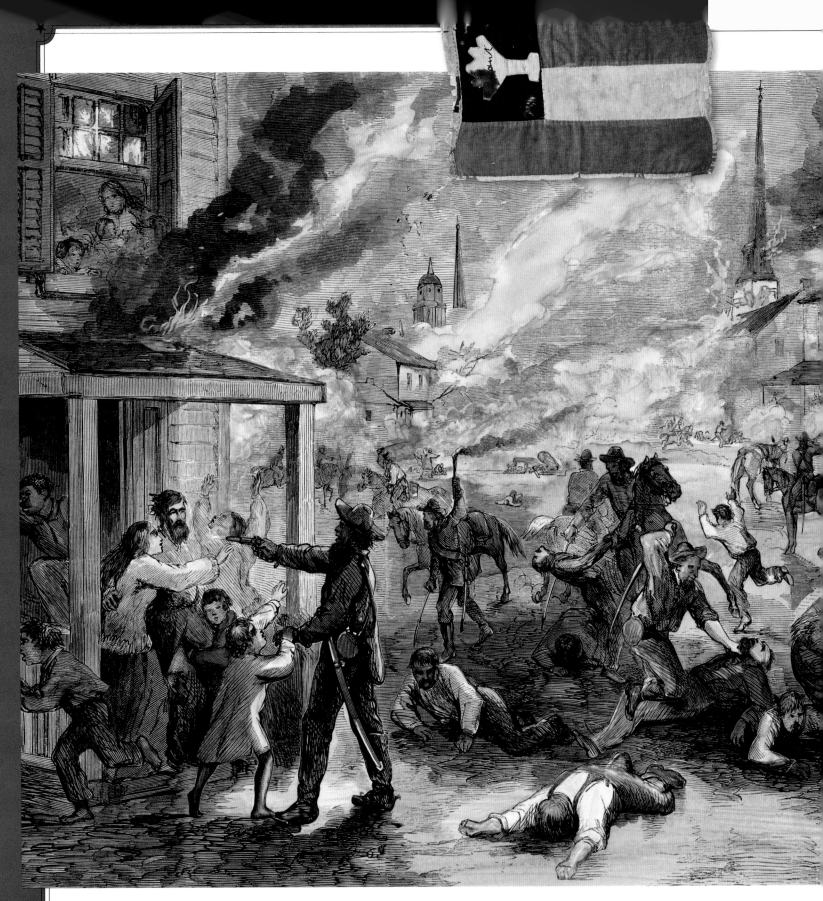

MURDER AND MAYHEM Flames engulf Lawrence, Kansas, a Union stronghold attacked on August 21, 1863, by Confederate guerrillas. Those partisans slaughtered many of the town's male inhabitants, as ordered by their leader, William Quantrill, who flew the flag at top.

BUSHWHACKERS VERSUS JAYHAWKERS

Guerrilla Warfare in Missouri and Kansas

Nowhere was the Civil War more savage or severe than along the Missouri-Kansas border, where much of the fighting was done not by regular troops but by partisans or guerrillas with little regard for military conventions such as sparing civilians. Partisans from Missouri who sided with the Confederacy were known as bushwhackers or border ruffians—a label for proslavery men who had crossed into Kansas in the 1850s and clashed with antislavery agitators like John Brown. Not all bushwhackers owned slaves, but most were Southerners by heritage and rebels by nature who would sooner kill Unionists than be bossed by them. Their foes in Kansas, called jayhawkers, were mostly of northern origins and included dedicated abolitionists as well as rowdies seeking plunder and vengeance. In September 1861, jayhawkers led by James Lane—a firebrand from Lawrence, Kansas, who vowed to cast bushwhackers "into a burning hell"—torched Osceola, Missouri, and executed nine Confederate sympathizers there.

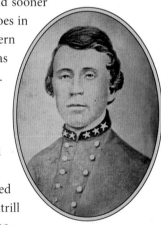

William Quantrill

Lane's nemesis was a former jayhawker turned bushwhacker named William Quantrill. Quantrill had fled Lawrence after betraying a plot by abolitionists, who were shot dead while attempting to free slaves in Missouri from their master, to whom Quantrill revealed the plan. In 1863, he set out to wreak havoc in Lawrence with fellow bushwhackers, including hardened killers like William "Bloody Bill" Anderson and a young gunman who would later gain notoriety, Cole Younger. Early on August 21, several hundred of those partisans approached Lawrence with orders from Quantrill to "kill every man big enough to carry a gun." His chief target was James Lane, who fled through the rear window of his home in his nightshirt. Had he captured Lane, Quantrill said later, "I would have burned him at the stake." Few others escaped the raiders, who killed 185 men and boys and left much of Lawrence in ashes. The terror they spread in Kansas soon came back to haunt Missouri, where Brig. Gen. Thomas Ewing ordered four counties near Kansas that harbored bushwhackers vacated. Jayhawkers attacked Missourians ousted from their homes and torched their property, leaving behind a wasteland called the Burnt District. ∎

TUMULT IN INDIAN TERRITORY

Civil Strife Within the Tribes

◆━●━◆

Wedged between Unionist Kansas and the Confederate states of Texas and Arkansas, tribes in Indian Territory were given little choice but to choose sides. Soon after the war began, Albert Pike, an Arkansas lawyer and author who served as Confederate Commissioner of Indian Affairs, sought treaties with representatives of the Five Civilized Tribes, which had been removed from the Southeast to Indian Territory in the 1830s. Many wealthy and influential members of those tribes owned black slaves, who made up nearly 15 percent of the territory's 100,000 or so inhabitants. Even some Indians who were not slaveholders favored the Confederacy over the Union, which had long pursued policies that favored white settlers at the expense of tribes.

Pike quickly reached agreement with the Choctaw and Chickasaw, who lived near Texas and had economic ties to their southern neighbors. He also induced prominent Seminoles, Creeks, and Cherokees to sign treaties allying them with the Confederacy, but they did not represent their tribes as a whole. Some chiefs objected to those treaties, including Billy Bowlegs of the Seminole and Opothleyahola of the Creek, both of whom fled to Kansas with their followers and backed the Union. John Ross, the principal chief of the Cherokee, favored neutrality but accepted the treaty with Pike to keep his rival Stand Watie, leader of the pro-Confederate faction, from breaking away. Watie had been among the minority of Cherokees who accepted removal to Indian

CHOOSING SIDES The flag above was carried by the Cherokee Mounted Rifles, a Confederate regiment commanded by Col. Stand Watie. The soldier at top was among those in Indian Territory who responded to Union recruitment efforts, including posters seeking "Indian Fighters" (opposite), and were sworn in to oppose Confederates.

territory while Ross and his followers resisted until they were forced into exile. That bitter dispute lingered, and Ross feared armed conflict within the tribe if he and Watie took opposing positions.

Although Pike's treaties with the five tribes did not require them to fight for the Confederacy outside Indian Territory, they came under pressure to do so. By 1862, Pike had been commissioned a brigadier general in the Confederate Army and was ordered by Maj. Gen. Earl Van Dorn of Texas to cross into Arkansas with his force—which included a Cherokee regiment led by Col. Stand Watie—and oppose Union troops advancing south from Missouri. The two sides collided in March at Pea Ridge in northern Arkansas, where the Cherokees captured a Union battery but were eventually repulsed along with the rest of Van Dorn's army. When Van Dorn learned that some Cherokees had scalped their Union enemies, he ordered Pike to prevent his Indian troops from committing any further "barbarities upon the wounded, prisoners, or dead who may fall into their hands." Indians were not the only ones to mutilate or massacre their enemies during the Civil War. Bloody Bill Anderson and other partisans in Missouri scalped their foes, and soldiers on both sides sometimes allowed their opponents no quarter and killed those who tried to surrender. Stung by Van Dorn's reproof, Pike later resigned rather than commit his forces to any more battles outside Indian Territory. Watie remained a dutiful Confederate officer, however, and

CHEROKEE FOES Longtime Cherokee rivals Stand Watie (near right) and John Ross (far right) became outright enemies in 1863 when Chief Ross backed the Union while Colonel Watie stood by the Confederacy.

rose to the rank of brigadier general in command of Indian troops.

In June 1862, Col. William Weer invaded Indian Territory from Kansas with Union forces that included Creeks, Seminoles, and Cherokees, returning from exile to break the Confederate grip on their tribes. John Ross offered no resistance when soldiers sent by Weer arrived at his home in Park Hill, near the Cherokee capital of Tahlequah, to arrest him. Conflict within the tribe could no longer be avoided, and Ross willingly sided with Cherokee Unionists. Weer's offensive faltered that summer, but Union forces soon reentered Indian Territory from Arkansas and

HISTORIC SITE

TAHLEQUAH: THE CONTESTED CHEROKEE CAPITAL

Founded in 1839 after Cherokees were evicted from Georgia by U.S. troops and forced down the Trail of Tears, Tahlequah served as capital of the resurgent Cherokee Nation in Indian Territory. By the 1850s, it had several schools, a National Hotel, and government buildings that included a council house and the Cherokee National Supreme Court (inset), which also housed the printing press of an official newspaper, the *Cherokee Advocate.*

During the Civil War, Tahlequah was fiercely contested by Cherokee Unionists known as Pins and opposing Cherokee Confederates led by Stand Watie, a relative of Major Ridge and his son John Ridge, who had signed the controversial treaty that removed the tribe from Georgia and were condemned to death for doing so. In July 1863, Watie's troops routed the Pins in Tahlequah and burned government buildings there. He described that attack matter-of-factly in a letter to his wife, Sarah: "Killed a few Pins in Tahlequah. They had been holding council. I had the old council house set on fire and burnt down."

The handsome Cherokee National Supreme Court building survived Watie's raid and emerged from the Civil War intact. The oldest government building in what is now the state of Oklahoma, it serves today as a museum in Tahlequah documenting the eventful history of the Cherokee Nation.

made Fort Gibson in Cherokee territory their stronghold. Stand Watie harried their supply lines and destroyed a train of 250 wagons carrying food and clothing to the fort, which served as refuge for hundreds of noncombatants. Fort Gibson held out, but Watie's troops scourged Cherokee Unionists in Tahlequah and torched buildings there.

DIVIDED LOYALTIES

The bitter strife within the Cherokee tribe was intensified by old resentments between those Unionists—who were known

GRAND COUNCIL Two decades before the Civil War engulfed Indian Territory and tore tribes apart, their leaders met at a peace council hosted by Chief Ross at Tahlequah in 1843, as depicted here by artist John Mix Stanley.

as Pins for an insignia they wore and were often full-blooded tribal traditionalists—and their opponents, many of them mixed-blood Cherokees who owned slaves and had ancestral ties to white Southerners. Hannah Hicks, the daughter of a white missionary, lost her Cherokee husband when Pins mistook him for a Confederate and killed him. "Alas, alas for this miserable people," she wrote, "destroying each other, as fast as they can: my heart cries out, O Lord, how long?"

Other tribes in Indian Territory whose leaders had sided with the Confederacy when the war began suffered similar convulsions and struggled to reunite and rebuild their communities when the fighting ended in 1865. The victorious Union required them not just to emancipate their slaves but to cede large tracts of land, which served as reservations for Plains Indians who were pressured by authorities into settling there after clashing with American settlers and soldiers. ■

THE UNION'S INDIAN WARS

Uprisings Across the West

Not all those who fought for the Union during the Civil War battled Confederates. Tens of thousands ended up fighting Indians in western conflicts that spread like wildfire. None was deadlier than the uprising by Dakota Sioux in Minnesota in 1862. They had given up much of their territory in exchange for a reservation along the Minnesota River and $475,000 in annuities—yearly payments in cash, food, and other essentials. More than $300,000 went to traders who made exorbitant claims against Dakotas for goods they had obtained on credit. In 1862, the tribe's diminished annuities were delayed because federal officials were preoccupied with the Civil War. Dakotas went hungry, but Indian agent Thomas Galbraith withheld food stored in the government warehouse and traders refused them further credit until the annuities arrived. "If they are hungry," said trader Andrew Myrick, "let them eat grass."

In August, some young Dakota men returned empty-handed from a hunting expedition and killed several white settlers living near the reservation. Rather than surrender them for punishment, tribal militants urged Chief Little Crow to lead an all-out attack on Americans. Once an avid warrior, Little Crow was now 52 and wary of challenging U.S. forces. "You will die like the rabbits when the hungry wolves hunt them down in the Hard Moon," he warned the militants. But he would not abandon them to their fate. Little Crow was "no coward," he said. "He will die with you."

Trader Myrick was among the first casualties of the uprising, found dead with grass stuffed in his mouth. In weeks to come, Dakota war parties killed several hundred settlers, many of them recent emigrants from northern Europe. Few of the men were spared,

DAKOTA WARRIORS Chief Little Crow (above) reluctantly agreed to lead an uprising by Dakota Sioux in western Minnesota in August 1862. He urged a concerted attack on U.S. troops at Fort Ridgely, but some warriors instead targeted settlers in New Ulm, where Dakotas fighting on foot and on horseback (right) wreaked havoc before retreating.

but many women and children were held captive. In the town of New Ulm, residents raised barricades and fought pitched battles with Dakotas, who retreated after killing or wounding nearly 60 settlers. Little Crow focused his attacks on a military target, nearby Fort Ridgely, but soldiers there repulsed his warriors with artillery fire.

In late August, 1,500 militiamen set out against the Dakotas from St. Paul, led by Henry Hopkins Sibley (not to be confused with Confederate officer Henry Hastings Sibley). A former trader who became governor of Minnesota, Sibley had a child by a Dakota woman. But his close ties to the tribe had not stopped him from claiming a sizable portion of its annuities, and he was intent on crushing the uprising. By late September, Sibley's forces had routed Little Crow's warriors, reclaimed the captives, and rounded up Dakota suspects, more than 300 of whom were sentenced to death by a military tribunal. Henry Benjamin Whipple, an Episcopal bishop who blamed the

PEACE CHIEF Cheyenne leader Black Kettle sought to avoid conflict in Colorado in 1864, only to be attacked by troops at Sand Creek along with his followers.

uprising on official corruption and incompetence, appealed to President Lincoln on their behalf. Whipple denounced "the rascality of this Indian business until I felt it down to my boots," said Lincoln, who reviewed the evidence and revoked most of the death sentences.

In December 1862, 38 men found guilty of murder or rape went to the gallows. By then, most Dakotas had fled Minnesota or been evicted from the state. Some later returned furtively like Little Crow, who was shot to death in 1863 by a settler who received a $500 reward. Many Dakotas joined forces with other Sioux in the newly organized Dakota Territory, which bore their name but offered them little refuge from pursuing troops or encroaching settlers in years to come.

CARNAGE IN COLORADO
Intent on suppressing Indian hostilities in their territory, two prominent figures in Colorado ended up causing mayhem. In April 1864, rumors of a mass uprising by Cheyennes and other Plains Indians prompted Governor John Evans to dispatch cavalry under Col. John Chivington with orders to "kill Cheyennes wherever and whenever found." Chivington, who had helped repulse the Confederate invasion of New Mexico, hoped to be elected to Congress when Colorado became a state, and Evans looked forward to serving in the U.S. Senate. Their political prospects would be enhanced if they crushed tribal resistance. Instead, Cheyennes retaliated against Chivington's punishing assaults by joining warriors of other tribes in attacking wagon trains, stagecoaches, and ranches in eastern Colorado. Evans put the bodies of settlers slain in one assault on display in Denver and authorized citizens to kill "all such hostile Indians."

As war fever gripped the territory,

MASS EXECUTION As shown here, 38 Dakotas were hanged in Mankato, Minnesota, on December 26, 1862, for assaults on settlers during the uprising. Many other condemned men were spared by President Lincoln, who found the evidence against them insufficient.

PACIFIC TELEGRAPH COMPANY.

NO. 1.] TERMS AND CONDITIONS ON WHICH MESSAGES ARE RECEIVED BY THIS COMPANY FOR TRANSMISSION.

The public are notified that, in order to guard against mistakes in the transmission of messages, every message of importance ought to be repeated, by being sent back from the station at which it is to be received, to the station from which it is originally sent. Half the usual price for repeating the message; and while this Company will, as heretofore, use every precaution to ensure correctness, it will not be responsible for mistakes or delays in the transmission or delivery of repeated messages, beyond an amount exceeding five hundred times the amount paid for sending the message; nor will it be responsible for mistakes or delays in the transmission of unrepeated messages from whatever cause they may arise, nor for the delays arising from interruptions in the working of its Telegraph, nor for any mistake or omission of any other Company, over whose lines a message is to be sent to reach the place of destination. All messages will hereafter be received by this Company for transmission, subject to the above conditions.

E. CREIGHTON, Sup't, Omaha, N. T.   J. H. WADE, Pres't, Cleveland, O.

To Col Chivington   Fly June 7 1864
          By Telegraph from Leavenworth 186

What troops have moved and where are they, What can you send forward The sending of supplies as well as Indian troubles makes it important to know. The Indians are very troublesome between Fort Lyon and the Kansas settlement

                         S R Curtis
                              Maj Genl

| 3g $\overline{Di}$ 415 pd σcs |

SAND CREEK MASSACRE Under pressure from Maj. Gen. Samuel Curtis—who sent the telegram at left in June 1864 and later wrote that "I want no peace till the Indians suffer more"—Col. John Chivington attacked Black Kettle's camp on November 29. Ignoring the American flag raised there to appease them (below), Chivington's men went on a murderous rampage.

Chief Black Kettle of the Southern Cheyenne sought to avoid bloodshed. When Chivington vowed to continue fighting Indians "until they lay down their arms and submit to military authority," Black Kettle and his followers submitted to Maj. Edward Wynkoop at Fort Lyon and remained there safely until Wynkoop was called to account for harboring and feeding those Indians. They were then told to return to their bleak reservation along Sand Creek near the Kansas border.

That gave Chivington, who was being criticized for inaction, an easy target. At dawn on November 29, his forces approached Black Kettle's vulnerable camp on Sand Creek.

The chief hurriedly displayed a U.S. flag and a white flag atop his lodge to signal his peaceful intentions. But Chivington was out for blood and told his men to take no prisoners. An Army interpreter later testified that they "used their knives, ripped open women, clubbed little children . . . mutilated their bodies in every sense of the word." Nearly 200 people were massacred. Black Kettle escaped the carnage, but he found no peace. In 1868, while camped along the Washita River in Indian Territory, he perished in an attack eerily similar to the nightmare he endured at Sand Creek, carried out by a brash young Civil War veteran, Lt. Col. George Armstrong Custer. ■

THE LONG WALK
Exile of the Navajos

In September 1862, Brig. Gen. James Carleton became military commander in New Mexico. He had arrived there with Union troops from California too late to help oust invading Confederates. So he waged war instead on Apaches and Navajos, who had long raided New Mexican settlements. Carleton relied mightily on Col. Kit Carson and his New Mexico volunteers. Carson was a tenacious Indian fighter, but when sent against Mescalero Apaches in late 1862 he refrained from carrying out Carleton's order to kill all men of that tribe "whenever and wherever they can be found." Instead, Carson pressured them into surrendering. By mid-1863, many were confined at Bosque Redondo, a dismal reservation along the Pecos River in eastern New Mexico, guarded by troops from nearby Fort Sumner. Bosque Redondo could barely support those Apaches, but Carleton intended to confine the entire Navajo population there as well.

Carleton denied Carson's request to resign from service and sent him to Navajo country along the Arizona–New Mexico border to evict that tribe from its rugged homeland. Waging total warfare even harsher than that used to deprive

Kit Carson

die-hard Confederates in the South of subsistence, Carson's troops destroyed the homes and crops of defiant Navajos and killed their sheep and other livestock. In January 1864, Carson's forces entered Canyon de Chelly, a place sacred to Navajos where red cliffs rose high above the valley floor. After showering the invaders with arrows and rocks hurled from the cliff tops, famished Navajo warriors surrendered, explaining to Carson that many of their women and children had already died of starvation.

More than 11,000 Navajos who survived the campaign were dispatched to Bosque Redondo—a grueling trek of some 400 miles known as the Long Walk because even elders and women with babies on their backs made the journey on foot. Hundreds died along the way, and others were seized by New Mexicans and reduced to servitude. Conditions for the 9,000 or so Navajos who settled at Bosque Redondo were so miserable that Lt. Gen. William Tecumseh Sherman—the supreme exponent of total warfare against Confederates and Indians—acknowledged their plight when he visited the reservation in 1868. Making a rare concession, he agreed to a treaty allowing those Navajos to return to their homeland. ∎

UPROOTED Navajos like those pictured above who were forced onto the bleak reservation at Bosque Redondo endured hunger and humiliation. Chief Manuelito (opposite) held out with his band against confinement there until 1866 and later signed the treaty that returned Navajos to their ancestral territory.

MARK TWAIN'S WESTERN FORAY
Adventures of an Ex-Confederate

In June 1861, when the Civil War was new and exciting and drawing thousands of young men into uniform, 25-year-old Samuel Clemens left his job as a Mississippi River steamboat pilot and formed an amateurish Confederate militia company called the Marion Rangers with some of his boyhood friends in Hannibal, Missouri. For many of them, he wrote, "this military expedition of ours was simply a holiday." They soon realized that soldiering was no picnic and disbanded. Clemens cared little which side won and was glad to be out of it. When his older brother Orion, a dedicated Unionist, was appointed secretary of the newly organized Nevada Territory and invited him along, he jumped at the chance. Like others in states consumed by the conflict, he found refuge in the Far West. His eventful journey there transformed little-known Sam Clemens into a gifted writer and budding celebrity called Mark Twain.

In August 1861, after a bone-jarring stagecoach ride that he later memorialized in his book *Roughing It* (inset), he and Orion arrived in Carson City, Nevada's capital. Like most who flocked to that territory after silver and gold were discovered there, he hoped to strike it rich but found digging for ore grueling and profitless. In September 1862, he set aside pick and shovel and went to work as a reporter for the Virginia City *Territorial Enterprise*. Situated atop the fabulously rich Comstock Lode, Virginia City was a rowdy town where men were quick to take offense. Adopting the pen name Mark Twain helped shield him from angry readers until he became too well known to escape them. Like many journalists in those days, Twain did not always stick to the facts. He sometimes fabricated stories to amuse his audience, but not everyone got the joke. One whopper of his that appeared in print caused the editor of a rival newspaper to brand him a "vulgar liar." Twain, who carried a pistol but could not shoot straight, nearly ended up in a duel. He concluded that he had outstayed his welcome in this rough mining district where, as he later quipped, a newcomer was not respected until he had "killed his man."

In May 1864, Twain left Virginia City for California and went on to win renown for his satirical prose. By fleeing the Civil War and heading west, he had found his calling as an author whose weapon of choice was his razor-sharp wit. ∎

TERRITORIAL-Enterprise
Mark Twain, Editor 1863
Virginia City, Nevada.

AUTHOR IN TRAINING
Mark Twain honed his skills as a writer in Virginia City, Nevada, by working as a reporter and editor for the *Territorial Enterprise*. A man resembling the young Mark Twain (opposite) stands at center in the picture at left, behind the stovepipe in the newspaper's office.

NEVADA'S COMSTOCK LODE
The Hard Life of Hard-Rock Miners

Beginning in 1860, Nevada's Comstock Lode yielded more than $300 million in silver and gold over the next few decades. Virginia City and nearby Gold Hill merged into one big boomtown, home to as many as 25,000 people by the mid-1870s, or roughly half the population of Nevada as a whole. Many of its inhabitants were miners, but they were not freewheeling fortune hunters like the forty-niners who had panned for gold along rivers and streams in California. These miners labored for wages deep underground, often wielding picks and sledgehammers to break rocks containing precious ore, which yielded nearly 60 percent silver on average and 40 percent gold. Men worked shirtless in sweltering heat, retreating periodically to cooling stations filled with buckets of ice before resuming their hazardous tasks, which included laying charges of black powder or dynamite that sometimes exploded prematurely, killing or maiming miners.

"If you wish to visit one of those mines," wrote Mark Twain after visiting several of them himself, "you may walk through a tunnel about half a mile long if you prefer it, or you may take the quicker plan of shooting like a dart

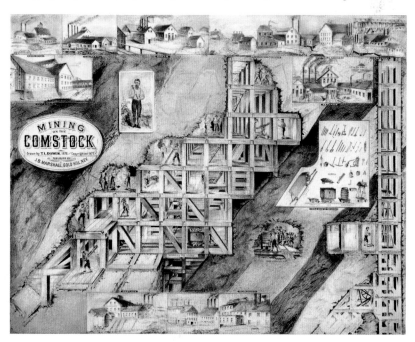

DIGGING DEEP Miners like those at left labored far below the surface on the Comstock Lode, shown above in a cutaway revealing the innovative square-set timber method, which supported deep mines in much the same way that steel frameworks supported tall buildings.

BOOMTOWN Pictured here in 1870, bustling Virginia City was one of the largest towns in the Far West before its mineral wealth was exhausted in the late 19th century.

down a shaft, on a small platform. It is like tumbling down through an empty steeple, feet first. When you reach the bottom, you take a candle and tramp through drifts and tunnels where throngs of men are digging and blasting; you watch them send up tubs full of great lumps of stone . . . you reflect frequently that you are buried under a mountain, a thousand feet below daylight . . . when your legs fail you at last, you lie down in a small box-car in a cramped 'incline' like a half up-ended sewer and are dragged up to daylight feeling as if you are crawling through a coffin that has no end to it."

When disaster struck, the deep mines of the Comstock Lode became death traps. On April 7, 1869, a fire erupted in the Yellow Jacket Mine 800 feet below the surface and raged for days, killing about 40 miners, many of them asphyxiated by smoke and toxic fumes that spread through tunnels to two other mines. The entire community was "shrouded in gloom at the ghastly occurrence," reported the *Territorial Enterprise,* which contrasted the calamity to earlier mine accidents that claimed one or two lives. "This time the story is not of a singular man precipitated down a shaft, or crushed by a falling mass of earth. It is a whole chapter of fire and suffocation—of mangled and blackened bodies—of two score of strong men desperately struggling for life, and finally perishing by fire, smoke and poisonous gases, hundreds of feet under ground." One boss, described by a reporter as a "simple yet kindly soul," notified the wife of a miner who perished by appearing at her door and inquiring, "Does the *Widow* Williams live here?"

EARNING A LIVING

Men took such risks because mining was their livelihood and paid well by 19th-century standards—at least four dollars an hour, which became the minimum wage for miners on the Comstock Lode after they unionized in opposition to pay cuts in the mid-1860s. Working eight-hour shifts six days a week, men made enough to support families, helped by wives who often earned income by cooking, sewing, or laundering when not performing their own household tasks. Virginia City and Gold Hill evolved during the 1860s from rough mining camps with few female inhabitants to respectable communities with hundreds of married couples and dozens of teachers, preachers, doctors, dentists, and nurses. Those who cared for the sick and wounded had their hands full, for mining the ore was no less dangerous than milling it, which involved pulverizing the rock and separating out the precious metal using mercury, which emitted toxic vapors as it boiled away.

A few venturesome miners became successful mine owners like John Mackay, an Irish immigrant who started out laboring belowground for the standard wage, rose to become superintendent of a mining company, and then

BOUNTY FROM BELOW Miners emerging from shafts on the Comstock Lode in the late 1860s push cars piled with rocks containing silver and gold.

began probing with partners for new veins of ore—one of which turned out to be the Big Bonanza, a mine that made him one of the wealthiest men in the world. Others who got rich exploiting the Comstock Lode were savvy veterans of the California gold rush like George Hearst, who profited hugely on his timely $3,000 investment in Virginia City's Ophir Mine and bequeathed a fortune to his son, publisher William Randolph Hearst.

By the late 1800s, the legendary Comstock Lode was all but exhausted. Virginia City and Gold Hill met the fate of other western mining districts that boomed spectacularly and ultimately went bust, reducing once flourishing communities to ghost towns. ■

SOCIAL HISTORY

WESTERN MINERS FROM ABROAD

The Comstock Lode was a magnet for immigrants. Some of the most experienced miners came from the British county of Cornwall, where tin and copper had been extracted for centuries. By 1870, about 10 percent of those living in Virginia City and Gold Hill were Cornish or British. Tensions arose between the Cornish and the Irish, who made up about 20 percent of the population and often had less mining experience but competed strenuously for jobs. On one occasion, a boxing match between Irish and Cornish contestants sparked a brawl between their fans. "While all who participated were badly whipped," a journalist reported, "no one was victorious."

Chinese immigrants made up about 7 percent of the population but were barred from working in the mines and often toiled for lower wages as servants or cooks. No foreign country lay closer to the Comstock Lode or had a larger corps of miners than Mexico, but Mexicans were not welcome here and comprised less than one percent of the population. More than five times that number came from Germany, among them engineer Philip Deidesheimer, whose square-set timber method, devised in Virginia City, was widely adopted to buttress deep mines and prevent cave-ins. Germans miners frequented a beer garden run by Jacob Van Bokkelen, a merchant of Dutch ancestry who died in 1873 when explosives stored in his room for use in the mines accidentally detonated.

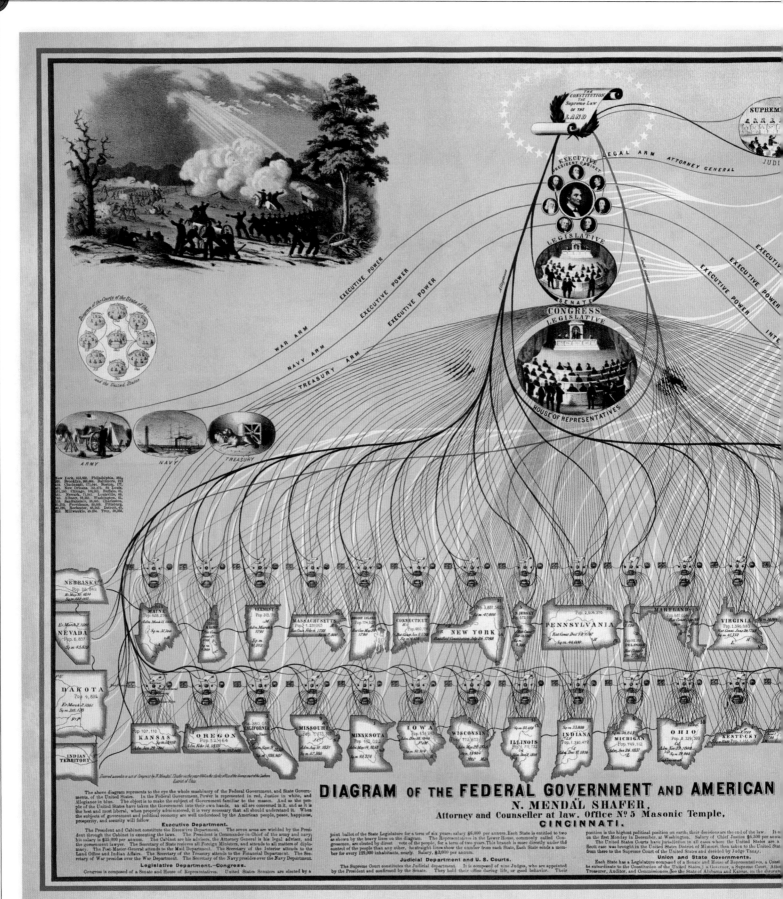

THE CONSTITUTION THE Supreme Law OF THE LAND

SUPREME

JUDI

EXECUTIVE PRESIDENT CABINET

LEGAL ARM   ATTORNEY GENERAL

EXECUTIVE POWER   INTE

LEGISLATIVE

SENATE

CONGRESS LEGISLATIVE

HOUSE OF REPRESENTATIVES

EXECUTIVE POWER

EXECUTIVE POWER

EXECUTIVE POWER

WAR ARM

NAVY ARM

TREASURY ARM

ARMY   NAVY   TREASURY

Diagram of the Courts of the State of Ohio
and the United States

New York, 813,669. Philadelphia, 565,
Brooklyn, 396,004. Baltimore, 213
Cincinnati, 171,041. Boston, 177,
New Orleans, 168,675. St. Louis,
Chicago, 109,263. Buffalo, 81,
Newark, 71,941. Louisville, 68,
Albany, 62,360. Washington, 61,
San Francisco, 56,600. Charleston,
Providence, 50,666. Pittsburg,
Rochester, 48,353. Detroit, 45,
Milwaukie, 45,254. Troy, 39,235.

NEBRASKA
Pop 28,882

NEVADA
Pop 6,857

DAKOTA
Pop 4,834

INDIAN TERRITORY

MAINE
Pop 628,276

VERMONT
Pop 315,

MASSACHUSETTS
Pop 1,231,065

RHODE ISLAND
Pop 174,6

CONNECTICUT

NEW YORK
Pop 3,887,542

N JERSEY

PENNSYLVANIA
Pop 2,906,310

MARYLAND

VIRGINIA
Pop 1,596,683

DELAWARE

KANSAS

OREGON
Pop 52,464

CALIFORNIA

MISSOURI

MINNESOTA

IOWA

WISCONSIN

ILLINOIS

INDIANA
Pop 1,350,470

MICHIGAN
Pop 749,112

OHIO
Pop 2,339,59

KENTUCKY

DIAGRAM of THE FEDERAL GOVERNMENT AND AMERICAN

N. MENDÄL SHAFER,
Attorney and Counseller at law. Office Nº 5 Masonic Temple,
CINCINNATI.

The above diagram represents to the eye the whole machinery of the Federal Government, and State Governments of the United States. In the Federal Government, Power is represented in red, Justice in white, and Allegiance in blue. The object is to make the subject of Government familiar to the masses. And as the people of the United States have taken the Government into their own hands, as all are concerned in it, and as it is the best and most liberal, when properly administered, it is very necessary that all should understand it. When the subjects of government and political economy are well understood by the American people, peace, happiness, prosperity, and security will follow.

Executive Department.

The President and Cabinet constitute the Executive Department. The seven arms are wielded by the President through the Cabinet is executing the laws. The President is Commander-in-Chief of the army and navy; his salary is $25,000 per annum. The Cabinet are his advisers, the Attorney General is his legal adviser, and the government lawyer. The Secretary of State receives all Foreign Ministers, and attends to all matters of diplomacy. The Post-Master-General attends to the Mail Department. The Secretary of the Interior attends to the Land Office and Indian Affairs. The Secretary of the Treasury attends to the Financial Department. The Secretary of War presides over the War Department. The Secretary of the Navy presides over the Navy Department.

Legislative Department.—Congress.

Congress is composed of a Senate and House of Representatives. United States Senators are elected by a joint ballot of the State Legislature for a term of six years; salary $6,000 per annum. Each State is entitled to two as shown by the heavy lines on the diagram. The Representatives in the Lower House, commonly called Congressmen, are elected by direct vote of the people, for a term of two years. This branch is more directly under the control of the people than any other, he straight lines show the number from each State, Each State sends a member for every 129,000 inhabitants, nearly. Salary, $3,000 per annum.

Judicial Department and U. S. Courts.

The Supreme Court constitutes the Judicial department. It is composed of nine Judges, who are appointed by the President and confirmed by the Senate. They hold their office during life, or good behavior. Their position is the highest political position on earth; their decisions are the end of the law. It is on the first Monday in December, at Washington. Salary of Chief Justice $6,500 per annum. The United State Courts have jurisdiction in all cases where the United States are a Scott case was brought in the United State District Court of Missouri, then taken to the United States from there to the Supreme Court of the United States and decided by Judge Taney.

Union and State Governments.

Each State has a Legislature composed of a Senate and House of Representatives, a Constitution be subordinate to the Constitution of the United States,) a Governor, a Supreme Court, Attorney Treasurer, Auditor, and Commissioners. See the State of Alabama and Kansas, on the diagram.

ORGANIZING THE WEST

Territories on the Path to Statehood

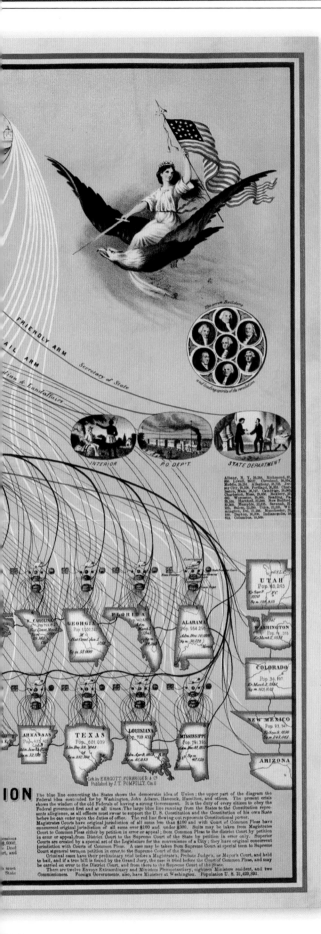

David W. Ballard

etween 1861 and 1864, the embattled Union tightened its hold on the West by admitting Kansas as a state and organizing six new territories: Colorado, Dakota, Nevada, Idaho, Arizona, and Montana. Nevada with its Comstock Lode was especially valuable to the Union and achieved statehood in October 1864, despite having a population of only about 40,000—less than any western state admitted previously. President Lincoln counted on Nevada to help him win reelection in November 1864 and push through Congress the 13th Amendment abolishing slavery.

After the Civil War, most western territories waited far longer than Nevada to achieve statehood. Nebraska, organized in 1854, entered the Union in 1867, followed by Colorado in 1876, but other applicants were put on hold as Republicans who dominated the White House vied with resurgent Democrats in Congress. Political partisanship sometimes caused trouble in the territories. In 1866, David W. Ballard became governor of Idaho and Solomon Howlett became secretary there. Like their counterparts in other territories, they were federal appointees, and both were loyal Republicans. The Idaho legislature, on the other hand, was chosen by voters there, many of them Democrats from Missouri with Confederate sympathies who had fled that state during the Civil War after Unionists took charge. Ballard clashed with Democratic legislators, and Howlett withheld their pay until they signed an oath of allegiance required of officeholders by Congress, pledging that they were loyal to the United States and had never aided or encouraged its enemies. Legislators refused to sign and protested by ransacking their chamber and tossing furniture out the window. Ballard then called in U.S. troops to maintain order.

In January 1867, the legislators backed down and signed the oath, but ill will between the governor and the legislature lingered for years. Not until 1890 did Idaho achieve statehood, along with Wyoming and four other western states admitted in a flurry the year before—North Dakota, South Dakota, Montana, and Washington. ∎

NATIONAL TIES An 1862 patriotic print for Unionists shows the 9 western territories of the time and all 34 states, including those in the Confederacy, attached to the United States in the form of the Lincoln Administration and the Constitution, Congress, and Supreme Court.

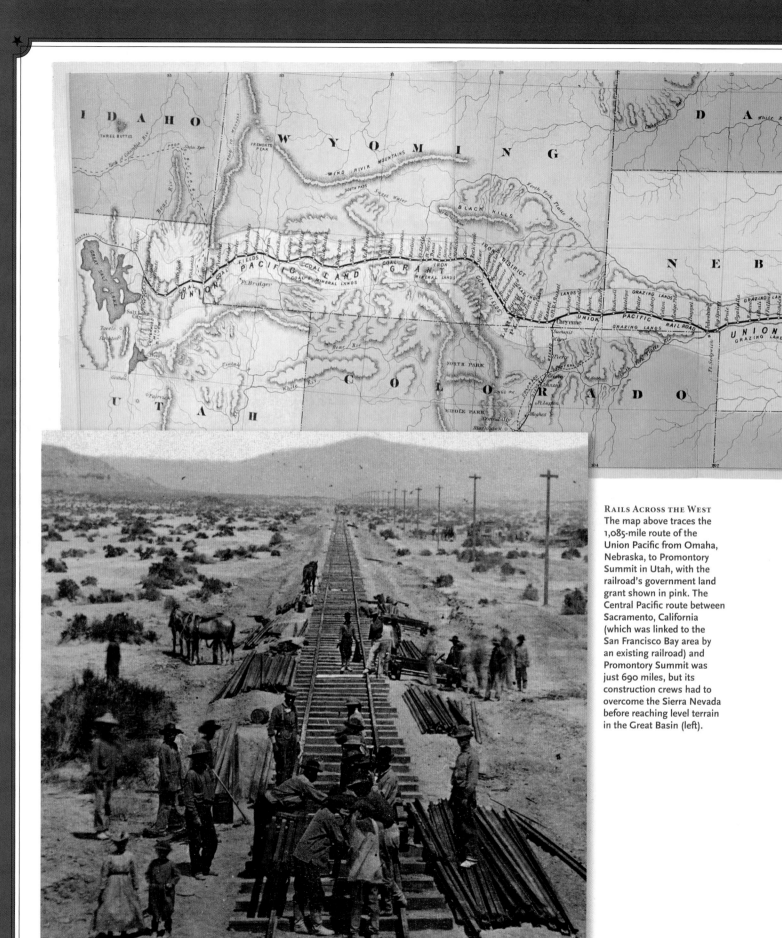

RAILS ACROSS THE WEST
The map above traces the 1,085-mile route of the Union Pacific from Omaha, Nebraska, to Promontory Summit in Utah, with the railroad's government land grant shown in pink. The Central Pacific route between Sacramento, California (which was linked to the San Francisco Bay area by an existing railroad) and Promontory Summit was just 690 miles, but its construction crews had to overcome the Sierra Nevada before reaching level terrain in the Great Basin (left).

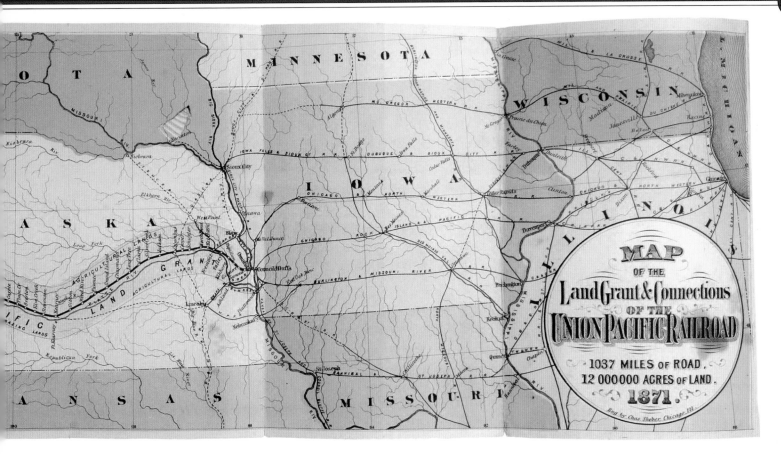

TRANSCONTINENTAL RAILROAD
Tracks and Ties That Bound the Union

◄●►

n December 2, 1863, dignitaries in Omaha, Nebraska, broke ground for the Union Pacific Railroad, which would help span the continent by laying tracks westward as the Central Pacific Railroad advanced eastward from Sacramento, California. The ceremony took place not long after Lincoln delivered his Gettysburg Address honoring the Union dead. Bolstered by hard-earned victories there and elsewhere in 1863, Unionists were determined not just to reclaim the South but to secure the West and bind it to the East by rail. "When this shall have been done," wrote Secretary of State William Seward to those breaking ground in Omaha, "disunion shall be rendered forever after impossible."

Planning for a transcontinental railroad went back to the early 1850s, when five routes were surveyed. Congress was unable to choose between them until representatives who favored the southernmost route left to join the Confederacy. Northerners remaining in Congress then settled on a central route from the Missouri River to California and passed the Pacific Railroad Act, which spurred construction by providing the Union Pacific (UP) and Central Pacific (CP) with hefty land grants and loans, ranging up to $48,000 a mile for challenging mountainous terrain.

Gifted surveyors such as Peter Dey and Grenville Dodge of the UP and Theodore Judah of the CP refined the transcontinental route, which paralleled the Oregon and California Trails partway but often departed from those wagon roads to follow straighter paths or avoid grades too steep for locomotives pulling heavy loads. Judah plotted an ingenious but laborious course over the Sierra Nevada for CP construction crews that involved carving rail beds out of mountainsides and digging 13 tunnels. He often clashed with rival investors in the CP known as the "Big Four"—Charles Crocker, Mark Hopkins, Collis Huntington, and Leland Stanford—who obtained larger government loans by prevailing on Lincoln to certify that the

GOLDEN SPIKE
This was used ceremonially to join the Union Pacific and Central Pacific Railroads in Utah in May 1869.

Sierra Nevada began in the foothills just east of Sacramento. "Abraham's faith moved mountains," one politician quipped. Judah feared that the Big Four would milk the CP dry and hoped to buy them out, but he died of yellow fever in late 1863 while crossing Panama to raise funds in the East.

Dey had similar conflicts with the UP's management and resigned as the railroad's chief engineer. He was replaced in 1866 by Dodge, a former Union general. Soon the UP, which had thus far made little progress, was advancing across Nebraska with military efficiency. Every day, a construction train chugged forward another mile or so to where new track was being laid, delivering equipment and laborers, including some ex-Confederates as well as Union veterans. One reporter likened the pounding of their hammers on spikes to a "grand Anvil Chorus playing across the plains." In their spare time, workers caroused in towns that sprouted up along the tracks to serve them. Known as "hell on wheels," most of those places withered after crews moved on. But some endured, either as little "jerkwater" towns—where

EAST MEETS WEST A cartoon commemorating completion of the transcontinental railroad shows locomotives representing the largest cities on the East and West Coasts joining hands while Indians and buffalo flee the scene.

railroad men pulled chains to obtain water from towers for steam-powered locomotives—or as substantial division points like Cheyenne, Wyoming, where rail yards and machine shops were located.

RACE TO THE FINISH

By 1867, as the UP tracks entered Wyoming, CP crews were still struggling over the Sierra Nevada. Unable to hire enough white laborers for the demanding task, CP construction boss James Strobridge reluctantly employed Chinese workers and found them more than equal to the task. Scores died in explosions while laying charges of black powder or dynamite or fell victim to blizzards or avalanches, but thousands remained hard at work through the bitter winter of 1867–68. By spring, tracks had been laid though Summit Tunnel and down along the Truckee River to Reno, Nevada. CP crews were now on level ground and surpassing the pace of UP crews, who had to excavate several tunnels through the Wasatch Range along the Wyoming-Utah border.

No junction for the two lines had yet been agreed upon. Bosses on both sides vied for federal subsidies by pressing crews ahead so fast that much of their work was slapdash and temporary. CP workers set a record on April 28, 1869, by laying more than ten miles of track in twelve hours. By then, Promontory Summit in northern Utah had been designated as the junction. Completion of the transcontinental railroad there on May 10 signaled that the nation was now firmly bound together, as expressed by an inscription on a golden spike used to join the tracks: "May God continue the unity of our country as this railroad unites the two great oceans of the world." ■

LAST SPIKE Leland Stanford, with hammer in hand at center, missed the spike at the ceremony joining his Central Pacific with the Union Pacific in 1869.

INDISPENSABLE IMMIGRANTS
Chinese Labor on the Railroad

The greatest obstacle for builders of the transcontinental railroad—the towering Sierra Nevada—was overcome largely by Chinese immigrants once deemed unfit for the task. "I will not boss Chinese!" declared James Strobridge when Charles Crocker, part owner of the Central Pacific (CP) and superintendent of construction, suggested hiring them to meet the CP's labor demands. Strobridge preferred bossing white workers and thought Chinese men were too frail to grade rail beds, excavate tunnels, and lay tracks. Crocker pointed out that men of similar stature had built China's Great Wall. Strobridge agreed to try a crew of 50 in early 1865. He was soon asking for more.

By 1867, more than 10,000 Chinese immigrants were working diligently on the railroad in the Sierra Nevada. Some had been in California since the gold rush. Others were recruited in China by labor contractors and transported across the Pacific specifically to build the railroad. At first, they earned less than white workers on the CP, who made only about $35 a month. Eventually, they earned the same amount but worked longer shifts—up to twelve hours a day, six days a week. Despite the grueling regimen, they were generally healthier than other workers because they drank hot tea, avoiding the risks posed by unboiled water. Early on, there was "no danger of strikes among them," wrote E. B. Crocker, Charles Crocker's brother and the railroad's legal counsel. But as their numbers and efficiency increased, they realized that their labor was worth more to their employer than they were paid to perform it.

In June 1867, they went on strike, demanding higher pay, a ten-hour workday, and the right to seek employment elsewhere unhindered. Charles Crocker refused and forced them back to work by cutting off their food supplies. "I don't think we will ever have any more such difficulties with them," wrote his brother, who paid belated tribute to those workers in a speech in 1869 after they laid tracks across Nevada to Promontory Summit in Utah: "I wish to call to your minds that the early completion of this railroad we have built has been in large measure due to that poor, despised class of laborers called the Chinese, to the fidelity and industry they have shown." Chinese immigrants went on to help build other railroads across the West in decades to come, but they remained a "poor, despised class," denied American citizenship until the mid-20th century. ∎

MANUAL LABOR Chinese workers grade a rail bed for the Southern Pacific on a hillside in California in the early 1880s using picks and shovels—the same basic tools wielded by those who built the Central Pacific over the Sierra Nevada in the 1860s.

PLATE 147   RAILWAYS

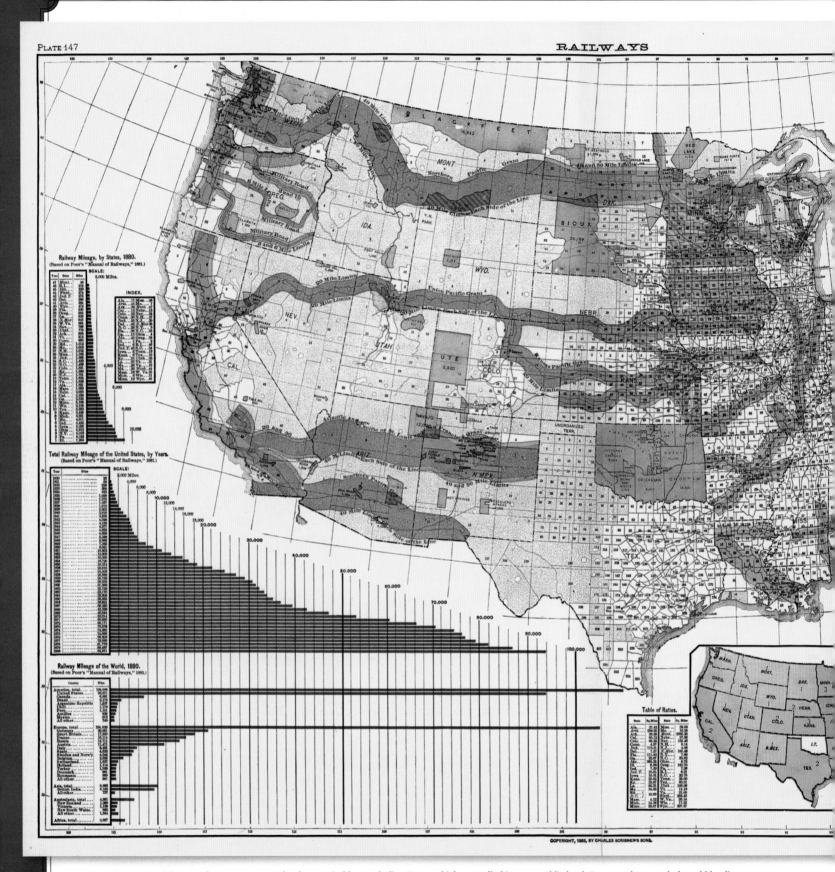

LAND LINES An 1880 map shows government land grants in blue, excluding Texas, which controlled its own public land. From north to south, broad blue lines extending to the West Coast indicate approximate routes of the Northern Pacific, Union Pacific, Central Pacific, Santa Fe, and Southern Pacific Railroads.

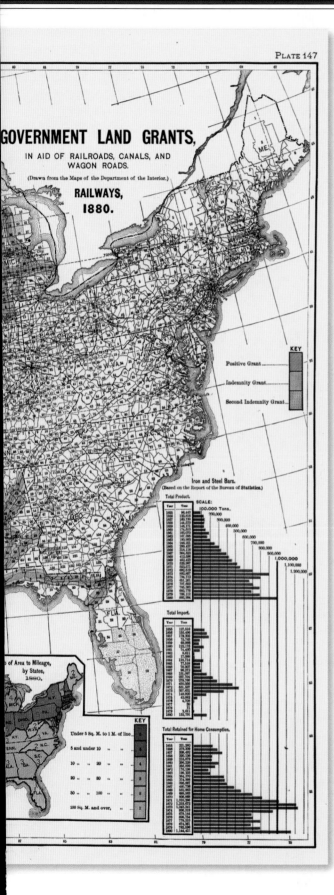

PLATE 147

GOVERNMENT LAND GRANTS,

IN AID OF RAILROADS, CANALS, AND
WAGON ROADS.

(Drawn from the Maps of the Department of the Interior.)

RAILWAYS,
1880.

RAILROAD LAND GRANTS

Laying Tracks and Luring Settlers

hile the Central Pacific and Union Pacific were gathering steam and advancing toward their historic junction in Utah in 1869, other railroads were starting up that would eventually cross the West. In 1863, the Atchison and Topeka Railroad in eastern Kansas was reorganized as the Atchison, Topeka and Santa Fe, which was later known simply as the Santa Fe Railroad and extended to Los Angeles. In 1864, the Northern Pacific Railroad was chartered to lay tracks from Lake Superior to Puget Sound. The Southern Pacific Railroad, founded in 1865 and acquired in 1868 by the Big Four who owned the Central Pacific, originated in California to link Sacramento with San Francisco and Los Angeles and gradually expanded across southern Arizona, New Mexico, and Texas to New Orleans. None of those railroads traversed mountainous Colorado, but Denver and nearby towns were linked to Kansas City by the Kansas Pacific Railway in 1870 and connected by rail to the Union Pacific at Cheyenne, Wyoming, a year later.

The federal government boosted western railroad construction with generous loans and huge land grants. The Union Pacific and Central Pacific each received 12,800 acres of land for every mile of track they laid. Together, they acquired more land than covered by New Jersey, Maryland, and Delaware combined. The government hoped to benefit by retaining lots on either side of the tracks that alternated with lots granted to the railroads. The plan was to sell those government lots to homesteaders for a fee that would rise from $1.25 an acre in the 1860s to $2.50 an acre as railroads lured settlers westward and towns developed, increasing the value of the land. But except for fertile areas such as eastern Nebraska and Kansas that were already attracting settlers when railroads received their grants,

ENGINE OF GROWTH By the late 1800s, the Santa Fe Railroad connected Los Angeles, whose population was approaching 100,000, with emerging towns in the San Bernardino Valley.

land along the tracks was often too dry for conventional farming and contested by Indians who would not yield their homelands and hunting grounds without a fight. Railroads advertised for settlers on both sides of the Atlantic, and many eventually answered that call. In the 1860s, however, few people other than ranchers were willing or able to make a living on the perilous Plains. Land grants settled sparsely by ranchers did not bring railroads much passenger or freight revenue.

SCHEMES AND SCANDALS

Hungry for quick profits, directors of the Union Pacific and Central Pacific siphoned cash from them by setting up construction firms that charged those railroads excessive rates to lay track. The directors made millions on construction while keeping their deeply indebted railroads going by selling bonds to unsuspecting investors and lining the pockets of officeholders who favored their companies and abetted their schemes. In 1872, a scandal erupted in the nation's capital when a document surfaced listing politicians who were offered stock in Crédit Mobilier, a construction

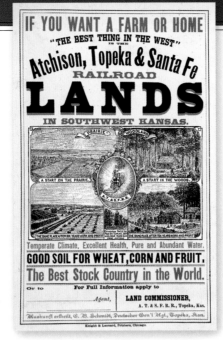

BUYER BEWARE A railroad poster luring settlers makes semiarid southwest Kansas look deceptively fertile.

company controlled by Union Pacific directors who were seeking "friends" in Washington. The public grew wary of the financial ploys of railroads and reluctant to invest in them. In 1873, banker Jay Cooke, who had taken on debt of the troubled Northern Pacific, was left holding bonds that were plummeting in value. Jay Cooke and Company collapsed, causing a financial panic that depressed the American economy for years and hampered railroad construction.

In the long run, western railroads prospered as settlers spread out across the Plains and shipped their produce by rail. Yet the great era of railroad-building that culminated in the late 1800s with the completion of a fifth line across the West—the Great Northern near the Canadian border—was a mixed blessing for settlers. Railroads were essential to the region's development, reducing journeys that once took days to hours and fostering towns that provided otherwise-isolated farmers and ranchers with precious communal institutions such as schools, churches, and hospitals. The dependence of Westerners on railroads caused resentment, however, particularly when settlers were served by only one line and could not bargain for better rates.

Henry George, an economic reformer who denounced the monopolistic power of the Big Four in California, wrote that a "railroad approaches a small town as a robber approaches his victim." Railroads charged much higher rates per mile for short hauls between towns with only one carrier than for long hauls between cities served by competing railroads. Political efforts to regulate railroads began among farmers in the Midwest who organized as Grangers in the 1870s. Their cause was later taken up by the Populist Party, which originated in Kansas and won broad support from Westerners, including railroad employees seeking better pay and safer working conditions. ■

BUSY HUB Horse-drawn cabs wait at the Atchison, Topeka and Santa Fe depot in Topeka, Kansas. Boosted by the railroad, Topeka grew from a population of under 1,000 in 1860 to more than 15,000 in 1880.

HOMESTEADERS AND SODBUSTERS
Pioneers on the Prairie

aniel Freeman could not wait for New Year's Day to dawn. He was ready to claim his land as soon as the clock struck midnight. On January 1, 1863, the Homestead Act, passed by Congress the previous May, went into effect. Any adult citizen or would-be citizen could claim 160 acres of public land and gain title to it by living there for six months and paying $1.25 an acre—or by living there for five years and making significant improvements, in which case the homesteader had to pay only a small registration fee. According to family lore, Freeman persuaded the land agent in Brownsville, Nebraska, to open for business as soon as the new year began and filed his claim at ten minutes past twelve. He would be remembered as the first homesteader.

Born in Ohio in 1826, Freeman studied medicine in Cincinnati and made his living both as a farmer on his homestead—located along a creek near the town of Beatrice in southeastern Nebraska—and as a physician to neighbors.

He settled there on his own, and homesteading without a spouse was hard, lonely work. In 1864, Freeman began a courtship in writing with Agnes Suiter of Iowa, who had been engaged to his brother before he died fighting for the Union. Freeman did not hide the fact that life on the Nebraska frontier could be dangerous. He told her of his service in a volunteer company organized to drive hostile Indians away. But he also described the rewards of life as a homesteader, using irregular spelling as many Americans did then: "I like the west well . . . we hav a rough but free and easy way that sutes me well and this is a good place to rase stock and make money . . . we hav a large yeald of wheat and oats this harvest and corn."

In late 1864, Freeman declared his intentions. "I love you and would be happy in trying to make you happy if you can love me in return," he wrote. "I would like to make you Misis Freeman some time this Winter." They wed in February 1865 and went on to have eight children. In 1868, after five years on his homestead, he received title to the land after submitting

EARTH LODGE Settlers like those living in the sod house at left either claimed land as homesteaders or purchased it. Well-watered land with trees like that in Iowa and eastern Nebraska advertised by the Burlington and Missouri River Railroad (opposite) cost more than land on the open Plains where sod houses were built. The railroad offered customers "exploring tickets" to inspect land and loans to purchase it.

PRODUCTS WILL PAY FOR LAND AND IMPROVEMENTS!

MILLIONS OF ACRES

View on the Big Blue, between Camden and Crete, representing Valley and Rolling Prairie Land in Nebraska.

IOWA and NEBRASKA LANDS

FOR SALE ON 10 YEARS CREDIT

BY THE

Burlington & Missouri River R.R. Co.

AT 6 PER CT. INTEREST AND LOW PRICES.

Only One-Seventh of Principal Due Annually, beginning Four Years after purchase.

.20 PER CENT. DEDUCTED FROM 10 YEARS PRICE, FOR CASH.

LAND EXPLORING TICKETS SOLD

and Cost allowed in First Interest paid, on Land bought in 30 days from date of ticket.

Thus our Land Buyers ☞ GET A FREE PASS in the State where the Land bought is located.

These TERMS are BETTER at $5, than to pre-empt United States Land at $2.50 per Acre.

EXTRAORDINARY INDUCEMENTS on FREIGHT and PASSAGE are AFFORDED TO PURCHASERS and THEIR FAMILIES.

Address GEO. S. HARRIS, LAND COMMISSIONER,
or T. H. LEAVITT, Ass't Land Comm'r, Burlington, Iowa.

Or apply to

FREE ROOMS for buyers to board themselves are provided at Burlington and Lincoln.

CIRCULARS are supplied GRATIS for distribution in ORGANIZING COLONIES and to induce individuals to emigrate WEST.

A SECTIONAL MAP, showing exact location of our IOWA LANDS is sold for 30 Cents, and of NEBRASKA LANDS for 30 Cents.

PROOF REQUIRED UNDER HOMESTEAD ACTS MAY 20, 1862, AND JUNE 21, 1866.

WE, *Joseph Graff & Samuel Kilpatrick* do solemnly *swear* that we have known *Daniel Freeman* for *over five* years last past; that he is *the head of a family* consisting of *wife* and *two* children *and is* ___ a citizen of the United States; that he is an inhabitant of the *S½ of NW¼, & NE of NW¼ and SW¼ of NE¼* of section No. *26* in Township No. *4 N* of Range No. *5 E* and that no other person resided upon the said land entitled to the right of Homestead or Pre-emption.

That the said *Daniel Freeman* ___ entered upon and made settlement on said land on the *1st* day of *January*, 1863, and has built a house thereon *part log & part frame 14 by 20 feet one story, with two doors two windows. Shingle roof board floors and is a comfortable house to live in*

and has lived in the said house and made it his exclusive home from the *1st* day of *January*, 1863, to the present time, and that he has since said settlement ploughed, fenced, and cultivated about *35* ___ acres of said land, and has made the following improvements thereon, to wit: *built a Stable. a Sheep Shed 100 feet long Corn Crib. and has 40 apple and about 400 peach Trees set out.*

Joseph Graff

Samuel Kilpatrick.

I, *Henry M. Atkinson, Register* do hereby certify that the above affidavit was taken and subscribed before me this *20th* day of *January*, 1865.

Henry M. Atkinson

Register

ERTIFY that *Joseph Graff & Samuel Kilpatrick* whose names ed to the foregoing affidavit, are persons of respectability.

Henry M. Atkinson , Register.

Jno. L. Carson , Receiver.

FIRST HOMESTEADER Daniel Freeman, pictured here in his later years, was in his early 40s when he signed the application above along with two neighbors and received title to his pioneering homestead in eastern Nebraska. He and his wife eventually moved from the original log cabin he built there to a two-story brick home to accommodate their growing family.

proof that he had made substantial improvements, including building a stable, as certified by two of his neighbors. He died there in 1909. Agnes Freeman remained on their pioneering homestead until her death in 1931.

BUSTING SOD

Few homesteaders were as fortunate as the Freemans. Many who had little experience as farmers, or were too poor to get by until their first crops could be harvested, forfeited their homesteads, which were often purchased at auction by wealthier landowners or speculators. By the late 1860s, most of the fertile, well-watered land east of the Great Plains was taken or too expensive for farmers of modest means. Those who settled on the open Plains, whether on government or railroad land, faced the challenge of building homes where there were no trees and tilling soil that had never been touched by a plow. Many of those sodbusters lived in sod houses that struck people accustomed to wooden houses as bleak and primitive. "You must make up your mind to see a very naked looking home at first," wrote Uriah Oblinger to his wife, Mattie, before she and their infant daughter joined him on their newly acquired homestead in Nebraska. "Nothing but the land covered with grass and a sod house to live in." They got by as farmers because their land was at the eastern edge of the Plains, which was not too dry, and possessed soil as "rich as the river bottoms of Indiana," in Uriah's words. The home he built was good enough for Mattie. "I expect you think we live miserable because we are in a sod house," she wrote her relatives, "but I tell you in solid earnest I never enjoyed my self better."

Settlers who ventured far beyond the 100th meridian, however, struggled to make a living off the hard, parched land there. As late as 1880, when Gage County in eastern Nebraska where the Freemans lived boasted a population of more than 13,000, Keith County in western Nebraska had fewer than 200 inhabitants. Advances such as James Oliver's sturdy iron plow helped well-situated sodbusters like the Oblingers reap bounty. But without irrigation, most of the land between the 100th meridian and the Pacific Coast was suitable only for mining or ranching. ■

JAMES OLIVER'S SODBUSTING PLOW

The 19th century witnessed rapid technological advances in the production of steel, an alloy stronger than pure iron. The steel plow devised in the 1830s by John Deere of Illinois was a great improvement over earlier cast-iron plows, which would chip or break against stones and would often become clogged with mud that had to be scraped clean repeatedly.

Deere's innovation did not render cast-iron plows obsolete, however. James Oliver, a Scottish immigrant who toiled as a farmhand and ironworker before becoming co-owner of a foundry in South Bend, Indiana, found a way of chilling hot, molten iron so that its surface cooled quickly and could be sharpened to a keen, hard edge on plowshares and moldboards (curved blades that turn earth over). Patented in 1868, Oliver's "chilled" plow (right) was strong enough to carve furrows in virgin soil but not too heavy or expensive for homesteaders and other settlers of limited means who plowed by hand.

While Deere's company began producing costlier riding plows, which eased the task of those with large areas to cultivate, Oliver continued to manufacture economical walking plows, handled by farmers on foot and pulled by a few horses or mules. He sold millions of them by the early 20th century. Like his customers, James Oliver was an enterprising traditionalist, who refined an age-old iron-casting process to expand agricultural production across America and around the world.

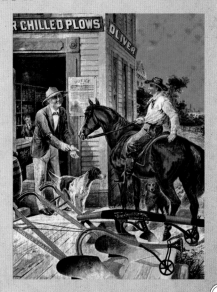

THE LONG DRIVES

Herding Cattle North From Texas

Unlike other Confederate states, which were devastated economically during the Civil War, Texas emerged from the conflict with a notable surplus of one of its most valuable commodities—beef on the hoof. Although many Texans had left their ranches in 1861 to fight for the Confederacy, their free-ranging cattle proliferated. By 1865, several million longhorns roamed Texas, ready to be rounded up and delivered to markets in the North, where beef supplies had been reduced by wartime demands and cattle fetched prices more than ten times higher than in Texas. Texans could not yet reach northern cities directly by railroad, so they began driving cattle up through Indian Territory to rail depots in Kansas, where the longhorns were shipped east to be processed in Kansas City, St. Louis, or Chicago. Those long drives made cowboys famous for enduring the grueling journeys and infamous for raising hell in cattle towns at the end of the trail.

The roundups that preceded those drives were often conducted jointly by neighboring ranchers and their cowboys. Although some wealthy cattlemen possessed huge tracts with vast herds like the sprawling King Ranch

CHOW TIME Cowboys gather around chuck wagons during a roundup along the Belle Fourche River in Dakota Territory, where cattle were introduced from Texas in the late 1870s.

To Dodge City   To Abilene

COUNTY MAP OF THE
STATE OF
TEXAS

Showing also portions of the

ADJOINING

STATES AND TERRITORIES

SCALE OF MILES

Drawn and Engraved by W. H. Gamble Philadelphia

Legend

m & McCoy or Eastern Trail (1867~1884)

r Trails

n or Dodge City or Texas Trail (1874~1893)

ght~Loving Trail (1866~1881)

e Trail (1840~1867)

eld Overland Stage Line (1857~1861)

rontier Forts

Trails North Beginning in the late 1860s, Texans drove cattle to Kansas on the Chisholm Trail (red) and to New Mexico and Colorado on the Goodnight-Loving Trail (orange).

HARD DRIVING Above, two cowboys keep temperamental longhorns in line during a cattle drive. Leather saddlebags like the one below carried a cowboy's personal possessions, such as tobacco and rolling papers for cigarettes.

in southeast Texas, many owned only the ground on which they lived and grazed their cattle on public land, where longhorns belonging to various ranchers commingled. Roundups usually took place in early spring and were referred to by Texans as "cow hunts." Many of the cattle captured on those hunts were young, unbranded animals known as mavericks for Samuel Maverick, a politically prominent rancher whose unbranded cattle roamed free after he moved from the Gulf Coast to San Antonio in the late 1840s. Typically, mavericks were divided evenly among the ranchers who joined in a cow hunt, but cattlemen sometimes played poker for them. One Texas rancher recalled that so many unbranded yearlings were rounded up after the Civil War that they were valued at only 50 cents a head. Those who had lost their cattle but still had "a little money," he said, could try their hand at poker and win "a stack of yearlings."

After the mavericks had been roped and branded and the cattle branded in earlier years had been sorted out, longhorns deemed ready for sale were driven north. Some ranchers remained at home to look after their calves and breeding stock and entrusted long drives to cowboys who worked for them or to independent drovers who delivered cattle to market for a fee. Texans could not drive cattle straight to Kansas City or St. Louis because laws designed to prevent the spread of Texas fever—a tick-borne disease that longhorns were immune to but that devastated other breeds of cattle—barred longhorns from passing through Missouri and eastern Kansas. Instead, many herds were driven north up the Chisholm Trail, pioneered by Jesse Chisholm, who was part Cherokee and developed a wagon road through Indian Territory to a trading post he operated near Wichita, Kansas. No railroad reached Wichita until the early 1870s, so cowboys following the Chisholm Trail in the late 1860s continued north to Abilene, which was served by the Kansas Pacific Railway and lay at the western end of the longhorn quarantine zone. A shrewd livestock trader and landowner there named Joseph McCoy appealed to the governor and obtained a quarantine exemption for Abilene, which shipped hundreds of thousands of longhorns east before it began losing business to rival cow towns in Kansas.

RIDING HERD

Life for cowboys on the trail was rigorous. Those not assigned to guard the herd at night slept fully clothed in bedrolls on the ground and were roused at dawn to gather at the chuck wagon, manned by a cook known as a sourdough or "bean-master" for the fare he dispensed. Some of those cooks were blacks or Mexicans, as were a number of cowboys from Texas. After a quick breakfast, they saddled up and headed out with their herd. The trail boss rode up front, followed by the chuck wagon and two veteran point men, assigned to keep the lead cattle in line. Swing men and flank men rode farther back on either side of the herd and inexperienced young drag men brought up the rear, prodding stragglers and eating dust kicked up by the longhorns. Indians demanded tolls from men driving cattle through tribal territory and sometimes made off with animals, but cowboys often had more trouble with white settlers in Kansas, who feared Texas fever and grew hostile when longhorns approached. Nothing caused cowboys more grief, however, than stampedes. To calm nervous cattle and keep them from bolting, men sang to them. Any song would suffice "so long as there was music to it," one cowboy recalled, "and it was not uncommon to hear some profane and heartless bully doling out camp-meeting hymns to soothe the ruffled spirits of a herd of Texas steers."

It could take two months or more to drive cattle from central Texas to Abilene, Kansas—and that was not the longest or most arduous journey of its kind undertaken by Texans in the late 1860s. Two enterprising ranchers on the frontier west of Fort Worth, Charles Goodnight and Oliver Loving, established an epic cattle trail that followed the Butterfield stagecoach route to the Pecos, ascended that river to Fort Sumner, New Mexico, and continued northward along the Front Range of the Rockies to Denver, Colorado—an odyssey of roughly 1,000 miles that exposed venturesome cowboys to greater risk of Indian attack than the Chisholm Trail. In 1867, Loving was attacked and gravely wounded on his way to Fort Sumner and died there. Undeterred, Goodnight continued to develop and exploit the Goodnight-Loving Trail, which delivered beef cattle from Texas to towns and forts in New Mexico and Colorado as well as breeding stock for new ranches on the northern Plains. ■

NATURAL HISTORY

TEXAS LONGHORNS

The Texas longhorn (left) is a descendant of the first cattle brought to America by Spanish colonists. In the early 1800s, Spanish longhorns in Texas interbred with cattle introduced by American settlers, yielding rugged hybrids that flourished even when they were untended and roamed free. Their long horns helped adults protect calves from predators, and they were well adapted to life on the open range, tougher and more tolerant of drought than tamer breeds. Long legged and relatively lean, they traveled well and withstood arduous journeys to market. One drawback of their wild, free-roaming heritage was that longhorn bulls were unusually fierce. As was customary, cowboys castrated young males that were not intended for breeding, and those steers grew up strong and sturdy but less ornery than bulls. Legendary cattleman Charles Goodnight summed up the virtues of Texas longhorns: "As trail cattle," he wrote, "their equal has never been known and never will be. Their hoofs are superior to those of any other cattle. In stampedes, they hold together better, are easier circled in a run, and rarely split off . . . No animal of the cow kind will shift and take care of itself under all conditions as will the longhorns. They can go farther without water and endure more suffering than others."

Geared Up A cowboy wearing long leather boots and spurs poses for his portrait armed with a revolver and knife. Some cattle towns in Kansas required cowboys to disarm when they arrived.

COWBOYS AND CATTLE TOWNS
Business and Pleasure at Trail's End

Contrary to the popular image of wild cowboys riding into town with guns blazing, raising hell was seldom the first order of business when trail-weary drovers from Texas reached their destinations in Kansas. Many first visited a barbershop to be shorn and shaved and then went shopping to replace worn-out boots, hats, or trousers. Cowboys earned about a dollar a day on the trail and had from $60 to $90 in hand at journey's end, much of which went for new clothing. One merchant in Abilene sold visiting Texans custom-made boots stamped with a Lone Star insignia for up to $20.

Once refreshed and refitted, cowboys were ready to do the town and entered into its saloons and gambling halls with gusto. The Alamo saloon on Texas Street in Abilene was unusually posh and lured many cowboys from the Lone Star State. "At night everything is 'full up,'" wrote one reporter who visited that establishment. "Here, in a well lighted room opening on the street, the 'boys' gather in crowds round the tables, to play or to watch others; a bartender, with a countenance like a youthful divinity student, fabricates wonderful drinks, while the music of a piano and a violin from a raised recess, enlivens the scene." Few thrill-seeking cowboys spent much time in such places without surrendering their loose cash to bartenders, professional gamblers, or prostitutes.

Whether armed or disarmed, drunken cowboys could cause trouble in town. As one observer put it: "When he feels well (and he always does when full of what he calls 'Kansas sheep dip'), the average cowboy is a bad man to handle." Fistfights were more common than shootouts, however, and the homicide rate in

FRONT STREET
Shown at left in the 1870s, Dodge City was a profitable cattle town for merchants like Peter Beatty and James Kelley, who owned a restaurant and adjoining saloon on Front Street. Kelley was elected mayor and hired Wyatt Earp and other enforcers to stop cowboys and gamblers from carrying firearms in violation of the law and engaging in shootouts like the one pictured above.

HAT Shielding cowboys against sun, rain, or hail, hats could also be waved to fan fires or doffed to greet ladies.

LARIAT Often made of braided rawhide, lariats had to be stiff enough to hold their shape when cast as loops to lasso mustangs or mavericks.

CHAPS Cowboys wore leather chaps over their pants to protect their legs from brush, nettles, and other obstruction.

SADDLE With stirrups to anchor his feet and a cantle to keep him from sliding backward, a cowboy rode firm enough in the saddle to cast his lariat or fire a pistol on target.

SPURS Ornamental as well as functional, spurs were used to prod horses and jingled when the rider dismounted and entered a store or saloon.

BOXED UP Wielding whips, cowboys in Abilene herd Texas longhorns into a boxcar for shipment east on the Kansas Pacific Railway.

tipsy and trigger-happy. "There are four things your cowboy must not do," a journalist commented. "He must not insult a woman; he must not shoot his pistol in a store or bar-room; he must not ride his pony into those places of resort; and as a last proposal he must not ride his pony on the sidewalks."

In Abilene, cowboys were relegated to the wrong side of the tracks, which divided the more respectable, residential district to the north from the hangouts frequented by visiting Texans to the south. Merchants whose livelihood depended on entertaining cowboys often ended up at odds with residents who wanted to clear out saloons, brothels, and other dens of iniquity. During the 1870s, Abilene and Wichita ceased to be raucous resorts for cowboys as rival cattle towns emerged, including Caldwell, situated just a few miles from Indian Territory and closer to Texas. Dodge City in western Kansas became one of the last resorts for Texans driving cattle to that state. Dodge remained a rowdy, whiskey-soaked cow town even after Kansas officially went dry in 1881. By then, however, Texans had the option of herding cattle to rail depots in their own state and fewer were entering Kansas. A district court judge there reported that the "festive cowboy" was becoming "conspicuous by his absence in Dodge, and ere long he will be seen & heard there, in his glory, no more forever." ∎

Abilene and other notorious cattle towns was surprisingly low, seldom amounting to more than a few violent deaths a year. Wichita, which began luring cowboys a few years after Abilene did thanks to the arrival of the Atchison, Topeka and Santa Fe Railroad, recorded just four homicides over four years. To keep bloodshed there to a minimum, signs were posted instructing visitors to "Leave Your Revolvers at Police Headquarters, and Get a Check." In towns without such restrictions, tough lawmen—some of whom had been lawbreakers in the past—cracked down on cowboys who became

CHARLES SIRINGO'S FAREWELL TO COWBOY LIFE

Born in Texas in 1855, cowboy Charles Siringo served as a trail boss for the LX Ranch in the Texas Panhandle and drove herds to Kansas for owner David Beals. He eventually settled with his wife and mother in the cattle town of Caldwell, Kansas, and became a merchant there, as described in this passage from his 1885 memoir, *A Texas Cow Boy or, Fifteen Years on the Hurricane Deck of a Spanish Pony:*

> I arrived in Caldwell September the first, and after shipping the herd, Mr. Beals ordered me to take the outfit back to the Panhandle and get another drove. This of course didn't suit, as I had only been at home a few days. But then what could I do? I hated to give up a good

job, with no prospects of making a living by remaining in town.

> I finally concluded to obey orders, so started the men and horses up the [Indian] Territory line, while I and Sprague went to town with the wagon to load it with chuck . . . After getting the wagon loaded and ready to start, I suddenly swore off cow-punching and turned everything over to Mr. Sprague, who bossed the outfit back to the Panhandle.

> The next day I rented a vacant room on Main street and, rolling up my sleeves and putting on a pair of suspenders, the first I had ever worn, started out as a merchant—on a six-bit scale. Thus one cow-puncher takes a sensible tumble and drops out of the ranks.

THROUGH THE GRAND CANYON

Explorations of John Wesley Powell

After losing his right arm fighting for the Union at Shiloh in 1862, 35-year-old John Wesley Powell performed one of the last great feats of western exploration in 1869 by leading a party down the Green River to the turbulent Colorado River and on through the Grand Canyon. He and nine other men set out in late May in four boats from Castle Rock on the upper Green River in southwestern Wyoming. Powell and two men led the way in a light, swift boat christened the *Emma Dean* for his wife, who had joined him on earlier expeditions, followed by three larger boats with watertight compartments fore and aft to make them buoyant. Entering the Flaming Gorge along the Utah border, they encountered the first of many rapids on their route. One boat was wrecked without loss of life in early June in a flume they dubbed Disaster Falls. Later that month, fire erupted in camp and consumed part of their gear and provisions.

John Wesley Powell

On July 5, a discouraged expedition member left before the rest continued downriver through Desolation Canyon and reached the Colorado River two weeks later, having traveled more than 500 miles to that point. In mid-August, they entered "the Great Unknown," as Powell referred to the Grand Canyon in his diary. "We are three quarters of a mile in the depths of the earth," he wrote, "and the great river shrinks to insignificance as it dashes its angry waves against the walls and cliffs that rise to the world above." Unnerved, three more men left the party on August 28—unaware that the worst of the rapids were behind them—and climbed the North Rim. They hoped to reach a Mormon settlement but were killed by Indians.

Powell then abandoned the battered *Emma Dean* and continued with his five remaining men in the last two boats. Soon they were safely out of the canyon. "All we regret now," wrote expedition member George Bradley, "is that the three boys who took to the mountains are not here to share our joy and triumph." Hailed for his feat, Powell led another party down the Colorado River in 1871 and published a vivid account that explained the geologic origin of the majestic canyons there. "The river preserved its level," he wrote, "but mountains were lifted up." ■

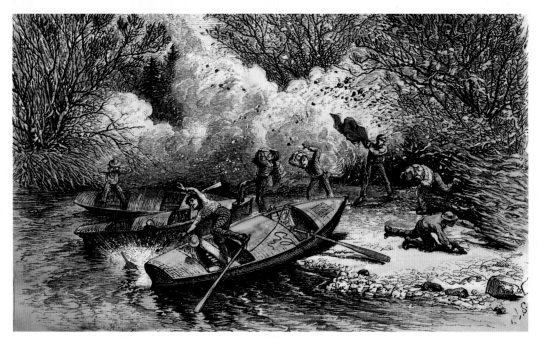

PERILOUS VOYAGE Two illustrations that accompanied an article by John Wesley Powell describing his daring 1869 expedition show the fire that engulfed his party's camp along the Green River in June (left) and two of their boats running rapids on the Colorado River through the Grand Canyon in August (opposite).

THE UNSETTLED PLAINS

Treaties Reached and Breached

❧━━━◆◆◆━━━❧

In March 1869, Ulysses S. Grant was inaugurated president and William Sherman succeeded him as commanding general of the U.S. Army. The war between North and South that raised those two leaders to prominence had been over for nearly four years, but peace remained elusive in the West. Tribes there had clashed with soldiers and settlers frequently during the Civil War and sporadically since then. Some warriors on the Plains attacked railroad surveyors, hoping to halt construction, during which buffalo were slaughtered in droves to feed workers.

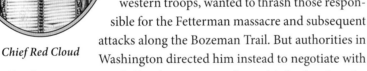

Chief Red Cloud

Other Indians sought to sever arteries like the Bozeman Trail, which ran from the Oregon Trail in Wyoming to goldfields in Montana through prime hunting grounds of the Lakota Sioux. In December 1866, Lakotas inspired by Chief Red Cloud and led by the warrior Crazy Horse targeted Fort Phil Kearny on the Bozeman Trail, where Capt. William Fetterman and 80 soldiers were lured into an ambush and annihilated.

Sherman, serving then as commander of western troops, wanted to thrash those responsible for the Fetterman massacre and subsequent attacks along the Bozeman Trail. But authorities in Washington directed him instead to negotiate with tribal leaders. In 1868, Red Cloud was among those chiefs who signed a treaty at Fort Laramie that established the Great Sioux Reservation in western Dakota Territory, closed the Bozeman Trail, and designated that area and other "unceded territory" on the northern Plains as hunting grounds for tribes, "so long as the buffalo may range thereon in sufficient number as to justify the chase."

Sherman doubted that the treaty would hold. A similar agreement with tribes of the southern Plains, negotiated at Medicine Lodge Creek in Kansas a year earlier, was already unraveling as Indians assigned to bleak reservations in western Indian Territory clashed with surrounding settlers and suffered reprisals by soldiers. Sherman believed that Plains Indians would have to be utterly subjugated or wiped out. "The more we can kill this year," he wrote, "the less will have to be killed the next war." ■

PEACE TALKS General Sherman (seated fifth from right) and other officials meet in 1868 with tribal leaders at Fort Laramie. Red Cloud declined to attend the talks but later signed the treaty, which did not bring lasting peace to the region.

"IN 1868, MEN CAME OUT AND
BROUGHT PAPERS. WE COULD NOT READ THEM
AND THEY DID NOT TELL US TRULY
WHAT WAS IN THEM."
—CHIEF RED CLOUD

CHAPTER FOUR

1870–1879

★ FOR THE ★

PLAINS

LAST STAND George Custer raises his saber against an Indian foe as warriors close in on him and his men in this idealized depiction of the chaotic Battle of the Little Bighorn on June 25, 1876. News of Custer's death and defeat reached the public in July as the nation was observing the centennial of its Declaration of Independence.

WAR FOR THE PLAINS

raveling as far as they could on the emerging Northern Pacific Railroad in November 1873, Lt. Col. George Armstrong Custer and his wife, Elizabeth "Libbie" Custer, detrained at the raw young town of Bismarck in Dakota Territory and crossed the Missouri River by boat to Fort Abraham Lincoln, where Custer's Seventh Cavalry Regiment was stationed. Lewis and Clark had passed that same spot in October 1804 during their historic expedition to the Pacific. For all the advances made since then by settlers and soldiers, the land beyond Fort Lincoln on the west bank of the Missouri was still Indian country. Among those who camped and hunted

there were the Lakota Sioux, who had tried to stop Lewis and Clark from proceeding upriver and dealing with the Arikara and other tribes that might become formidable rivals if allied with Americans. By 1873, Arikaras were in fact serving as scouts for the Seventh Cavalry against Lakotas, who viewed the fort and the railroad surveyors its soldiers protected as threats to their hunting grounds. After arriving there, Libbie Custer learned that those Arikaras, or "Rees," had recently

been attacked by Lakotas. "They fought all day, and finally the Rees succeeded in driving their enemies away," she wrote. "All this took place right at the post, where the firing could be seen from the windows."

By the early 1870s, the vast expanse between the Mississippi River and the Pacific Ocean had been organized into American states or territories, but those stationed at outposts like Fort Lincoln knew that the West was not yet won. The war

Yellowstone National Park

Gold nuggets

Quanah Parker

1870 President Grant pushes ahead with his Indian peace policy following the massacre in Montana of Piegans of the Blackfeet tribal group by U.S. troops.

1872 Chief Cochise of the Chiricahua Apache obtains a reservation for his people in their homeland, the Chiricahua Mountains along the Arizona–New Mexico border. Yellowstone National Park is established.

1874 Comanches, Kiowas, and allied Indians attack buffalo hunters at Adobe Walls in Texas, triggering the Red River War. Prospectors invade the Great Sioux Reservation following discovery of gold in the Black Hills during Custer's expedition there.

1871 General in Chief Sherman narrowly escapes attack by Kiowas in Texas and has Kiowa war leader Satanta and two others arrested and charged with murder for raiding a wagon train and killing teamsters.

1873 Captain Jack and other Modoc resistance leaders in California are executed for killing U.S. commissioners sent to negotiate with them. Wholesale slaughter of bison on the Plains continues.

1875 Comanche war leader Quanah submits to authorities and reports to the Comanche and Kiowa reservation in Indian Territory, where he takes the name Quanah Parker in honor of his mother.

for the Plains, which had begun in the 1850s, was approaching its climax and would come to define this decade on the frontier. Armed resistance to soldiers and settlers among assertive Plains tribes like the Lakota and Comanche increased as their territory diminished, resulting in battles that overshadowed efforts by President Grant and others in Washington to reform the nation's Indian policies and promote peace. Those reformers made little headway because progress to them meant confining Indians on reservations and abolishing tribal traditions and ceremonies that celebrated hunting and fighting as honorable pursuits. Unwilling to purchase peace at that price, Plains warriors chose instead to reckon with foes like George Custer who shared their belief that riding into battle was magnificent. When the 1870s came to an end, no American of the era would be as renowned in memory as the ill-fated Custer, whose sensational death at the hands of defiant Lakotas and Northern Cheyennes ensured that their heroes would long be remembered as well.

DIVIDING AND CONQUERING

By the time he took charge of the U.S. Army under President Grant, William Sherman had divided Plains Indians by assigning the Lakota and Northern Cheyenne and Arapaho

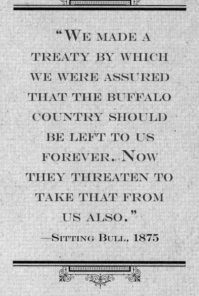

"WE MADE A TREATY BY WHICH WE WERE ASSURED THAT THE BUFFALO COUNTRY SHOULD BE LEFT TO US FOREVER. NOW THEY THREATEN TO TAKE THAT FROM US ALSO."
—SITTING BULL, 1875

to reservations in and around western Dakota Territory and the Comanche, Kiowa, and Southern Cheyenne and Arapaho to reservations in Indian Territory, nearly 700 miles away. That left a broad corridor between reservations for railroad-building, settlement, farming, and ranching. Sherman and his officers let professional hunters slaughter bison even in places reserved by treaty as tribal hunting grounds, calculating that Indians would have little reason to leave their reservations if buffalo became scarce or nonexistent. Any bands that left without permission or failed to report to reservations would be pursued and defeated, a task Sherman entrusted to his avid field commander in the West, Philip Sheridan. Officers directed by Sheridan crushed resistance on the southern Plains during the Red River War of 1873 and on the northern Plains during the so-called Great Sioux War of 1876–77, which included the Battle of the Little Bighorn and subsequent campaigns to subdue Custer's foes.

Concerted Indian resistance to the Army was rare because western tribes were divided into bands and had numerous chiefs or leaders, who sometimes met in council but seldom agreed to wage war or make peace in unison. Few tribes had principal chiefs, and many bands had war leaders as well as peace chiefs or civil chiefs. Prominent tribal leaders who came

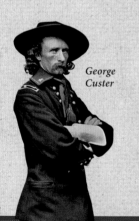

George Custer

1876 Lakotas and Northern Cheyennes who have fled agencies around the disrupted Great Sioux Reservation clash with pursuing U.S. forces in Montana along the Rosebud River and the Little Bighorn, where Custer and five companies are annihilated.

1878 Comanches and Kiowas led by Quanah Parker receive permission to hunt off the reservation and find no bison on the southern Plains.

Buffalo herds

1877 Attacks on Lakotas and Northern Cheyennes force them back to their agencies, where Crazy Horse is arrested and killed. Chief Joseph surrenders in Montana with several hundred Nez Perce fugitives.

Nez Perce headdress

1879 Carlisle Indian Industrial School, the first government boarding school located off Indian reservations, is founded in Pennsylvania.

to terms with the government were often credited with more influence than they possessed. Red Cloud was regarded as a great Sioux chief, but he represented only the Oglala, one of seven bands of the Lakota, who were in turn one of three branches of the far-flung Sioux. As conflict loomed in the mid-1870s, the Oglala war leader Crazy Horse eclipsed Red Cloud and lent muscle to a resistance movement inspired by Sitting Bull, a Hunkpapa Lakota chief who no longer went into battle but drew many Lakotas and Northern Cheyennes into a potent but fleeting military alliance.

Some war leaders made successful transitions to peace chiefs after yielding to authorities, notably Quanah Parker, the son of a Comanche chief and a white woman captured by the tribe. Others who surrendered after heroic resistance like Chief Joseph of the Nez Perce, whose epic flight from his homeland in Oregon in 1877 ended in northern Montana, spoke eloquently not just for their band or tribe but for all Indians placed under American rule on reservations but denied the same rights as other people born on American soil. As Chief Joseph declared, "I have asked some of the Great White Chiefs where they get their authority to say to the Indian that he shall stay in one place, while he sees white men going where they please. They cannot tell me." ∎

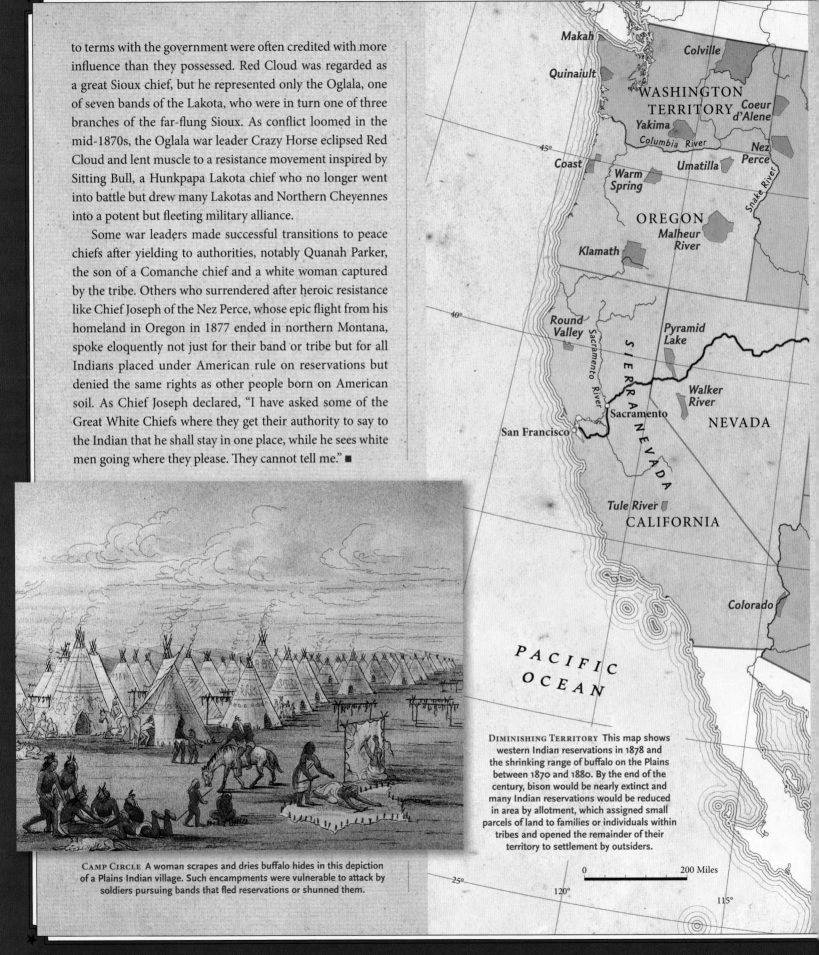

CAMP CIRCLE A woman scrapes and dries buffalo hides in this depiction of a Plains Indian village. Such encampments were vulnerable to attack by soldiers pursuing bands that fled reservations or shunned them.

DIMINISHING TERRITORY This map shows western Indian reservations in 1878 and the shrinking range of buffalo on the Plains between 1870 and 1880. By the end of the century, bison would be nearly extinct and many Indian reservations would be reduced in area by allotment, which assigned small parcels of land to families or individuals within tribes and opened the remainder of their territory to settlement by outsiders.

0   200 Miles

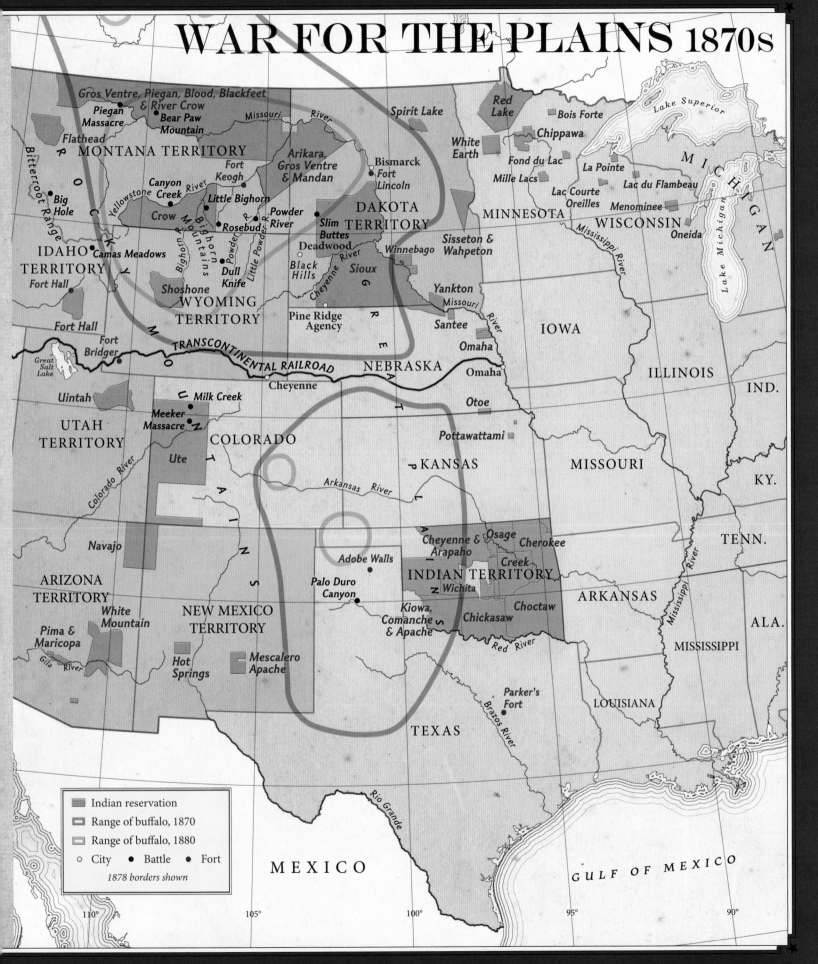

WAR FOR THE PLAINS 1870s

Lake Superior

MICHIGAN

Lake Michigan

Red Lake

Bois Forte

Chippawa

White Earth

Fond du Lac

La Pointe

Lac du Flambeau

Mille Lacs

Lac Courte Oreilles

Menominee

MINNESOTA

WISCONSIN

Oneida

Spirit Lake

Gros Ventre, Piegan, Blood, Blackfeet & River Crow

Piegan Massacre

Bear Paw Mountain

Missouri   River

Bismarck
Fort Lincoln

Flathead

MONTANA TERRITORY

Fort Keogh

Arikara, Gros Ventre & Mandan

Canyon Creek

Yellowstone   River

Little Bighorn

Powder River

DAKOTA TERRITORY

Sisseton & Wahpeton

Big Hole

Bitterroot Range

Crow

Rosebud

Bighorn River

Bighorn Mountains

Powder R.

Little Powder R.

Slim Buttes

Mississippi River

Deadwood

Black Hills

Cheyenne River

Sioux

Winnebago

Yankton

Missouri

IOWA

IDAHO TERRITORY

Camas Meadows

Dull Knife

Shoshone

WYOMING TERRITORY

Pine Ridge Agency

River

Santee

Omaha

Fort Hall

Fort Bridger

Great Salt Lake

Fort Hall

TRANSCONTINENTAL RAILROAD

Cheyenne

NEBRASKA

Omaha

Omaha

ILLINOIS

IND.

Uintah

Milk Creek

Meeker Massacre

Ute

UTAH TERRITORY

COLORADO

Otoe

KANSAS

Pottawattami

MISSOURI

KY.

Colorado River

Arkansas   River

ARIZONA TERRITORY

Navajo

MOUNTAINS

GREAT

PLAINS

Cheyenne & Arapaho

Osage

Cherokee

TENN.

White Mountain

NEW MEXICO TERRITORY

Adobe Walls

Palo Duro Canyon

Creek

INDIAN TERRITORY

Wichita

Choctaw

ARKANSAS

Pima & Maricopa

Gila   River

Hot Springs

Mescalero Apache

Kiowa, Comanche & Apache

Chickasaw

Red   River

Chisasaw

MISSISSIPPI

ALA.

TEXAS

Parker's Fort

Brazos River

LOUISIANA

Mississippi River

Rio Grande

MEXICO

GULF OF MEXICO

Legend
- Indian reservation
- Range of buffalo, 1870
- Range of buffalo, 1880
- ○ City   ● Battle   ● Fort

1878 borders shown

110°   105°   100°   95°   90°

GRANT'S PEACE POLICY
Good Intentions Gone Awry

lysses S. Grant entered the White House in 1869 determined to end government abuses that fueled tribal resentments and hostilities. Corrupt Indian agents and contractors were cheating tribes of funds they were owed and delivering shoddy goods to reservations. "I wish to know why agents are sent out to us who do nothing but rob us," declared Chief Red Cloud, who visited Grant in Washington in 1870 and gave a speech in New York, asking to have "men sent out to my people whom we know and can trust." Grant responded by heeding the advice of Quakers who urged him to appoint Indian agents with religious convictions, including members of their own Society of Friends whose pacifist beliefs might help pacify defiant tribes. "If you can make Quakers out of the Indians it will take the fight out of them," Grant reportedly told them. "Let us have peace."

Grant instituted his peace policy by appointing Quakers and other devout Christians as reservation agents. Part of their job, in his words, was to help Indians become "useful and productive members of society" through training and education, which included instilling Christian values and beliefs in students at mission schools like the one attended by Ely Parker, an accomplished Seneca Iroquois appointed by Grant to head the Indian bureau. Grant's peace policy was aimed not just at educating Indians, but at taking "the fight out of them." That meant detribalizing them and discouraging or forbidding many of their traditional practices. Under Grant and his successors, government efforts to pacify and assimilate Indians would include banning sacred dances and ceremonies, taking children from their parents and sending them to boarding schools, and ultimately breaking up reservations and shattering communal bonds within tribes. Such coercive measures proved as disruptive as the earlier abuses of Indian agents and did not end tribal resistance to authorities. A more pressing problem for Grant was that he could not take the fight out of American soldiers or settlers, who continued to clash with Indians. When the fighting intensified, Grant responded as he warned he would when he became president. Those Indians who did not accept his peace policy, he said, would find him "ready for a sharp and severe war policy." ■

RED CLOUD SPEAKS Standing amid other chiefs, Red Cloud of the Lakota Sioux addresses an audience at Cooper Union (left) in New York City in 1870 after meeting with President Grant at the White House. "I have tried to get from the Great Father what is right and just," Red Cloud said through an interpreter. "I have not entirely succeeded." He returned east in 1872 and posed with William Henry Blackmore (opposite), a British philanthropist who commissioned photographer Alexander Gardner to portray Red Cloud and other tribal leaders visiting Washington that summer.

SHERMAN'S PUNISHING OFFENSIVE

Total War Against Defiant Tribes

Shortly before he became commanding general of the U.S. Army under President Grant, William Tecumseh Sherman wrote a letter to Senator Edmund Ross of Kansas recommending that Congress place the Indian bureau under the War Department. That would make the Army responsible not just for waging war against Indians but for keeping peace and overseeing reservations. As matters stood, Sherman complained, Indian agents were "ridiculously impotent with drunken or warlike savages," whereas he and his officers could "punish with one hand and caress with the other." He believed that by using a firm hand he could prevent tribal conflicts from arising. "Indian wars never bring honors or reward," he wrote, adding that he had done all he could to avert hostilities by discouraging soldiers and settlers from wantonly attacking Indians. "I have never labored harder than I have done the past two years to avoid war," he claimed.

Sherman did try to restrain settlers from provoking Indian conflicts, but he was hardly the reluctant warrior he claimed to be in his letter to Senator Ross. While commanding forces in the West in the late 1860s, he had ordered his trusted subordinate, Maj. Gen. Philip Sheridan, to launch merciless attacks on Plains Indians who ventured beyond the bounds allowed them by treaty. "All who cling to their old hunting grounds are hostile and will remain so until killed off," Sherman wrote. Like Sherman, Sheridan had been instrumental in crushing Confederate resistance during the Civil War by fulfilling General Grant's strategy of depriving

ARMY CHIEF Portrayed as a Union general by photographer Mathew Brady in 1864 (opposite), Sherman was as stern in action as in appearance. He wore the forage cap at top while overseeing relentless campaigns against Plains Indians fighting to preserve their traditional way of life, represented above by a beaded gaiter and moccasins.

the enemy of "everything that could be used to support or supply armies." In 1864, while Sherman was blazing a fiery path across Georgia, Sheridan swept like a scythe through Virginia's fertile Shenandoah Valley, seizing all the food and livestock that his forces could use and destroying the rest. That was total warfare, but it was not as thorough and devastating as the attacks Sheridan carried out for Sherman against Indians who fled their assigned reservations or refused to report to them. At no time during the Civil War had Sherman or Sheridan advocated slaughtering civilians, but their campaigns against Indians involved assaults on villages that killed women and children as well as warriors and left the survivors without shelter or sustenance. Sheridan commended George Custer for his devastating assault in November 1868 at Washita that killed Black Kettle—a Cheyenne peace chief who was seeking the Army's protection—along with his wife and other women and children in his village. When Sherman went to Washington to take charge of the U.S. Army, he left Sheridan in command on the Plains to continue punishing defiant tribes.

AN EMBATTLED CHIEF

After contending with Indians on the Plains, Sherman faced opposition of a different sort when he moved to the nation's capital. His efforts to gain control over reservations and Indian policy were thwarted in January 1870 by a massacre in Montana, where troops led by Maj. Edward Baker attacked Piegan Indians of the Blackfeet tribal group, many of whom were suffering from smallpox. More than 170 people were slain,

PHILIP SHERIDAN
1831–1888

Known as "Little Phil," Sheridan (shown above in camp during the Civil War) was over a half foot shorter and a decade younger than his fellow Ohioan William Sherman, but otherwise they had much in common and made a formidable tandem. Both were highly temperamental—Sheridan was suspended from West Point after flashing his bayonet at a cadet sergeant who offended him—and both harnessed their nervous energy as commanders and rode roughshod over their foes. Hailed in the North and reviled in the South for their scorched-earth tactics during the Civil War, they went on to campaign with even greater severity against tribal foes in the West. Sheridan offered no apology for launching blistering assaults on Indian camps such as the one carried out by his subordinate Custer at Washita. "If a village is attacked and women and children killed," he said, "the responsibility is not with the soldiers but with the people whose crimes necessitated the attack."

Sheridan followed Sherman up the chain of command and succeeded him as general in chief after he retired in 1883. Together, they ensured that western tribes remained under relentless pressure until they were confined to reservations once and for all. Although Sheridan denied ever saying that the "only good Indian is a dead Indian," he came close to endorsing that dismal maxim when engaged in hostilities. Yet he also recognized that his tribal foes had ample reason to fight. "We took away their country and their means of support," he wrote, "broke up their mode of living, their habits of life, introduced disease and decay among them, and it was for this and against this they made war."

and many others later perished in the bitter cold. Afterward, Congress refused to entrust Indian affairs to the U.S. Army and barred its officers from serving as Indian agents or filling any other nonmilitary posts. Grant then pushed ahead with his plan to appoint devout Christians as Indian agents. Sherman disapproved of Grant's peace policy and other presidential initiatives but remained loyal to his commander in chief, preserving the bond forged between them early in the Civil War when Sherman was considered mentally unstable and Grant was accused of drinking on duty. "He stood by me when I was crazy," Sherman later remarked, "and I stood by him when he was drunk; and now, sir, we stand by each other always."

In May 1871, Sherman visited Texas to investigate Indian raids there and narrowly avoided being attacked by Kiowa warriors, waiting in ambush. They let his coach and the cavalrymen escorting it pass unhindered and raided a wagon train on the same road a short time later, killing several teamsters. Sherman went after the leaders of that war party—Satanta, Satank, and Big Tree—arrested them in Indian Territory, and

A FAIR EXCHANGE—AND LESS ROBBERY.
ZACH CHANDLER—"I don't see why you take away my pets from me. I never harmed them. That was before my day!"
GENERAL SHERMAN—"I will take good care of the Indians, sir, and will see that their rights are fully protected."
UNCLE SAM—"That I know you will, General; and I shall save $3,000,000 a year by the change, myself!"

MILITARY OPTION Standing between Uncle Sam and a warrior representing the corrupt "Indian ring," Sherman promises to protect Indians in a cartoon drawn in 1876 when Congress again considered placing the War Department in charge of Indian affairs rather than the Department of the Interior, headed by Zachariah Chandler (far left). Chandler's predecessor, Columbus Delano, resigned over scandals involving the Indian bureau.

sent them to be tried for murder in Texas. Satank died in a desperate attempt to escape, but Satanta and Big Tree were convicted and sentenced to death. Much to Sherman's annoyance, Governor Edmund Davis then commuted those sentences and paroled them in 1873. "I believe Satanta and Big Tree will have their revenge" Sherman wrote Davis, and "if they are to have scalps, that yours is the first that should be taken." Satanta was later sent back to prison for violating his parole and committed suicide.

HUMAN TARGETS Tribal winter camps like this one in Montana were sometimes attacked by troops sent by Sherman and Sheridan to force Indians back onto reservations. Those who survived such assaults risked freezing or starving to death if they did not submit.

Although Sherman was capable of being merciful toward defeated tribes, as he was toward the Navajo when he allowed them return to their homeland, he believed that Plains Indians must give way before the advancing tide of settlement, much as the buffalo they relied on did. Late in life, he likened the displacement of bison by cattle to the displacement of Indians by "white men and women who have made the earth blossom as a rose . . . This change has been salutary and will go on to the end." ■

SLAUGHTERING THE BISON

The Near Extinction of the American Buffalo

Soon after becoming general in chief, Sherman said that the best way to force Indians to settle down on reservations would be to "send ten regiments of soldiers to the plains, with orders to shoot buffaloes until they became too scarce to support the redskins." Sherman could not spare enough troops to decimate the millions of bison still roaming the Plains in 1870, but some officers serving under him encouraged soldiers to kill any buffalo they encountered, and civilians joined in the slaughter. An account in *Harper's Weekly* described how a train on the Kansas Pacific Railway would slow down when it approached a herd, allowing passengers to get out guns stored for defense against Indians and blast away. "Frequently a young bull will turn at bay for a moment," the reporter noted. "His exhibition of courage is generally his death-warrant, for the whole fire of the train is turned upon him."

A far greater threat to the species emerged in the early 1870s when a new industrial process for converting buffalo hides into leather was devised. Professional hunters with high-powered rifles fanned out across the Plains. By some estimates, they killed a million or more bison annually for their hides alone, although the bones were later collected and used to make fertilizer. "The air was foul with a sickening stench," wrote Col. Richard Irving Dodge in carcass-strewn Kansas, "and the vast plain, which only a short twelvemonth before teemed with animal life, was a dead, solitary, putrid desert."

Officers did not stop riflemen from moving south of the Arkansas River into areas designated by treaty as Indian hunting grounds. Comanches and allied Indians resisted those intrusions, triggering the Red River War. When legislators in Texas proposed curbing the slaughter of bison there, Sheridan defended the white hunters: "They are destroying the Indians' commissary," he said. "Send them powder and lead, if you will; but for a lasting peace, let them kill, skin and sell until the buffaloes are exterminated."

Other factors contributed to the near extinction of bison, including disease and the disruption of migratory routes and grazing grounds as railroads were constructed and cattle ranches proliferated. By the time government efforts to preserve the species began around 1890, only a few hundred buffalo remained at large in America. ∎

BONEYARD A man stands atop a huge mound of buffalo skulls collected on the Plains in the mid-1870s after the animals were gunned down by professional hunters for their hides.

The Red River War

Adobe Walls to Palo Duro Canyon

nce lords of the southern Plains, Comanches numbered only about 3,000 by the early 1870s. Some lived permanently on the reservation assigned them in western Indian Territory or left there periodically to hunt or raid. Others held out in canyons along the Red River and its tributaries in the Texas Panhandle, where they defied troops sent to subdue them and lived as their ancestors had, relying on bison for sustenance, clothing, and other essentials. Incursions by white buffalo hunters with long-range weapons infuriated them. In 1874, they formed a war party of several hundred men, including allied Kiowas as well as some Southern Cheyennes and Arapahos, and went after hunters housed near a crumbling fort in the panhandle called Adobe Walls. The warriors were urged on by Isa-tai, a visionary who claimed that bullets would not harm them. But the attack was led by a man who knew what bullets could do and fought without flinching—Quanah, who later took his white mother's last name and became Quanah Parker.

When the battle began at Adobe Walls around dawn on June 27, a few dozen hunters holed up in a trading post there took deadly aim at the warriors approaching on horseback. Some were shot down before they got within a half mile. Quanah reached the building and backed his horse into the door but was unable to break though. Wounded as he and other attackers fell back in disarray, he survived the defeat with his reputation for bravery enhanced. Afterward, the warriors split into smaller bands and attacked stagecoaches, ranch houses, and other vulnerable targets in and around Texas.

Sheridan then set in motion a systematic campaign to destroy the villages of the hostile bands in the panhandle and force survivors onto the reservation. The crowning blow was delivered by Col. Ranald Mackenzie, a West Pointer from New York who pursued Indians as tenaciously as a Texas Ranger. On September 28, 1874, he led dismounted cavalrymen down into Palo Duro Canyon, the last great refuge for defiant Comanches and their allies, and routed the inhabitants of five villages nestled in its depths. Most escaped with their lives, but Mackenzie destroyed their lodges, food, and horses, leaving them no recourse other than the reservation. By the spring of 1875, only one sizable band remained at large—several hundred Comanches led by the elusive Quanah. ■

DAWN RAID Warriors attack white buffalo hunters at Adobe Walls in an artist's impression of the battle there in June 1874. "We tried to storm the place several times," war leader Quanah Parker recalled, but the fast-firing hunters forced them to retreat.

QUANAH PARKER'S JOURNEY
From War Leader to Peace Chief

uanah and his people were weary and hungry. Among the last Comanches to resist confinement on the reservation, they had spent the bitter winter of 1874–75 on the run. "The soldiers were after us," he recalled, "and many times they were almost upon us." In April, Col. Ranald Mackenzie sent physician and interpreter Jacob Sturm with three Comanches from the reservation to persuade these holdouts to give up and come in. When they located Quanah's camp in the Texas Panhandle, Sturm and his fellow "peace messengers" offered Indians they met with there tobacco, coffee, and sugar, which "pleased them immensely having had none of the luxuries for a long time."

Described by Sturm as a "young man of much influence with his people," Quanah had been an implacable war leader in recent years, but his isolated band of Comanches now had no hope of prevailing against Mackenzie's forces. Seeking omens of what lay ahead, Quanah saw a wolf scurry off to the north and an eagle fly away in that direction, toward the reservation. He saw that as signaling the future for his people. "They say they will abandon their roving life and try to live as white people do," Sturm reported.

When Quanah reached Fort Sill, an Army post in western Indian Territory that also served as the reservation agency, Colonel Mackenzie was there to meet him. He realized that Quanah might be particularly well suited to serve as an intermediary between Comanches and American authorities because his beloved white mother, Cynthia Ann Parker, had been seized and adopted by Comanches before giving

MOTHER AND SON Pictured above long after he came in to the reservation in 1875, Quanah Parker last saw his mother Cynthia Ann Parker when she was recaptured from Comanches in 1860. She sat for the portrait opposite a year later.

birth to him. Mackenzie wrote to an Army officer in Texas on Quanah's behalf, stating that he was "very desirous of finding out the whereabouts of his mother, if still alive, who was captured by the Indians near the falls of the Brazos nearly forty years ago, while yet a girl."

That attack occurred in Texas in May 1836 at Parker's Fort, established by Cynthia Ann's grandfather John Parker. He and her father, Silas, were among several men killed in that raid, and she was carried off with other women and children. Around 11 at that time, she later became the wife of Chief Peta Nocona, whose camp was attacked by Texas Rangers in December 1860. Young Quanah, born around 1848, fled that assault and remained with Comanches, but the Rangers took charge of his mother and baby sister, Prairie Flower. By then a fully assimilated Comanche, Cynthia Ann once again endured captivity, this time by whites who meant well but were foreign to her. One witness saw her with tears "streaming down her face," muttering in an Indian language. She made futile attempts to flee with her daughter and rejoin her tribe before Prairie Flower died in 1864. By the time Quanah inquired about his mother in 1875, she too had passed away. Yet he honored her memory by becoming Quanah Parker, a respected Comanche leader who dealt skillfully with white officials on the reservation.

COMING TO TERMS

Quanah embarked on his new role as peace chief by gaining the trust of his old foe Mackenzie, who sent him out with a white flag to bring in those few Comanches who remained holdouts. Among them was Herman Lehmann, a child of German immigrants in Texas who was captured and adopted by Apaches and later taken in by Comanches. "Quanah told us that it was useless for us to fight longer," Lehmann recalled, "for the white people would kill us all if we kept fighting." Quanah looked after Lehmann before he returned reluctantly to his family in Texas, where he felt sadly out of place.

In 1878, Indians were allowed to leave the reservation to hunt buffalo under Quanah's guidance. Finding no bison in Indian Territory, they crossed into Texas without permission and descended into Palo Duro Canyon, where cattle were now grazing instead of buffalo. Rancher Charles Goodnight, who had moved in there after Indians were driven out, confronted angry men in Quanah's party who resented his presence and were killing his cattle. Goodnight and Quanah averted conflict by reaching an agreement that allowed the Indians to kill two cows a day while they hunted in vain for buffalo.

PLURAL WIVES Quanah poses with the two of the seven women he wed while on the reservation, where polygamy was discouraged.

They returned empty-handed to the reservation, where Quanah adapted to the expanding cattle trade by negotiating grazing rights on the reservation with surrounding ranchers. As he said when he met Goodnight, he now had "two names—Quanah and Mr. Parker." Some on the reservation felt that Mr. Parker was too close to white men, who in return for his cooperation granted him fees and favors that allowed him to build a handsome residence called the Star House. Yet he never ceased to be Quanah, a chief who upheld Comanche traditions by maintaining several wives while reservation agents preached monogamy, by lobbying to prevent the government from claiming valuable tribal grazing lands for barely a dollar an acre, and by defending Indian spiritual practices, including the ritual use of peyote. When he brought his mother's remains home from Texas and buried her on the reservation, he was honoring her not just as his white mother but as the Comanche woman who nurtured him and helped him become that accomplished man of two worlds called Quanah Parker. ∎

ENDURING CAPTIVITY

REDEEMED Olive Oatman bears a tattoo after being ransomed from Mohaves in 1856.

Cynthia Ann Parker was one of many captives reclaimed from tribes that held them. Some told of harrowing abuse like her pregnant cousin Rachel Parker Plummer, who was raped and had her son taken from her and the infant she later gave birth to killed. Others were so thoroughly assimilated by their captors that they never readjusted to the society they later rejoined.

Warlike western tribes tended to view all those they captured alive as despised enemies. Men were often tortured and killed, and women were often assaulted and treated as little better than slaves.

Children and some adolescents, on the other hand, were frequently transformed from foes into full-fledged members of the tribe through adoption, which often involved initiation rites. After being captured as a boy by Apaches, Herman Lehmann thought he was about to be scalped but instead had his head shaved. His ears were then pierced with a hot iron, which was also applied to his arms. He found the ordeal excruciating and passed out, but he was then "washed, bathed, and oiled" and brought up as an Apache.

Olive Oatman (left) was seized by Yavapai Indians in Arizona around the age of 14 and was later sold to Mohaves, who tattooed her chin. Although an account published after she was ransomed from Mohaves claimed that the tattoo branded her as their slave, it probably signified her admission into the tribe, whose members had similar tattoos.

AMBASSADOR Pictured above, standing at far right beside his host in Washington and fellow Indian delegates, Quanah Parker represented Comanches in talks there. His Star House (right) was completed in 1890 without approval or aid from Indian Commissioner T. J. Morgan, a staunch foe of polygamy.

"NO ASSISTANCE WILL BE GRANTED PARKER IN THE CONSTRUCTION OF HIS HOUSE, UNLESS HE WILL AGREE, IN WRITING, TO MAKE A CHOICE AMONG HIS WIVES."
—T. J. MORGAN

INVADING THE GREAT SIOUX RESERVATION
Custer and the Black Hills Gold Rush

nown to Indians as Long Hair, Lt. Col. George Armstrong Custer stirred up trouble when he set out across Dakota Territory with his Seventh Cavalry and other troops on July 2, 1874, to reconnoiter the Black Hills. Under the 1868 Treaty of Fort Laramie, the Black Hills were set aside for the "absolute and undisturbed use and occupation" of the Lakota Sioux. General Sheridan wanted to establish a fort there, within the Great Sioux Reservation, and the treaty did not deny the Army access. But Custer had an ulterior motive—to investigate reports of mineral wealth in the area, which if confirmed would draw prospectors to the reservation in violation of the treaty. His adjutant and brother-in-law, James Calhoun, wrote that Custer was eager "to explore the Black Hills, believing that it would open a rich vein of wealth calculated to increase the commercial prosperity of this country." To that end, he allowed two miners to accompany the expedition.

When Custer and his men ascended into the Black Hills in late July, they left behind a "hot, dry, burned-up landscape," in the words of Capt. William Ludlow, and found the air cool, the water pure, and the grass "knee-deep and exceedingly luxuriant and fresh." A prized refuge and hunting ground for Lakotas, those hills were soon swarming with white fortune hunters, lured by reports exaggerating the amount of gold discovered there by the miners Custer brought along. The Army was obliged by treaty to prevent civilians from trespassing on the reservation and evicted some who did so, but Custer and other commanders contributed to the influx by publicly touting the merits of the Black Hills for prospectors as well as settlers.

In September 1875, officials met with Lakotas and tried in vain to purchase the Black Hills. Tribal resistance to the government was mounting, led by Chief Sitting Bull and others who denounced the Fort Laramie Treaty and threatened hostilities if any further concessions were made. Officers blamed such "nontreaty" Indians for attacks on civilians who invaded the Black Hills. In November, Grant met with General Sheridan and agreed that the Army would no longer prevent people from trespassing on the reservation and would instead concentrate on corralling the nontreaty bands. Grant's peace policy was defunct, and Sheridan was now free to wage war. ■

FATEFUL JOURNEY Numbering more than 1,000 men, Custer's expedition camps in July 1875 on the way to the Black Hills, where the discovery of gold (inset) caused unrest and led to war.

RECKONING AT THE LITTLE BIGHORN

Sitting Bull, Crazy Horse, and Custer's Last Stand

As prospectors invaded the Black Hills, many Lakotas fled the Great Sioux Reservation and joined hunting bands near the Bighorn Mountains along the Wyoming-Montana border. In late 1875, messengers warned that unless they reported to agencies by January 31, 1876, they would "be deemed hostile and treated accordingly." Many who refused and held out were in unceded territory, where they were entitled by treaty to camp and hunt as long as enough buffalo remained "to justify the chase." Few white hunters dared intrude there, and the buffalo still roamed, sustaining the holdouts. Sitting Bull, their inspirational leader, taunted Indians who clung to the agencies and relied on government rations: "You are fools to make yourselves slaves to a piece of fat bacon, some hard-tack, and a little sugar and coffee."

Born around 1831, Sitting Bull began hunting buffalo as a boy. Like other Plains Indians, he considered that animal a great gift from the spirits. His name evoked the proud image of a buffalo bull on its haunches, refusing to budge. An accomplished warrior as a young man, he now exercised moral leadership by upholding Lakota traditions in defiance of *Wasichus* (whites). In early June 1876, as troops approached, he performed the Sun Dance, an offering to spirits that sustained the tribe. Shedding blood from lacerations in his arms as he danced, he faced the blazing sun until he went into a trance and had a triumphant vision of soldiers falling head-down into his camp.

Fulfilling Sitting Bull's dream by defeating the oncoming troops was a task for resolute war leaders like Crazy Horse. Nearly a decade younger than Sitting Bull, he inherited his name from his father when he came of age, but he earned it partly by stealing horses from rival tribes—a coup prized by Plains Indians, who depended as much on horses as on bison. Like

Sitting Bull

HERO OR GOAT A prodigious Union officer in his mid-20s when pictured at near left around 1865, Custer was a controversial figure when he entered the Great Sioux War in 1876 and met his fate at the Battle of the Little Bighorn (far left). Some suspected him of seeking military glory to enhance his political prospects.

Sitting Bull, Crazy Horse was esteemed both by his fellow Lakotas and by allied Northern Cheyennes. Among the 7,000 or so Lakotas and Northern Cheyennes who held out against the Army along with small numbers from other tribes were about 2,000 warriors. Many were at Sitting Bull's camp along the Rosebud River in southeastern Montana when he had his vision. Some had been attacked by troops and heeded his warning: "We must stand together or they will kill us separately."

HEADSTRONG COLONEL

Custer nearly missed this campaign. He had so annoyed the president by criticizing his administration that Grant wanted him replaced. After pleading with Grant in writing "to spare me the humiliation of seeing my regiment march to meet the enemy and I not share its dangers," he retained command of the Seventh Cavalry but was placed under Brig. Gen. Alfred Terry. Urged by Sherman to "advise Custer to be prudent," Terry instead informed the impulsive colonel that he had "too much confidence in your zeal, energy and skill to give you directions

Chief Gall

which might hamper your freedom of action."

In mid-June, Terry's column moved westward up the Yellowstone River as Col. John Gibbon's column moved eastward to link up with him where the Rosebud enters the Yellowstone. Meanwhile, Brig. Gen. George Crook's column was advancing north from Wyoming toward Sitting Bull's camp. Crook was a seasoned Indian fighter, but he had never encountered warriors as formidable as those who rode into battle against him along the Rosebud on June 17. Led by Crazy Horse, they were the "best cavalry on earth," wrote one opposing officer. A Cheyenne who lost his mount was rescued valiantly by his sister, Buffalo Road Woman, who dashed in on horseback and galloped off with him. The hard-fought Battle of the Rosebud ended inconclusively, but it left Crook short of ammunition and unwilling to risk another fight trying to link up with Terry and Gibbon. Terry, now the senior officer in charge, was unsure of enemy strength. Scouts told him that Indians were moving westward from the Rosebud to the Little Bighorn River and had about 800 warriors, barely half the actual number. Terry set Custer

> ## "Our hearts were bad, and we cut and shot them all to pieces."
> —Chief Gall

on their trail with about 600 men while Gibbon swung around from the north to support him and trap the holdouts. "Don't be greedy, Custer," said Gibbon, who figured that Custer might start the battle without him.

Custer was indeed in a hurry, concerned that his foes would slip away. His Indian scouts, including Crows and Arikaras long at odds with Lakotas, saw signs that numerous bands were gathering along the Little Bighorn. "We are going to have a damn big fight," one scout warned. Yet on the morning of June 25, when Custer approached the sprawling encampment of holdouts, situated on the west side of the Little Bighorn, he remained confident of defeating them unless they bolted. Gibbon was not yet in place to the north, so Custer divided his forces, sending three companies under Maj. Marcus Reno across the shallow river south of the camp to launch the assault while he swung around to the north with five companies to attack at the far end. That reckless effort to trap his foes allowed his numerically superior foes to repulse Reno's thrust before turning to reckon with Custer.

Decades later, old warriors would recall how Sitting Bull urged them into battle on that fateful day. "We are here to protect our wives and children, and we must not let the soldiers get them," he said. "Make a brave fight!" As Custer forged ahead with two companies, seeking a place to ford the river,

HOT PURSUIT Troopers under Major Reno are shot down as they retreat across the Little Bighorn in a painting by Lakota artist Amos Bad Heart Buffalo.

Crazy Horse drove a wedge between him and his three trailing companies. Hopelessly divided and vastly outnumbered, Custer and the 210 men in those five companies were annihilated by their foes and many of their bodies were mutilated. Including Reno's casualties, 263 men of the Seventh Cavalry were killed and 59 wounded that day. It would be remembered as a massacre, but the warriors who prevailed did not seek this battle. For some, it was their last stand as well as Custer's, for the Army would redouble its efforts to track them down and force them onto reservations. ∎

NATURAL HISTORY

HOW HORSES TRANSFORMED PLAINS INDIAN CULTURE

Before they had horses, Plains Indians traveled on foot, using dogs to pull their belongings in sleds called travois. In the late 1600s, horses spread from the Spanish Southwest across the Plains, where they were sometimes called "big dogs." Unlike canines, they could be ridden and could haul much heavier loads over greater distances, greatly increasing the mobility of tribes. The mustangs Plains Indians rode (above) were relatively small and swift and were well suited for hunting buffalo, which they could outrun. That in turn lured tribes from the woodlands along the Mississippi and lower Missouri Rivers out onto the Plains to pursue bison on horseback, which increased conflict between tribes. Like other equestrians throughout history, Plains Indians found that stallions, which competed fiercely for dominance in the wild, could be as brave and stalwart as the men who rode them into battle. Warriors were known to paint their horses for combat, as they did themselves, and a man's worth could be measured in the size of the horse herd he acquired. A suitor sometimes paid a "bride price" of several horses to the family of a woman he wished to marry to show he was worthy of her.

LIBBIE CUSTER AND JESSIE FRÉMONT

Women Who Shaped Their Husbands' Legends

More than a week elapsed before word of Custer's disastrous defeat at the Little Bighorn reached Fort Abraham Lincoln, on the Missouri River in Dakota Territory, where soldiers' wives anxiously awaited news of the Seventh Cavalry. Among them was Elizabeth "Libbie" Custer, who since her marriage in 1864 had spent as much time as possible with her husband, often joining him in the field. When he left on campaign in May 1876, she wrote later in her book *Boots and Saddles,* "a premonition of disaster that I had never known before weighed me down." In early July, men wounded at the Little Bighorn returned to the fort by steamboat and confirmed her worst fears and those of other wives. "This battle wrecked the lives of twenty-six women at Fort Lincoln," she wrote. Fatherless children were left weeping beside "their bereaved mothers."

Widowed at 34, Libbie Custer lived to be 90. She had no children and never remarried, supporting herself by writing and lecturing about her life with her husband. She staunchly defended Custer, viewed by some as a valiant martyr and by others as a reckless glory seeker who sought a "personal victory" at the Little Bighorn, as one newspaper put it, rather than waiting for reinforcements and sharing credit with others. Libbie Custer helped counter such criticism by portraying him as a conscientious officer and loving husband, who gave her a rare opportunity to witness and chronicle Army life in the West from a woman's perspective. The three books she wrote about their years together were

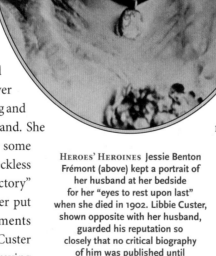

HEROES' HEROINES Jessie Benton Frémont (above) kept a portrait of her husband at her bedside for her "eyes to rest upon last" when she died in 1902. Libbie Custer, shown opposite with her husband, guarded his reputation so closely that no critical biography of him was published until after her death in 1933.

tributes not just to him but to the Army wives who shared her anxieties when apart from their husbands and her anguish when lives were lost. "I think of the sympathy shown me," she wrote, "and I feel the soft touch of their hands as they came to comfort me, even when their own hearts were wrung."

Jessie Benton Frémont faced a different challenge—marriage to a hero whose later years lacked the luster of his early feats. She helped John Frémont achieve fame not just by providing him with a powerful patron in her father, Senator Benton, but also by contributing to vivid and widely read reports of his western expeditions, which he dictated to her and she refined. When President Lincoln later relieved him of command in Missouri during the Civil War, she took up his cause by writing a book that praised the battlefield exploits of Frémont's Guard, an elite corps of 150 men he organized, and argued that their good service, like his, had gone unrewarded.

After the war, he promoted a western railroad that became mired in scandal and failed, damaging his reputation and finances. To help support him and their children, Jessie wrote popular magazine articles about her travels and experiences while continuing to defend his record. When he died in 1890, she was 66 and had been his wife for more than 48 years. "Time will vindicate General Frémont," she declared, adding that his "name can never be erased from the most colorful chapters of American history. From the ashes of his campfires, cities have sprung." ∎

SCALE

Constitutional Population
Under 2 inhab. to the Sq.Mile

2 ... 6
6 ... 18
18 ... 45
45 ... 90
90 and over

Cities over 8000 inhabitants in solid color,
in circles proportionate to population.

Indian Reservations

Range or Hunting Ground.

NOTE.

Centre of Population: 39° 12' N.
                                              63° 53.7' W.
Disregarding population
West of 100° the centre
would be: 39° 52.5' N.
                                              32° 41' W.

MAP

SHOWING, IN FIVE DEGREES OF DENSITY, THE DISTRIBUTION,
WITHIN THE TERRITORY OF THE UNITED STATES, OF THE

CONSTITUTIONAL POPULATION
(i.e. excluding Indians not taxed)

Compiled from the Returns of Population at the Ninth Census
OF THE UNITED STATES, 1870,
BY
FRANCIS A. WALKER.
To which is added a sketch of the principal
INDIAN RESERVATIONS AND RANGES
from information furnished by the Office of Indian Affairs
of date 1871.

Pl. XIX

FROM TRIUMPH TO DEFEAT

The Bitter Aftermath of the Little Bighorn

Soon after the Battle of the Little Bighorn, the combined bands that overwhelmed Custer separated to hunt and evade the pursuit that was sure to follow their stunning victory. Civilians were shocked and alarmed by that massacre. But Sherman and Sheridan had overcome worse defeats during the Civil War, and they now had support in Congress, which dropped its opposition to military control of reservations temporarily in order to punish the Lakota Sioux and their allies. Army officers replaced civilians as agents overseeing "hostile" Indians. They were to be disarmed and their rations withheld until chiefs agreed to cede the Black Hills and surrounding areas.

To foil Crazy Horse, Sitting Bull, and other tribal resistance leaders, Sheridan called on commanders who were quick and decisive without exhibiting what he called the "superabundance of courage" that led Custer to throw caution to the wind and court disaster. Two seasoned veterans of the Red River War who had subdued Comanches and their allies on the southern Plains—colonels Ranald Mackenzie and Nelson Miles—were assigned to crush resistance on the northern Plains under the direction of General Crook. At dawn on November 25, 1876, Mackenzie attacked a large village of Northern Cheyennes led by Chiefs Dull Knife and Little Wolf, situated along a fork of the Powder River in northeastern Wyoming. Warriors fought back, killing or wounding more than two dozen soldiers. But Cheyenne casualties were steeper, and the villagers fled as Mackenzie's men torched their lodges. Nearly a dozen infants froze to death before the fugitives joined Cheyennes and Lakotas led by Crazy Horse in southeastern Montana. In January 1877, Miles caught up with those holdouts along the Tongue River and battled them in a blizzard, adding to their losses. Hungry, cold, and weary, the survivors lost heart and began returning to their agencies. In May, Crazy Horse yielded and lay down his weapons. Arrested four months later while trying to leave the reservation, he struggled with his captors and was bayoneted to death.

Sitting Bull crossed into Canada with his band and held out until 1881, when buffalo were too scarce to sustain them and they yielded to the commander at Fort Buford in Dakota Territory. The battle was lost, and the Great Sioux Reservation had been broken up. Sitting Bull asked to be remembered as the "last man of my tribe to surrender my rifle." ∎

LOST LAND An 1870 map shows population densities and tribal areas, including the Great Sioux Reservation in western Dakota Territory, the largest area retained by any one tribe. Lakotas lost the Black Hills when the conflict called the Great Sioux War ended in 1877.

COPING WITH CONFINEMENT
Reservation Life and Strife

<img_1>

In March 1879, Valentine McGillycuddy took charge of the Pine Ridge Agency, the administrative center of a smaller reservation assigned to the Oglala band of Lakotas after their Great Sioux Reservation was broken up. A former Army surgeon, he had tended to the dying Crazy Horse, whom he later praised as "the greatest leader of his people in modern times." Yet like many Americans, Indian Agent McGillycuddy found it easier to appreciate dead or defeated chiefs than to tolerate those who remained alive and defiant. The Pine Ridge Agency was originally called the Red Cloud Agency in honor of that Oglala chief. Red Cloud had renounced hostilities, but he was still a proud and determined leader, reluctant to defer to the agent. Removing Red Cloud's name signaled that the Pine Ridge Reservation would be firmly under the control of McGillycuddy, whose mission was to detribalize the Oglala.

One of the agent's first steps was to replace warriors called *akicitas,* who were appointed by chiefs to maintain order within the tribe, with a reservation police force that he hired and equipped. Their tasks included enforcing prohibitions against the Sun Dance and other "heathenish rites and customs." Offenders could be jailed for up to 30 days, a harsh penalty for Lakotas, who had no prisons before the reservation era. It was dread of imprisonment that caused Crazy Horse to grapple with the guard who killed him. To make matters worse, McGillycuddy asked police officers to serve as judges. A lieutenant named Standing Soldier thought that was asking too much of officers who were resented by Oglalas for enforcing stringent rules and were paid considerably less than white soldiers. "In protecting life and property and adopting the white man's ways we have risked our lives and incurred the enmity of many of our people," declared Standing Soldier, who warned that acting as judges and sending offenders to jail would expose lawmen to further hostility. "We do not think that it is well to have the same man that acts as judge also act as policeman and perform the punishment," he

ACCOMMODATION American flags displayed in Red Cloud's bedroom (left) signal that the chief had come to terms with the U.S. government, but he was often at odds with Valentine McGillycuddy, the Indian agent at the Pine Ridge Reservation. Despite the agent's efforts to abolish tribal traditions, some on the reservation continued to live in tepees (opposite) and carry sacred objects like the Lakota shield above, adorned with a hawk, kestrel, and feathers— charms that were believed to empower and protect warriors.

DRESSED UP Students assemble in uniform at the Carlisle Indian Industrial School. Children at such schools were taught to regard traditional dress and customs, represented by the Plains Indian doll below, as backward.

concluded. "They tell me that is not the way the white man manages his own court."

INDOCTRINATION AND RESISTANCE

Most reservation dwellers avoided prison, but few were spared the wrenching impact of an educational system that disrupted families and taught children to reject their parents' way of life. Schooling offered youngsters benefits, but it came at a steep price. Boys had their hair cut short, which many found humiliating. Students learned English but were frequently scolded or punished for speaking their native language.

In 1879, the first of many government boarding schools for Indian children located off reservations was founded at Carlisle, Pennsylvania, by Col. Richard Henry Pratt, who believed that only by removing boys and girls from their families and tribes could they be properly raised as Americans. Pratt's formula for detribalizing and assimilating a child was stark: "Kill the Indian in him, and save the man." When parents resisted schooling

the reservation with several hundred Modocs. They returned to their homeland in California around Tule Lake, where they later sought refuge in lava beds from troops sent to capture them and waged war on those soldiers.

Apaches of various bands in and around Arizona Territory resisted confinement to reservations long after most tribes had given up the fight. In a rare concession, Brig. Gen. Oliver Howard met with Chief Cochise of the Chiricahua Apache in 1872 and granted him the reservation he asked for, embracing the Chiricahua Mountains, long home to his people. But that settlement was later scrapped when authorities decided to lump Apaches together at the woefully inadequate San Carlos Reservation, triggering further conflict. ∎

LAVA BEDS NATIONAL MONUMENT

Formed by ancient volcanic eruptions that left a tortured landscape gouged with craters and caves, the lava beds below Tule Lake in northern California served as the stronghold for Modocs who resisted troops sent in 1872 to force them back onto a reservation they despised. Fighting began late that year and intensified in January 1873 when more than 300 soldiers and volunteers were repulsed by some 70 Modoc warriors led by Captain Jack. Brig. Gen. Edward Canby was then sent with other commissioners to negotiate with the Modocs. Meeting in council beforehand, the warriors decided to attack the commissioners. Captain Jack warned of retaliation by the Army but abided by that decision. On April 11, as the two sides met for talks, he shot Canby dead. In the ensuing gunfight, another commissioner was killed.

Captain Jack escaped to rejoin his forces hiding in caves in the lava beds (inset), where they were besieged by nearly 1,000 troops and eventually subdued. Arrested and convicted of murder, Captain Jack and three others were executed in October 1873. Many of the men, women, and children who had held out with them were exiled to Indian Territory. Lava Beds National Monument preserves the volcanic battleground where Modoc warriors fought for independence.

for their children, Indian agents withheld their rations and sometimes sent reservation police to remove youngsters to boarding schools.

Reservations were meant to restrain and pacify Indians, but some were so bleak or poorly managed that tribes fled them and clashed with pursuing troops. Rather than assigning each tribe a distinct reservation in its homeland, authorities often placed Indians on land foreign to them and among people alien to them. The Modoc of northern California were forced onto the reservation of the Klamath in southern Oregon, where Modocs were unwelcome and outnumbered. In 1870, a tribal leader known to whites as Captain Jack left

Manning the Forts
Soldier Life on the Frontier

Amid the vast expanse of the West and its sundry towns and camps, forts and the soldiers who manned them were relatively few and far between. By the early 1870s, the U.S. Army had been reduced to 26,000 men, some of whom were still stationed in the South, upholding federal authority in former Confederate states. Soldiers in the West had to perform nearly all the tasks required to sustain their outposts, including building them. While construction was ongoing, they lived in tents or dugouts. They also had to keep their forts stocked with fuel, a major task in winter. Men at Fort Laramie, one of the bigger western garrisons, stripped the vicinity of firewood and had to travel up to 50 miles to fell trees.

When not busy sawing or hammering, troops spent hours drilling or performing guard duty. One day in the life of William Drown, a bugler at Fort Laramie who kept a diary there, consisted of serving as orderly bugler for his commanding officer in the morning, after which he "saddled up and rode two miles and assisted in digging a grave. Returned at half past twelve—started again at one with the funeral procession, after which was marched home, dressed myself for evening parade, marched back again to the corral, assisted in flogging a deserter, came home, ate supper, and here I am scratching it down in the old journal." Those who thought soldiers had it easy, he and others in uniform concluded, should try being soldiers.

Desertions—and floggings for those caught in the act—were common among men whose starting pay was just $13 a month, less than half what a typical cowboy earned. Although life in camp could be monotonous, those who served in the Army in one capacity or another were a remarkably diverse lot. Some were recent emigrants from Europe. Others were so-called buffalo soldiers: black troops serving in separate regiments. On patrols, troops were often accompanied by Indian auxiliaries, who functioned not just as scouts but as fighting men. Most forts contained more than a few women, including the wives of officers and enlisted men, laundresses, and nurses who aided Army surgeons or tended patients in their absence. Fort Laramie had a school at which 20 children were enrolled in 1877. Soldiers who served as teachers there received a bonus—the princely sum of 20 cents a day. ∎

SIX-GUN The United States purchased more than 5,000 of these Smith & Wesson Schofield revolvers, introduced in the 1870s and issued mainly to cavalrymen.

GUARDIANS Below, soldiers in buffalo coats patrol Fort Keogh in Montana Territory in 1879. Guarding forts against attack was of particular concern for those who had wives and children with them like the officers at right, posing with family members at Fort Walla Walla in Washington Territory.

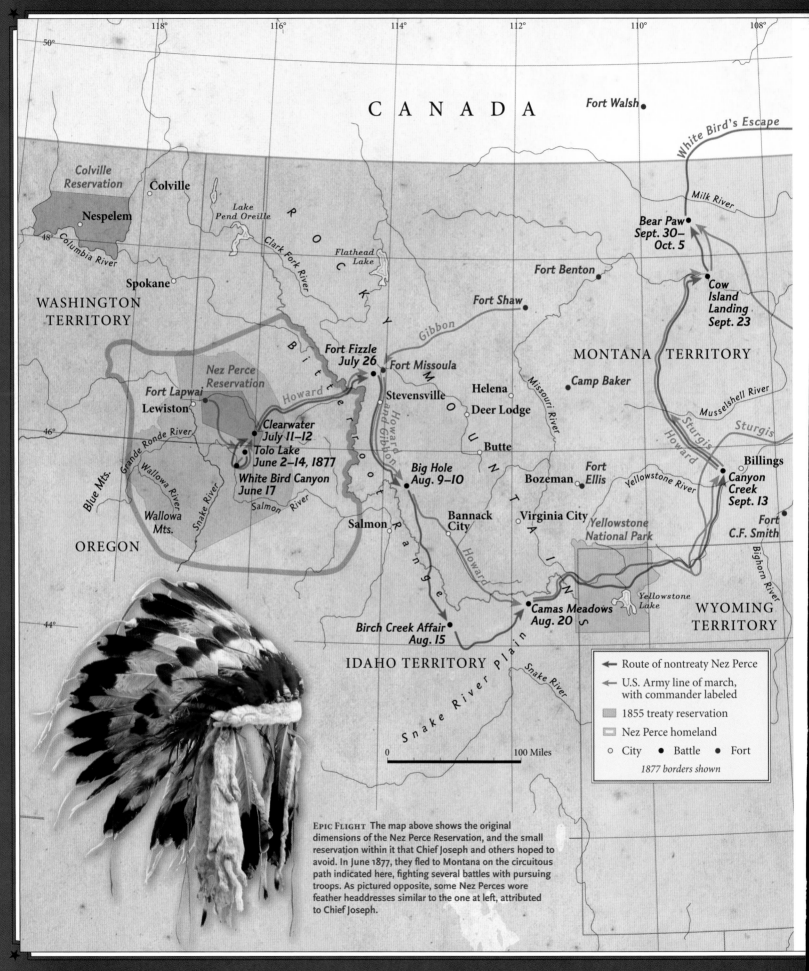

CANADA

Fort Walsh

White Bird's Escape

Milk River

Colville
Reservation

Colville

Nespelem

Lake
Pend Oreille

Bear Paw
Sept. 30–
Oct. 5

Cow
Island
Landing
Sept. 23

Fort Benton

Spokane

WASHINGTON
TERRITORY

Flathead
Lake

Fort Shaw

MONTANA   TERRITORY

Clark Fork River

Gibbon

Fort Fizzle
July 26

Fort Missoula

Camp Baker

Nez Perce
Reservation

Stevensville

Helena

Missouri River

Musselshell River

Sturgis

Fort Lapwai

Lewiston

Deer Lodge

Howard

Sturgis

Clearwater
July 11–12

Tolo Lake
June 2–14, 1877

White Bird Canyon
June 17

Grande Ronde River

Wallowa River

Snake River

Salmon River

Big Hole
Aug. 9–10

Butte

Billings

Yellowstone River

Canyon
Creek
Sept. 13

Blue Mts.

Bozeman

Fort
Ellis

OREGON

Wallowa
Mts.

Salmon

Bannack
City

Virginia City

Yellowstone
National Park

Fort
C.F. Smith

Bighorn River

Camas Meadows
Aug. 20

Yellowstone
Lake

WYOMING
TERRITORY

Birch Creek Affair
Aug. 15

IDAHO TERRITORY

Snake River Plain

Snake River

Howard

Howard and Gibbon

ROCKY

MOUNTAINS

Bitterroot Range

Legend

← Route of nontreaty Nez Perce

← U.S. Army line of march,
with commander labeled

■ 1855 treaty reservation

□ Nez Perce homeland

○ City   ● Battle   ● Fort

1877 borders shown

0   100 Miles

EPIC FLIGHT The map above shows the original
dimensions of the Nez Perce Reservation, and the small
reservation within it that Chief Joseph and others hoped to
avoid. In June 1877, they fled to Montana on the circuitous
path indicated here, fighting several battles with pursuing
troops. As pictured opposite, some Nez Perces wore
feather headdresses similar to the one at left, attributed
to Chief Joseph.

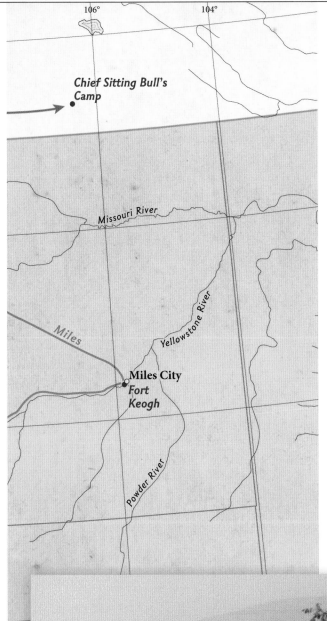

106°   104°

Chief Sitting Bull's
Camp

Missouri River

Yellowstone River

Miles

Miles City
Fort
Keogh

Powder River

FLIGHT OF THE NEZ PERCE
Chief Joseph's Odyssey

ithin the space of a single lifetime, Nez Perce Indians who had welcomed Lewis and Clark in 1805 and helped sustain that historic expedition found themselves besieged by white settlers and pressured into surrendering their land. Among the chiefs who resisted that pressure was a leader named Joseph, whose band inhabited the Wallowa Valley in northeastern Oregon. He had converted to Christianity and dealt cordially with Americans, but he refused to sign a treaty that reduced the original Nez Perce Reservation, which included his homeland, to a small area along the Clearwater River in Idaho. As he lay dying in 1871, he urged his son and successor, known thereafter as Chief Joseph, to cling to the Wallowa Valley. "This country holds your father's body," he said. "Never sell the bones of your father and mother."

In 1877, Chief Joseph was asked to do just that. The government conceded that his band and other Nez Perces who rejected the treaty were entitled to compensation but insisted that they sell their land and move to the reservation, which meant surrendering not just their territory but their cultural identity. They want to "live as free and unrestricted as their fathers," one official wrote. "They aspire to be Indians and nothing else." When talks in May failed to sway them, Brig. Gen. Oliver Howard warned that they would be attacked if they did not report to the reservation within a month.

Chief Joseph and his people sorrowfully abandoned the Wallowa Valley and joined other holdouts in Idaho. They were about to depart for the reservation when impulsive young men with scores to settle killed four settlers nearby. Chief Joseph remarked that it was difficult for him and other Nez Perce leaders to prevent such violence against those who intruded on their territory and taunted them. "We have had a few good friends among the white men, and they have always advised my people to bear these taunts without fighting," he said. "Our young men are quick tempered and I have had great trouble in keeping them from doing rash things."

Fearing retaliation for the attack on the settlers, Joseph and more than 700 Nez Perces of various bands fled southward, away from the reservation, and camped in White Bird Canyon on the Salmon River. Troops went after them, rebuffed Indians seeking a truce under a white flag, and charged recklessly into the canyon, where warriors were waiting and killed 34 soldiers without losing a single man of their own.

PROUD LEADER Born in 1840, Chief Joseph stood for this portrait sometime after he succeeded his father in 1871.

FLIGHT TO THE PLAINS

Having thrashed American troops, Chief Joseph and other leaders of the fugitives had no hope of coming to terms with the government and continued their flight. Circling back northward, they held off soldiers sent by General Howard in a two-day battle along the Clearwater River in early July. Some chiefs then proposed in council that they cross the Bitterroot Range and seek refuge among the Crow in Montana, who had welcomed them in the past. Unaware that many Crow warriors were now serving in the U.S. Army against traditional foes such as the Lakota Sioux and could no longer be counted on as their friends, the Nez Perces trekked eastward over

INDIAN FIGHTER During his long career as an Army officer in the West, Nelson Miles helped subdue Quanah Parker, Sitting Bull, and Geronimo as well as Chief Joseph.

the mountains, foiling their pursuers time and again. Howard attributed their military prowess to Chief Joseph, who was touted in newspapers as the "Red Napoleon," a misleading label for a man who had tried to avoid hostilities and left the fighting now to war leaders like his younger brother, Ollokot. General Sherman, who seldom had kind words for tribes at odds with the Army, wrote later that the Nez Perces displayed remarkable courage and fought "with almost scientific skill."

On August 9, however, they suffered a grievous setback when cavalrymen led by Col. John Gibbon, a veteran of the Great Sioux War, attacked their camp in western Montana's Big Hole Valley and killed more than 70 people. Warriors fought back with a vengeance and made Gibbon pay dearly, but the fugitives grew increasingly desperate and clashed with civilians as well as soldiers. Passing through the recently established Yellowstone National Park at month's end, they relieved some startled tourists of their horses and provisions and assailed others before continuing northward through Montana, harried by troops and Crow warriors as well as scouts from other tribes.

Their only hope now was to cross into Canada, as Sitting Bull did, but cavalrymen led by Col. Nelson Miles hurried from Fort Keogh to head them off. A decorated Civil War veteran, Miles was as keenly ambitious as Custer but more methodical and calculating. He applied relentless pressure to his tribal foes but remained open to talks, giving them a chance to yield without suffering utter devastation. When he cornered the Nez Perces at Bear Paw Mountain, 40 miles below the Canadian border, they made one last stand, inflicting heavy casualties on Miles but failing to break out of the trap he set for them. A small group led by Chief White Bird managed to escape to Canada, but Chief

Joseph chose to spare the remainder further suffering as winter closed in. He was assured by Miles that they would be sent to the reservation in Idaho if they gave up, but that promise would not be fulfilled. As he prepared to submit, he had no way of knowing that he and his people would be exiled first to Kansas and then to Indian Territory. Many of them would never see their homeland again.

On October 5, 1877, Chief Joseph surrendered to Miles and General Howard, using memorable words that brought to an end to one of the last great struggles by American Indians against coercion and confinement. "I am tired of fighting," he said. "Our chiefs are killed . . . It is cold, and we have no blankets. The little children are freezing to death. My people, some of them, have run away to the hills, and have no blankets, no food. No one knows where they are—perhaps freezing to death. I want to have time to look for my children, and see how many of them I can find. Maybe I shall find them among the dead . . . My heart is sick and sad. From where the sun now stands I will fight no more forever." ■

LAST STAND In their final battle, the Nez Perce fugitives killed dozens of cavalrymen, but Chief Joseph remained hemmed in by his pursuers and surrendered (top). He is pictured above riding off in the company of Colonel Miles (left) and General Howard.

CAMERAMAN Pioneering Western photographer William Henry Jackson, shown here with rifle in hand, joined Ferdinand Hayden on expeditions to Yellowstone in 1871 and the Tetons in 1872.

FOUNDING YELLOWSTONE
America's First National Park

Long before Yellowstone National Park was established "for the benefit and enjoyment of the people" in 1872, Indians hunted there and mountain men seeking beaver pelts marveled at its geysers. Trapper Daniel Potts provided the first eyewitness account to appear in print, published by a newspaper in Philadelphia in 1827. He told of "hot and boiling springs, some of water and others of most beautiful fine clay, resembling a mush pot," which gushed up to 30 feet in the air. As one man in his party was standing by a sulfur spring, Potts related, the earth began to tremble, "and he with difficulty made his escape when an explosion took place resembling that of thunder."

Many readers assumed this was another tall tale from mountain men, who were known to stretch the truth to the breaking point, but subsequent accounts confirmed that Yellowstone was indeed a place where nature worked miracles. In 1871, Congress commissioned geologist Ferdinand Hayden to survey the region. Accompanied by photographer William Henry Jackson and landscape painter Thomas Moran, Hayden concluded that the Yellowstone Basin had once been "one vast crater," forged by volcanic forces as powerful as that found in "any portion of the globe." The result of that intense geothermal activity, which continued to fuel geysers and hot springs, was a landscape so spectacular that he recommended it be preserved for its scientific and scenic value. The Northern Pacific Railroad also pressed to have the area declared a national park, although it would be another decade before that troubled railroad came close enough to deliver tourists there. Until then, Yellowstone remained a wilderness park, fully accessible only on foot or on horseback. Visitors entered at their own risk, as demonstrated by their harrowing run-ins with Nez Perce fugitives in 1877. By 1883, however, the park was considered safe enough for President Chester A. Arthur to camp there, and construction began on a hotel at Mammoth Hot Springs. Americans were beginning to view what remained wild in the West not as something to be extinguished or exploited but as a national asset to be preserved and cherished. When homegrown wonders like Yellowstone beckoned, asked the *New York Times,* "Why should we go to Switzerland to see the mountains, or to Iceland to see the geysers?" ∎

ARTIST'S VIEW Thomas Moran produced this watercolor of Sulphur Mountain and Tower Falls during Hayden's expedition in 1871, a year before Yellowstone became America's first national park. Congress had earlier voted to preserve the Yosemite Valley, but it was administered by California until it became a national park in 1890.

FEDERAL LAWMEN U.S. marshals gather with rifles in hand at Fort Smith, Arkansas. Assigned to bring outlaws in Arkansas and neighboring Indian Territory to justice at federal court in Fort Smith, many U.S. marshals serving there died in the line of duty.

LAW AND DISORDER

In 1880, when Arizona was a sparsely settled territory of 40,000 inhabitants, the worst thing you could say about someone there was to call him a cowboy. As a newspaper editor in Tucson explained, "cowboy is a name which has ceased in this Territory to be a term applied to cattle herders. The term is applied to thieves, robbers, cutthroats and the lawless class of the community generally." Many of those troublemakers were in fact ranchers or ranch hands, and their misdeeds sometimes resembled the wild pranks of earlier cowboys who blew off steam in Kansas cattle towns like Abilene after long drives from Texas. The manager of a mine in Galeyville, Arizona, for example, complained of

cowboys who had the annoying habit of "saluting us with an indiscriminate discharge of firearms, and after indulging in a few drinks at the saloons, practice shooting at the lamps, bottles, glasses, etc." Some went so far as to shoot "the cigar out of one's mouth," he added, which caused "a nervous feeling among the visitors especially." One newcomer forced to dance at gunpoint by an unruly cowboy in an Arizona saloon returned later with six-shooter in hand and ordered his tor-

mentor to do likewise: "Now you dance a while, damn you."

People could laugh at such antics, but there was nothing funny about the crimes committed by so-called cowboys along the Arizona-Mexico border. Their raids into Sonora, where they stole livestock and engaged in shootouts with Mexicans, nearly ignited a border war. And when not stealing cattle, they sometimes robbed stagecoaches and killed the drivers or the armed guards riding alongside them. Many

Bank robbery by the James-Younger gang

Fence-cutters

1882 Jesse James is slain at home in St. Joseph, Missouri, by Bob Ford, a member of his gang.

1883 Fence-cutters clash with Texas cattlemen who are using barbed wire to close off pastures.

1880 Wyatt Earp becomes deputy sheriff of Tombstone, Arizona.

1881 Sentenced to death, Billy the Kid breaks out of jail in New Mexico and is tracked down and killed by Sheriff Pat Garrett.

Sheriff Pat Garrett

1884 Vigilantes led by rancher Granville Stuart execute many suspected rustlers in Montana.

sheriffs or marshals in the vicinity lacked the will or capacity to bring such offenders to justice. Those lawmen who did act forcefully, such as Wyatt Earp of Tombstone, Arizona, took such harsh measures that some people considered them worse than the outlaws they targeted. Others felt that wayward cowboys deserved no mercy and should be wiped out. "They are worse than the Apache and should be treated as such," declared the *Arizona Star* in February 1881; "wherever found let them be shot down like the Apache."

Those were strong words at a time when Apaches confined to the miserable San Carlos Reservation in southeastern Arizona broke out periodically and clashed with soldiers and settlers. In the frontier West as a whole, however, Indian conflicts were subsiding even as lawlessness persisted and came to define the region. Criminality was not, of course, an exclusively western phenomenon. Yet nowhere in America were outlaws more brazen in their attacks or lawmen more hard-pressed to stop them than on the western frontier, where saloons in seething boomtowns like Tombstone bred mayhem and offenders had vast areas in which to evade justice.

Some western gunmen who gained notoriety in the late 1800s were Civil War veterans who continued to wield weapons after the conflict ended. Several former Union

> "WHEN THE CIVIL AUTHORITIES ARE INSUFFICIENT OR UNWILLING TO PROTECT THE COMMUNITY THE PEOPLE ARE JUSTIFIED IN TAKING THE LAW INTO THEIR OWN HANDS."
> —EDITOR, *TOMBSTONE EPITAPH*

soldiers or scouts—including James Butler "Wild Bill" Hickok and Virgil Earp, who fought alongside his brother Wyatt in Tombstone's infamous O.K. Corral gunfight in 1881—served as lawmen in western states or territories, where Union veterans or men appointed by former Union commanders like Presidents Ulysses S. Grant and Rutherford B. Hayes often called the shots. Ex-Confederate soldiers or guerrillas who stuck to their guns like Jesse James and his cohort Cole Younger, on the other hand, were more inclined to defy postwar authorities and remain in rebellion as outlaws, often aided by people with ties to the Old South who admired their defiant stance.

LAWMEN AS LAWBREAKERS

Die-hard Rebels were not the only ones at odds with the law in the West. Many people came to resent and resist marshals or sheriffs who acted as partisans rather than peacekeepers, aggravating conflicts such as the so-called Lincoln County War in New Mexico, which thrust into prominence an elusive young gunfighter named Billy the Kid. Worse still were vigilantes who claimed to be dispensing justice to evildoers while carrying out vendettas against those who challenged their right to appropriate public land or mineral wealth. In the late 1880s, cattle barons in Wyoming launched a campaign

Ellen "Cattle Kate" Watson

Geronimo

1885 Chiricahua Apache leader Geronimo breaks out of the San Carlos Reservation with followers, pursued by troops.

1886 A hot, dry summer followed by a severe winter causes "great die-up" of cattle on the northern Plains.

1887 Graham-Tewksbury feud rages in Arizona's Pleasant Valley. Congress passes the Dawes Act, leading to allotment and breakup of Indian reservations.

1888 Dalton brothers turn from enforcing the law in Indian Territory to defying it.

1889 Lynching of Wyoming homesteaders Jim Averell and Ellen Watson (alias "Cattle Kate") foreshadows the Johnson County War. Oklahoma land rush begins.

to brand small ranchers there as rustlers and eliminate such competitors, culminating in the so-called Johnson County War, which ended when federal troops intervened.

The lavish attention paid in newspapers to western outlaws such as Belle Starr, whose exploits as a "bandit queen" in Indian Territory were embellished by journalists, heightened the impression that lawlessness was rampant in the 1880s. Yet this was also a time when lawmen, judges, and higher officials began to tame the Wild West and suppress bloodshed there. In the first few years of the decade, both Jesse James and Billy the Kid were targeted by authorities and killed, while the Earp brothers and Doc Holliday were doing away with some of the worst offenders in Arizona. U.S. troops, including black recruits known as buffalo soldiers, not only forced the surrender of feared warriors such as Geronimo and his fellow Apache fugitives but also helped keep peace by guarding Indian lands against illegal intrusions.

By 1890, much of what was once open range had been fenced in—a process that caused conflict initially but provided stability in the long run by placing barriers between competing owners and rival interests. Men who once drove cattle hundreds of miles across land unbounded by barbed wire lamented the change. "Fences, sir, are the curse of the country!" complained one old ranch hand. But if the new West that emerged toward the end of the 19th century was less adventurous and heroic, it was also less villainous and violent—a change welcomed by settlers, including many in Arizona weary of depredations by those outlaws called cowboys. ∎

U.S. states
U.S. territories
○ Towns
● Jesse James crime sites

WASHINGTON TERRITORY

Columbia River

OREGON

NEVADA

CALIFORNIA

G R
B A
M O J A
D E S E

PACIFIC OCEAN

TROUBLE SPOTS Charted here are places where law gave way to disorder between the 1870s and early 1890s, including towns where Jesse James and his gang staged robberies, cattle towns in Kansas where marshals cracked down on unruly cowboys, counties in New Mexico and Wyoming where disputes deadly enough to be called wars occurred, and sites in Arizona where showdowns and shootouts occurred.

AMBUSHED Taken by surprise, bandits return fire in a painting evoking the days when men called cowboys were saddled with a sinister reputation.

THE OLD WEST IN 1880

MONTANA TERRITORY

Butte

Virginia City

IDAHO TERRITORY

Johnson County War (1892)

WYOMING TERRITORY

Casper

Rawlins

Cheyenne

UTAH TERRITORY

Leadville

COLORADO

Snake River

Green River

Colorado River

Missouri River

Yellowstone River

DAKOTA TERRITORY

Deadwood

Badlands

NEBRASKA

Platte River

MINNESOTA

Northfield

WISCONSIN

MICHIGAN

Lake Superior

Lake Michigan

IOWA

ILLINOIS

Mississippi River

St. Joseph

Gallatin

Winston

Clay County

Centralia

Topeka

Nicodemus

Abilene

Lawrence

Independence

Kansas City

KANSAS

MISSOURI

Arkansas River

Dodge City

Caldwell

Coffeyville

KY.

TENN.

ARIZONA TERRITORY

NEW MEXICO TERRITORY

Lincoln County War (1878)

San Carlos Reservation

Pleasant Valley

Galeyville

Fort Huachuca

Tombstone

INDIAN TERRITORY

Fort Smith

ARKANSAS

Red River

MISSISSIPPI

LOUISIANA

TEXAS

Brazos River

Langtry

SONORA

MEXICO

GULF OF MEXICO

GREAT PLAINS

ROCKY MOUNTAINS

GREAT BASIN

DESERT

110°   105°   100°   95°

0   200 Miles

THE LAST DAYS OF JESSE JAMES

Downfall of a Deadly Rebel

Jesse James was a marked man. In late July 1881, Missouri governor Thomas Crittenden offered rewards of $10,000 for the capture and conviction of 33-year-old Jesse and his brother Frank, whose gang had recently carried out a train robbery near Winston, Missouri, that claimed the life of the conductor and a passenger. Crittenden hoped that the hefty rewards would induce underlings in the James gang to betray Jesse and Frank, who was five years older than his notorious brother but deferred to him as kingpin.

In defiance of the governor, the gang soon struck again. On the night of September 7, they forced the engineer of a train heading east from Independence, Missouri, to come to a halt by piling rocks on the tracks then relieved passengers and crew of their valuables at gunpoint. "They can't stop us from robbing trains," their leader said. "It's our business." To make sure that everyone knew who pulled this heist, he announced before

REWARD!
- DEAD OR ALIVE -

$5,000.00 will be paid for the capture of the men who robbed the bank at

NORTHFIELD, MINN.

They are believed to be Jesse James and his Band, or the Youngers.

All officers are warned to use precaution in making arrest. These are the most desperate men in America.

Take no chances! Shoot to kill!!

J. H. McDonald,
SHERIFF

leaving, "This is the last time you will ever see Jesse James."

Those words proved prophetic, for this would be the last exploit in his criminal career, which began two decades earlier when the Civil War tore Missouri apart and made him a hardened killer. The son of a roving preacher from Kentucky who left his family for the goldfields of California and died there in 1850, Jesse James was raised by his mother and her second husband in Clay County, Missouri, home to many transplanted Southerners who owned slaves as the James family did. During the Civil War, he joined Frank in a Confederate guerrilla band led by William "Bloody Bill" Anderson, a ruthless bushwhacker whose men took scalps as trophies. On September 27, 1864, they stopped a train in Centralia, Missouri, looted the baggage car, and seized nearly two dozen unarmed Union soldiers, heading home on furlough. "You are all to be killed and sent to hell," Anderson said. The ensuing massacre made him and his band prime targets for Union

WANTED FOR MURDER Portrayed opposite in a colorized photographic portrait, Jesse James emerged as one of the nation's most notorious outlaws for crimes that included an attempted bank robbery in Northfield, Minnesota, in September 1876. That raid claimed the life of a bank teller and led to a deadly shootout in the street (left) and a manhunt for Jesse and his cohorts, for whom rewards were offered (top).

forces. Anderson died fighting. Jesse James took a bullet through his lung but survived, emerging from the war as an avid gunman and renegade.

FROM GUERRILLA TO GANGSTER

For many years to come, Jesse and Frank carried out a long string of robberies with accomplices, including the notorious Cole Younger, another ruthless Confederate veteran. Some of their heists were intended not just to gather loot but to punish old foes. During a bank robbery in Gallatin, Missouri, in December 1869, Jesse killed the cashier, whom he mistakenly blamed for Anderson's death. In September 1876, his gang targeted a bank in Northfield, Minnesota, owned in part by Adelbert Ames, a notorious Yankee who had served as governor of Union-occupied Mississippi after the war and was reviled by white Southerners as a carpetbagger. Armed citizens foiled the robbery, killing two gang members and

NOTORIOUS SIBLINGS Brandishing revolvers, Jesse James (left) and his brother and criminal sidekick Frank sat for this portrait around 1870.

wounding Cole Younger and his brothers Bob and Jim, who were captured while Jesse and Frank slipped away.

Jesse's brutal exploits were glorified by John Newman Edwards, editor of the *Kansas City Times*. An ex-Confederate devoted to the Old South and its Lost Cause, he published an anonymous letter that readers assumed was from Jesse, although Edwards probably spiffed it up. In it, the outlaw portrayed his gang of thieves as Robin Hoods who "rob the rich and give to the poor" and claimed that their criminality was child's play compared with the corrupt administration of President and former Union commander Ulysses S. Grant. "It hurts me very much to be called a thief," wrote the gang leader, who complained that the title equated him unfairly with "Grant and his party."

Some Missourians who had backed the Confederacy considered Jesse a hero and shielded him, but public support waned when he formed a new gang and resumed his deadly crime spree in 1881. His nemesis, Governor Crittenden, had sided with the Union during the Civil War, but many former Rebels now agreed with Crittenden that it was time to clean up the state and crack down on its worst offenders. Although the governor offered rewards for both James brothers, he knew that Jesse was the instigator. In January 1882, Crittenden met privately with gang member Bob Ford and promised to reward and pardon him and his brother Charley if they eliminated their boss. On April 3, they entered his home in St. Joseph, Missouri, and Bob Ford shot Jesse James in the back of the head. Convicted of that murder, the Ford brothers were pardoned as promised. ■

BAND OF BROTHERS
Cole Younger (far left) and his brother Bob stand behind the seated Jesse James (second from left) and brother Frank in this portrait of the gang taken not long before the Northfield bank robbery in 1876. Jesse later formed a new gang that included Charley and Bob Ford, who shot him dead on April 3, 1882, as he was hanging a picture at home (below).

"JESSE AND I NEVER WENT INTO A PLACE THAT DIDN'T HAVE A BACK DOOR."
—FRANK JAMES

GOD BLESS OUR HOME

YOUNG HOTSHOT
Billy the Kid holds a
rifle in this unique
portrait of him.
He was best known
for his quick work
with a six-gun.

BILLY THE KID

An Elusive Gunslinger

Few western outlaws gained greater notoriety at a younger age than Billy the Kid. Born Henry McCarty in New York City in 1859, he moved west with his widowed mother, who died in Silver City, New Mexico. Left to his own devices by his stepfather, William Antrim, he was jailed for theft at 15 but climbed out through the chimney—the first of many escapes he made. He later killed a man in a saloon and took the alias William Bonney. A boyish figure with a buck-toothed grin, Billy became known as "the Kid."

In the late 1870s, he took part in a red-hot feud in New Mexico known as the Lincoln County War. Sheriff William Brady fanned that fire by backing the politically powerful merchant James Dolan, who supplied beef to the Army, against ranchers John Chisum and John Tunstall. They accused Dolan of dealing in stolen cattle and hoped to drive him out of business and make their own lucrative deals with the government. Billy the Kid fought for Chisum and Tunstall, who was murdered in February 1878 by a posse Brady sent. Brady

LAWMAN'S BADGE Sheriff Garrett wore this as a deputy U.S. marshal while chasing Billy.

and a deputy were then ambushed and killed by Billy and his cohorts in the town of Lincoln. Several of them died there in July when they were pinned down in a burning building, but Billy escaped. His fight against the unpopular Dolan faction won him admirers in New Mexico. Governor Lew Wallace considered pardoning him but found him too reckless to deal with. Complaining that John Chisum had failed to pay him as promised, Billy stole livestock from the rancher, adding to his list of enemies.

Captured in late 1880 by Pat Garrett, Lincoln County's new sheriff, and sentenced to death for killing Brady, Billy got away by snatching a revolver from his jailer and killing him and another lawman. One newspaper called him the "terror and disgrace of New Mexico." Garrett went after Billy and faced him in a dark room at Fort Sumner on the night of July 14, 1881. When the Kid made a move, Garrett pulled the trigger. Dead at 21, Billy's daring run had come to an inescapable conclusion. ∎

BROUGHT TO JUSTICE A posse led by Sheriff Pat Garrett (above) captured Billy the Kid in December 1880 and brought him in to Lincoln, New Mexico, as portrayed at left. Tried and sentenced to death, Billy made a bloody getaway and was again pursued by Garrett, who killed him at Fort Sumner in July 1881.

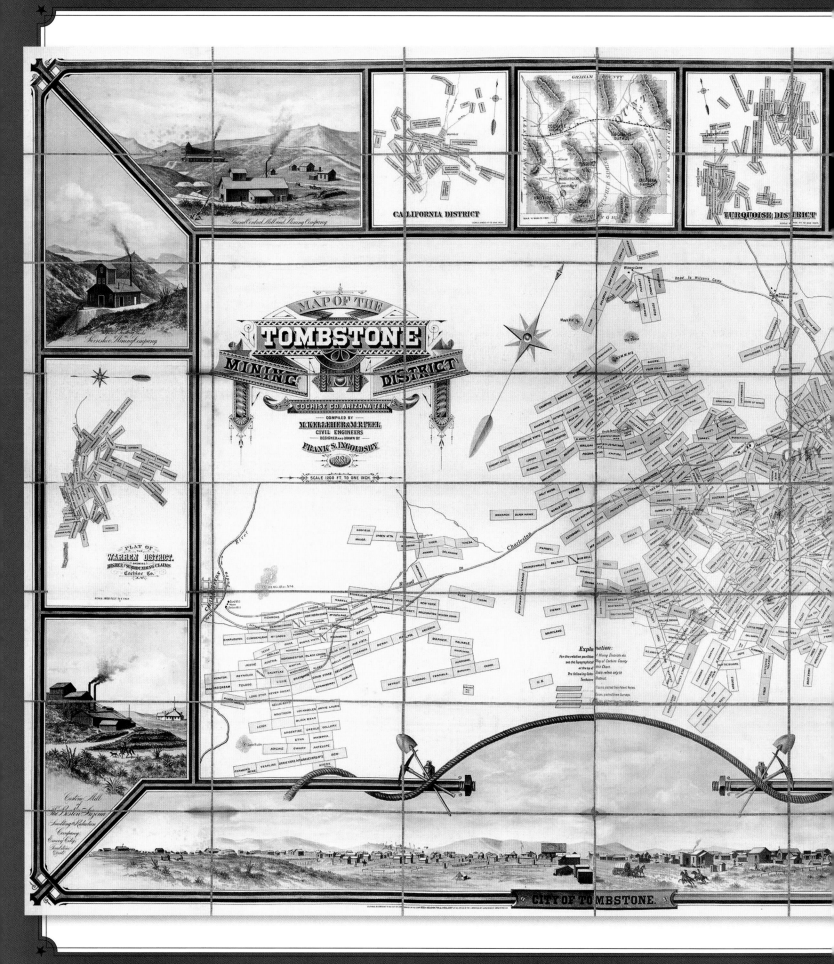

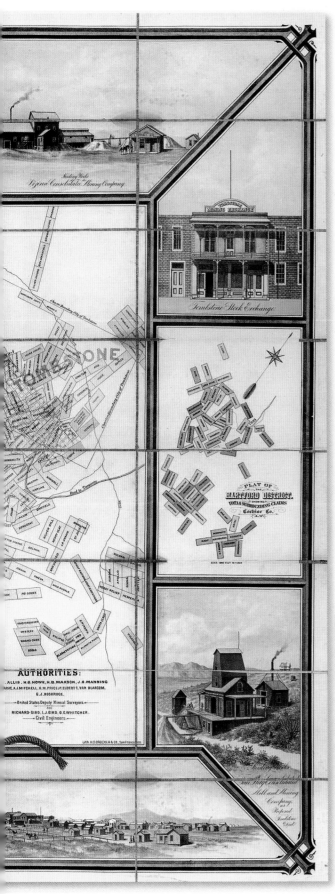

TROUBLE IN TOMBSTONE
Wyatt Earp's Rough Brand of Justice

L ike other renowned western lawmen, Wyatt Earp could be as ruthless in the pursuit of outlaws as they were in the pursuit of crime. When he became deputy sheriff in Tombstone, Arizona, in 1880, he took on a task that no one who was too scrupulous or soft-hearted could have handled. Founded by prospectors who discovered a deep vein of silver on a desolate hilltop in southern Arizona, Tombstone swelled to a population of 10,000, including hard-drinking, hard-rock miners who frequented saloons haunted by professional gamblers. Compounding the fights that occurred there were crimes committed by wayward ranchers and cowboys living around Tombstone, who crossed into Mexico to steal cattle or robbed stagecoaches north of the border.

Earp had not always been on the right side of the law. Born in Illinois in 1848, he was accused of defrauding authorities of a small sum while serving as constable in Lamar, Missouri, and was later charged with horse theft in Indian Territory before slipping away to Kansas and using his grit to police rowdy cattle towns. As assistant marshal in Dodge City, he won praise for his "quiet way of taking the most desperate characters into custody." He seldom drew his gun and relied largely on threats or his fists.

Wyatt Earp

BRIEF BONANZA The illustrated map at left shows the bustling mining town of Tombstone in 1881, when the notorious O.K. Corral gunfight took place. By 1891, when the photograph above was taken, Tombstone was declining. The town would lose much of its population by the early 1900s.

Wyatt Earp kept order in Tombstone with the help of his older brother Virgil—who served as both town marshal and a deputy U.S. marshal—and his younger brother Morgan, who had also been a lawman in Kansas. Allied with the Earps was John Henry "Doc" Holliday, a former dentist turned gambler and sharpshooter who was said to have killed several men before arriving in Tombstone. Doc was Wyatt's alter ego—the notorious figure he might have become had he not gone straight. Holliday was quick to respond when the Earps faced rough customers and needed help.

One such occasion in 1881 made Tombstone and its lawmen legendary. On October 26, Doc Holliday joined Wyatt, Virgil, and Morgan Earp in a vacant lot near the O.K. Corral where they took on five angry men—Ike and Billy Clanton, Frank and Tom McLaury, and Billy Claiborne. The Clantons and McLaurys were ranchers suspected of foul play who hated the lawmen. Moments after Holliday and the Earps confronted their foes and ordered them to drop their weapons, both sides began blazing away. Within a half minute, some 30 shots rang out. The McLaury brothers and Billy Clanton were fatally wounded. Ike Clanton and Billy Claiborne fled while Doc and Wyatt tended to the stricken Virgil and Morgan, who survived their wounds.

The deadly gunfight left Tombstone sharply divided between those who favored law and order as imposed by the Earps and those who thought they were engaged in a brutal vendetta. The *Tombstone Epitaph* hailed the Earps for showing the lawless "cowboy element that they cannot come into the streets of Tombstone, in broad daylight, armed with six-shooters and Henry rifles to hunt down their

CHARRED RUINS In 1882, fire destroyed the O.K. Corral and much of Tombstone. The town was rebuilt, but subterranean water flooded the mines repeatedly and contributed to Tombstone's decline.

victims." The rival *Tombstone Nugget* proudly reported that the funeral for Billy Clanton and the McLaurys was the "largest ever witnessed" in town, attended by hundreds of mourners accompanied by a brass band, playing "a solemn and touching march for the dead."

ATTACKS AND REPRISALS

In December 1881, Virgil Earp was severely wounded in the street at night by unidentified assailants. Four months later, Morgan Earp was shot and killed in a pool room by someone who fired through the window and got away. Wyatt blamed Ike Clanton and his cohorts, including outlaws Frank Stilwell and William "Curly Bill" Brocius, but he despaired of bringing

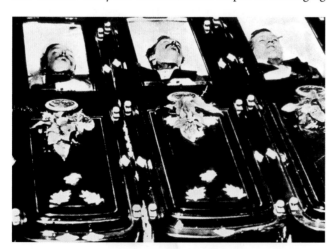

BURIED IN STYLE Three men killed in the 1881 shootout—Tom and Frank McLaury and Billy Clanton—were placed in handsome coffins and mourned by hundreds in Tombstone who blamed the Earp brothers for precipitating the gunfight.

them to justice in Tombstone, which was now controlled by the anti-Earp faction. So he enlisted Doc Holliday and other gunmen as vigilantes. Ike Clanton escaped their grasp, but Wyatt killed Stilwell and Brocius, who were probably guilty but had no chance to plead their case. His posse also took the life of Florentino Cruz, a Mexican suspected of complicity in the murder of Morgan. Cruz's employer, mine owner J. S. Browder, asked how law-abiding citizens could "sanction the kind of justice which is administered from the muzzle of guns in the hands of Doc Holliday and the Earp party."

Wyatt Earp was long dogged by charges that he violated the law when he took it into his own hands. Not until after his death in 1929 did writers and filmmakers celebrate him as one who dispensed swift justice on a savage frontier. An old admirer in Tombstone may have overstated the case when he claimed that Wyatt "never killed a man who did not richly deserve it." But he lived in trying times and turbulent places, where it was hard to enforce the law without sometimes bending or breaking it. ∎

BOOTHILL GRAVEYARD

Founded in 1878 when the town was just getting started, the Tombstone cemetery became known as Boothill because a number of men buried there were shot dead with their boots on. Many western towns have similar burial places, with crosses marking the graves of those who died peacefully or otherwise. But Boothill Graveyard in Tombstone has special historical significance because three men slain in 1881 by Doc Holliday and the Earp brothers in the Old West's most famous gunfight rest there—Billy Clanton, Frank McLaury, and Tom McClaury. Also buried in Boothill Graveyard are Newman Haynes "Old Man" Clanton, who fathered the notorious Clanton brothers and was killed by Mexicans following a cattle raid below the border; Billy Claiborne, who survived the 1881 gunfight only to be shot dead a year later in Tombstone; and Florentino Cruz, targeted for his alleged role in the murder of Morgan Earp.

Some of those interred at Boothill have epitaphs inscribed on their grave markers, including this one for Lester Moore, a Wells Fargo agent who died in a shootout: "Here lies Lester Moore / Four slugs from a .44 / No Les, no more." George Johnson, who unwittingly bought a stolen horse and was hanged as a rustler in 1882, received a belated apology from the citizens of Tombstone in this epitaph: "He was right / We was wrong / But we strung him up / And now he's gone."

ARMED AND INFAMOUS
Belle Starr, shown at
right with one revolver
in hand and another at
her side, was arrested on
the warrant above and
convicted of horse theft
in Fort Smith, Arkansas,
in 1883 along with her
Cherokee husband, Sam
Starr. After doing time
and returning to Indian
Territory, she was charged
with the same offense
in 1886 but acquitted,
which did not diminish
her notoriety as a pistol-
packing "bandit queen."

BELLE STARR
The Alleged "Bandit Queen"

On February 15, 1883, Belle Starr—born Myra Maybelle Shirley in Missouri in 1848—appeared with her Cherokee husband, Sam Starr, in federal court in Fort Smith, Arkansas, charged with stealing two horses from a neighbor in Indian Territory. For a small case, it drew a big crowd. As one reporter wrote, "The very idea of a woman being charged with an offense of this kind and that she was the leader of a band of horse thieves and wielding power over them as their queen and guiding spirit, was sufficient to fill the courtroom with spectators." Although there was no proof that Belle actually led such a gang, she reinforced her reputation as a "bandit queen" when she appeared in Fort Smith on horseback packing a rifle and two revolvers. "Next to a fine horse," she said by one account, "I admire a fine pistol."

Belle, who once described herself as "a friend to any brave and gallant outlaw," had long defied authorities and consorted with renegades. During the Civil War, a beloved older brother of hers served as a Confederate guerrilla in Missouri. She was credited with riding through enemy lines to aid him and his fellow bushwhackers before he died in action. After the war, she associated with the notorious Cole Younger and wed another ex-Confederate desperado, James Reed, who was killed by a lawman in Texas in 1874. Six years later, she and Sam Starr married and became partners in crime. Found guilty of horse theft in 1883, they were sentenced to brief terms at a reformatory—mild punishment considering that their judge, Isaac Parker, was renowned for sending outlaws to the gallows.

Belle and Sam remained on the wrong side of the law in Indian Territory and came to bad ends. He died in a gunfight, and she was shot in the back by an unknown assailant on February 3, 1889. Her violent death enhanced her legend as a bandit queen. One journalist tried to puncture that myth by stating that she was "merely a companion of thieves and outlaws," but Belle Starr was a renegade in her own right. ∎

BACK IN CUSTODY At left, a well-armed Belle Starr appears in 1886 beside a deputy U.S. marshal who brought her in to face charges in Fort Smith, Arkansas, where she had been convicted three years earlier. Typical of the press coverage she received was the picture above, which ran in the *National Police Gazette* with a caption describing her as a "wild western amazon" who vanished on horseback after being released on bail. In fact, she stood trial for horse theft in 1886 and got off, avoiding a second jail term.

Belle Starr
Shot Feb 3 1889 from ambush

READ AND REFLECT!

In view of the fact that CRIME has run riot to such an alarming extent in the Territory of Montana, (particularly East of the Missouri River,) during the past six months, and that

Murders and High-handed Outrages

Have been of such frequent occurrence as to excite the just indignation of all good citizens, it is believed that it is now time that the GOOD WORK should be re-commenced. Therefore,

THIS IS TO NOTIFY ALL WHOM IT MAY CONCERN!

That CRIME MUST AND WILL BE SUPPRESSED! and to that end, all OFFENDERS

WILL BE SUMMARILY DEALT WITH!

AND PUNISHED AS OF OLD!

BY ORDER OF   VIGILANCE COMMITTEE.

ROUGH JUSTICE

Vigilantes, Crooked Lawmen, and Hanging Judges

Granville Stuart was a tireless pioneer who worked variously as a miner, merchant, lumberman, banker, rancher, and politician in the territory that later hailed him as "Mr. Montana." He also gained lasting notoriety as the leader of "Stuart's Stranglers"—vigilantes who strung up or shot to death many suspected rustlers in 1884.

Born in western Virginia in 1834, Stuart followed in the path of the forty-niners and prospected in California with little success before finding gold in Montana as the rush there was beginning in the late 1850s. Stuart made his fortune by supplying the needs of other miners and settlers who flocked to the newly organized territory in the 1860s. By 1884, he was co-owner and general manager of the sprawling DHS Ranch in central Montana. He and other Montana ranchers were accustomed to losing cattle to blizzards and other natural hazards, but they would not tolerate losses to thieves,

Granville Stuart

who hid out in badlands like the Missouri Breaks, along the upper Missouri River.

Stuart had witnessed vigilantes in action in the unruly mining camps of California and Montana, where some self-appointed "regulators" were conscientious and gave offenders hearings before punishing them and others were mere lynch mobs, blinded by hatred and bias. Stuart's Stranglers lay somewhere between those extremes. Intent on eliminating confirmed outlaws, they did not target small ranchers or homesteaders, who were sometimes labeled rustlers and wrongfully attacked by large ranchers who resented their presence. But neither did Stuart's vigilantes grant those they suspected of stealing cattle or horses a trial before condemning them. In effect, they waged war on them and gave them no opportunity to defend themselves other than in combat.

In a few cases, Stuart's volunteers caught thieves and

ENFORCERS The deputy U.S. marshals opposite were among those who responded to the murder of a fellow deputy in 1887 by tracking down and killing the accused Ned Christie. He was one of many suspects slain in the West without receiving a trial or due process, often by vigilantes like those in Montana who posted the warning at top opposite. George "Big Nose" Parrott, shown at right holding up a stagecoach, was hauled from jail and lynched in 1881 after being convicted of murder in Wyoming and attempting to escape.

PUT TO DEATH Three men lynched for undisclosed offenses hang from a bridge in Kansas. Some lynchings in the West were racially motivated, but many of the victims were white men suspected of serious crimes.

hanged them on the spot, including two men found in possession of horses and cattle hides bearing the brands of ranchers from whom livestock was stolen. In other instances, the vigilantes engaged in shootouts with fugitives holed up in cabins. Four suspected rustlers who escaped from one such gunfight were later apprehended by a deputy U.S. marshal, who intended to deliver them for trial before Stuart's vigilantes overtook him and seized his prisoners. Nearby stood two uninhabited log cabins "close together," Stuart related. "A log was placed between the cabins, the ends resting on the roofs, and the four men were hanged from the log." The cabins were then set afire and the bodies cremated.

Estimates of the number executed by Stuart's Stranglers varied widely, from fewer than 20 to more than 70. Livestock losses to thieves declined noticeably as a result of the crackdown, but no one could be sure that innocent men were not among the victims. Some Montanans deplored the lynching of suspects in their territory, which aspired to statehood and respectability. Even in western states such as Kansas and Nebraska that were fairly well settled by the 1880s, however, lynchings sometimes occurred. In 1887, a man awaiting trial

on charges of murdering his daughter was taken from jail and strung up in Nebraska City.

Vigilantes were not the only enforcers who dispensed rough justice or broke the law. Suspects like Ned Christie, a Cherokee accused of killing a deputy U.S. marshal in Indian Territory, were sometimes killed by law officers before their guilt was proven in court. And innocent victims were sometimes targeted by crooked lawmen who bore grudges like the Dalton brothers of Indian Territory, who went on to become notorious criminals. Those charged with murder or other capital crimes without much evidence might nonetheless receive the death penalty if they came before harsh judges who

THE DALTON GANG

Among those who crossed the line between enforcing the law and breaking it were several members of the Dalton family—a brood of 15 children raised by a saloon keeper and his wife who moved to Indian Territory in the early 1880s. One of the boys, Frank Dalton, served conscientiously as a marshal under Judge Isaac Parker and died in the line of duty in 1887. Frank's brother Grattan then took his place, aided by two siblings, Bob and Emmett. Those three were soon violating laws they had sworn to uphold, beginning in 1888 when they murdered a man who was consorting with Bob's girlfriend and claimed he had resisted arrest. Their brother Bill later joined them, but he declined to take part when they and two other gang members set out to rob both banks in Coffeyville, Kansas, on a single day in 1892. Informed of the plot, men in Coffeyville took up arms and battled the outlaws, wounding Emmett and killing the other four men (below). Bill Dalton then formed a new gang and was slain by lawmen in Oklahoma.

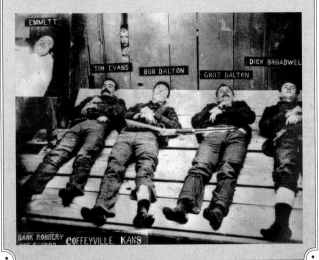

favored prosecutors, issued instructions to juries that impugned the accused, and showed no mercy to those found guilty. The West's most renowned "hanging judge," however, was in fact a man of firm legal principles—Isaac Parker. His grim reputation stemmed largely from the fact that he presided over a large, crime-ridden district that included western Arkansas and Indian Territory, where many non-Indian renegades sought refuge from the law. Judge Parker had good reason to regard such fugitives as menaces to society, for a number of deputy marshals were killed while pursuing them.

In 21 years as the federal court judge in Fort Smith, Arkansas, Parker sentenced to death 156 men and 4 women, or roughly half of those who stood trial there for their lives. Like Belle Starr, to whom he gave a light sentence for horse theft, Parker was sensationalized in press accounts, which portrayed this stern but equitable judge

IN SESSION Billed as the "Law West of the Pecos," Judge Roy Bean (inset) holds court on the porch of his saloon in Langtry, Texas. Bean admired actress Lillie Langtry, but the town was named for a railroad boss who laid tracks there.

MISJUDGED Called a hanging judge, Isaac Parker was required by law to hand out death sentences.

as one who enjoyed sending people to the gallows. "I never hung a man," he said in his own defense. "It is the law." Federal law required him to condemn to death those found guilty by juries of murder or rape.

Another western magistrate who was sometimes portrayed as a hanging judge, Roy Bean, had little claim to that title, other than the fact that he once barely escaped death by hanging before becoming justice of the peace in the 1880s in remote Langtry, Texas, where he held court in his saloon. A quirky frontier character who became something of a celebrity, Bean issued rulings that were bizarre but not unusually severe. One odd judgment of his that was widely reported involved a man who was found dead near Langtry with a pistol in his pocket and $40 in his possession. Bean fined the deceased that same amount for carrying a concealed weapon and used the proceeds to pay for his funeral. ■

THE PINKERTON AGENCY
Private Detectives and Spies

At a time when the nation possessed no federal bureau devoted to fighting crime, Pinkerton's National Detective Agency helped fill the breach. Founded in 1850 by Allan Pinkerton, an enterprising detective who foiled an assassination plot against President Lincoln in 1861 and served as intelligence chief for Maj. Gen. George McClellan of the Union Army, his agency loomed large in western law enforcement in the late 1800s.

Often hired by railroads or express companies that suffered losses when trains or stagecoaches were looted, Pinkerton agents risked their lives pursuing outlaws. After two of his detectives were killed in Missouri while investigating Jesse James and his gang, Pinkerton approved a controversial nighttime raid in 1875 that failed to snare the outlaws but badly injured Jesse's mother and killed his little half brother Archie. Jesse swore vengeance. "Pinkerton, I hope and pray that our Heavenly Father may deliver you into my hands," he wrote. Allan Pinkerton died of natural causes in July 1884,

however, and bequeathed the detective agency to his sons.

Pinkerton agents helped break up several outlaw gangs, including Butch Cassidy and his Wild Bunch. Agents also spied on railroad and mine workers' unions at the request of management. Among those spies was Charles Siringo, a former Texas cowboy who served on a posse that pursued Billy the Kid in New Mexico before becoming a Pinkerton agent in 1886. Assigned to infiltrate a mine workers' union in Idaho, he joined that brotherhood at considerable risk. "I had to take a Molly McGuire oath to bleed and die for my noble order," he wrote, "and if I ever turned traitor and gave the secrets of the union away death would be my reward." When union members discovered what he was up to, he fled for his life. Siringo later denounced both the union's radical firebrands and the organization that sent him to spy on them in a book he entitled *Two Evil Isms: Pinkertonism and Anarchism*. The detective agency got wind of his exposé and obtained a court order suppressing it. ■

MIXED RESULTS Allan Pinkerton, pictured opposite in camp on horseback during the Civil War, provided General McClellan with flawed intelligence reports that overstated the strength of Confederate forces. He proved more effective at tracking down outlaws after the war, using the telegraph to communicate with his far-flung agents (right).

FRONTIER FOLLIES

Drinking, Dancing, and Gambling

aldwell, Kansas, owed its livelihood largely to cowboys who drove cattle to the rail depot there and spent their hard-earned cash in the town's shops, saloons, dance halls, gambling dens, and brothels. When ornery cowboys shot up Caldwell in December 1881 and killed two prominent residents, however, the town council closed the saloons and outlawed prostitution and professional gambling. Instead of winning praise for their bold stand against vice and disorder, the councilmen received a petition protesting the crackdown and heard dire testimony from the owner of a gambling parlor, who stated that as "a direct result of their enforcement, trade had fallen off, and people would soon begin to leave the city." Caldwell risked ruin, he warned, if it failed to follow the example of Dodge City, a rival cow town that continued to ply cowboys with liquor and other diversions. The council soon reversed itself. Caldwell was once again in the business of providing customers with whatever cheap thrills or costly pleasures they could afford.

Whiskey bottle, circa 1885

Many towns across the West catered to cowboys, miners, and other men who liked to gamble, craved strong drink, and longed for intimate female company in frontier communities that were largely male. Like Caldwell, those towns often found it difficult to

DOUBLE JEOPARDY Saloons like the one at left in the mining town of Telluride, Colorado, doubled as gambling parlors. The notoriety of places like Deadwood, pictured above in 1876 soon after a gold rush began there in Dakota Territory, owed much to the volatile combination of gambling and whiskey.

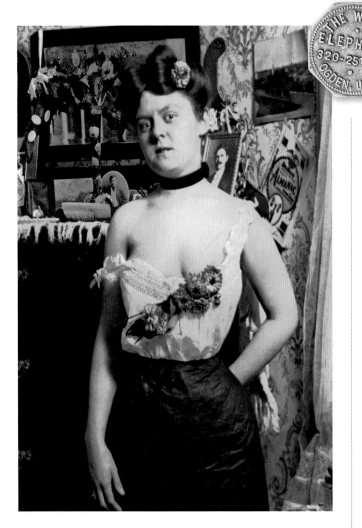

Saloon token, circa 1885

TOKEN PAYMENT Dressed in a way that left no doubt as to their vocation, prostitutes such as this woman in a Colorado saloon were sometimes paid with tokens, offered as change by saloons or brothels to encourage customers to return to the place that issued them.

roulette wheels, musical entertainment, and dancing girls, who kept business flowing by encouraging men to buy drinks. A cowboy told of his visit to one such emporium in Abilene, Kansas, where "a girl came up and put her little hand under my chin, and looked me square in the face, and said 'Oh you pretty Texas boy, give me a drink.' I asked her what she wanted and she said anything I took, so I called for two toddies." Many who kept men company in such places were indeed girls, still in their teens, and their services were not limited to dancing with customers or soliciting drinks. A journalist in Dodge City described the typical saloon there as "a long frame building, with a hall in front and sleeping rooms in the rear. The hall was nightly used for dancing, and was frequented by prostitutes, who belonged to the house." They and their customers used the rooms in back "both day and night," he added.

Whether prostitutes operated on their own in hovels called cribs or worked together in saloons, brothels, or so-called hog ranches that catered to soldiers at nearby forts, their lives were often brutal and brief, cut short by disease, violence, or suicide. Some escaped their dismal occupation through marriage, and a few rose to become madams of lucrative houses visited by men of means. Jennie Rogers of Denver ran

provide such profitable entertainment while at the same time preserving civic order and decency. In some places, the saloons and gambling dens far outnumbered all the shops, restaurants, and other public places combined. The boomtown of Leadville, Colorado, which grew to a population of 40,000 in 1880 following the discovery of rich silver deposits there a few years earlier, boasted 120 saloons, 118 gambling halls, 35 brothels, and a reputation for rowdiness surpassing that of Dodge City, where a newspaper correspondent wrote: "Leadville is 40 degrees nearer hell than any City in the Union. You Dodge City folks are Sunday-school children in comparison."

ADDED ATTRACTIONS

Some western saloons not only offered patrons whiskey, beer, and other stimulants but also furnished card tables and

---

SOCIAL HISTORY

TAXING RED-LIGHT DISTRICTS

Saloons and brothels were cash cows that some western towns milked regularly to meet municipal expenses. Although most places had laws against prostitution and organized gambling, offenders were usually fined rather than jailed. Monthly fines of five or ten dollars might be collected by lawmen from prostitutes or professional gamblers, and owners who shared in their proceeds often had to pay steeper fines. That revenue lowered the tax burden on lawful businesses, which made it difficult for civic reformers to eliminate red-light districts. One resident in Virginia City, Montana, who lived near a brothel billed as a "dance house," complained in writing of being roused from sleep regularly "by the shouts of drunken prostitutes and their partners" and stated that if authorities were reluctant to shut down the house for fear of losing the fines collected there, "I and my unfortunate neighbors will agree to make up to the city what would be lost if the vile place was cleaned out." Some municipal authorities got rid of cheap dives or bordellos that caused offense to residents by raising fines to levels that only the more discreet and profitable houses of ill repute could afford.

> "ONCE THE HERD IS OFF HIS HANDS, THE COWBOY UNBUCKLES... HE BECOMES DEEPLY AND FAMOUSLY DRUNK."
> —JOURNALIST ALFRED HENRY LEWIS

several such establishments in that city, including the glittering House of Mirrors on Market Street, which opened in 1889 and was frequented by police officers, city officials, and state legislators.

Brawls and assaults sometimes occurred in brothels, but nothing produced more notorious gunplay than gambling in saloons, where alcohol fueled the grievances of those who felt cheated. Some avid gamblers who haunted western bars—including Doc Holliday and his nattily attired acquaintances Luke Short and Bat Masterson—were also keen gunmen. John Wesley Hardin, a temperamental Texan who once shot a stranger through a thin hotel-room wall for snoring too loudly, killed several of his 20 or more victims in gambling disputes. Wild Bill Hickok, adept both as a lawman and as a

CARD GAME Faro, played with cards on a board, using a device resembling an abacus to keep score, rivaled poker in popularity as a game of chance in the late 1800s.

card player, was done in by another gunslinging gambler named Jack McCall in a saloon in Deadwood in 1876. After losing repeatedly to Hickok at cards, McCall began drinking heavily and shot him in the back of the head while he was playing poker with others. Legend has it that when Hickok drew his last breath, he was holding aces and eights, known to posterity as the "deadman's hand." ■

ORNERY CUSTOMER Heated arguments in saloons over cards like the incident portrayed here sometimes turned deadly when gamblers were armed and rendered dangerous by liquor.

Surrender of Geronimo

Fugitive From "Hell's Forty Acres"

In May 1885, the Chiricahua Apache war leader Geronimo fled the San Carlos Reservation in Arizona with a band of more than 100 men, women, and children. Unlike some earlier Indian resistance leaders, he was widely regarded as an outlaw. "Geronimo gained a reputation for cruelty and cunning never surpassed by that of any other American Indian chief," the *New York Times* stated later in his obituary. When evading pursuit by troops, Geronimo and his warriors often plundered and killed settlers, but desperate circumstances had led them to resist confinement and become renegades. In 1872, their esteemed leader Cochise had obtained a large reservation for them in southwestern Arizona that included their beloved Chiricahua Mountains. Not long after Cochise died in 1874, authorities reneged on that deal and removed Chiricahua Apaches to low-lying San Carlos, known as "Hell's Forty Acres."

"They had been driven into this barren waste at San Carlos with no provision for their self-support," wrote Lt. Britton Davis, who pursued Geronimo but understood what led him

George Crook

and his followers to rebel. "Their principal occupation was gathering once a week at the Agency to receive the rations doled out to them." Geronimo fled and returned to San Carlos several times before making his final breakout in 1885. The Army sent 5,000 troops after him, led by first by Brig. Gen. George Crook—a renowned officer who was relieved of command after Geronimo eluded him—and then by Brig. Gen. Nelson Miles, who finally obtained his surrender in September 1886.

Confined with other Apache warriors at Fort Pickens in Florida, Geronimo felt more like a convicted felon than a prisoner of war. "Here they put me to sawing up large logs," he later recalled. "For nearly two years we were kept at hard labor." Eventually, the prisoners were reunited with family members and settled at Fort Sill in Oklahoma Territory. He died there in 1909 around the age of 80, barred from returning to the mountains from which his people were evicted. "It is my land, my home, my fathers' land," he said. "I want to spend my last days there, and be buried among those mountains." ∎

DEFIANT STANCE
Portrayed opposite on a postcard based on a photograph for which he posed defiantly with rifle in hand in 1882, Geronimo long evaded capture before surrendering with his followers in 1886. The picture at right, taken before he and other prisoners left Arizona under guard in rail cars, shows Geronimo seated in the front row, third from right.

AFRICAN AMERICANS ON THE FRONTIER

Buffalo Soldiers and Exodusters

Among the U.S. forces who tracked down Geronimo and compelled him to surrender were black troopers of the 10th Cavalry, based at Fort Huachuca in Arizona. Known as buffalo soldiers, a term first applied to them by Indians, such African American recruits made up a fair share of those serving in uniform in the West in the late 1800s. Organized in four regiments—the 9th and 10th Cavalry and the 24th and 25th Infantry—they did hard duty at bleak outposts and had little opportunity for advancement, seldom rising above the rank of sergeant in an army that kept them separate and unequal. Nevertheless, they had higher morale and a lower desertion rate than white units on the frontier.

Artist Frederic Remington, who accompanied the 10th Cavalry on campaign in Arizona in the 1880s, paid tribute to those buffalo soldiers. "They may be tired and they may be hungry," he wrote, "but they do not see fit to augment their misery by finding fault with everybody and everything . . . As to their bravery, I am often asked, 'Will they fight?' That is easily answered. They have fought many, many times. The old sergeant sitting near me, as calm of feature as a bronze statue, once deliberately walked over a Cheyenne riflepit and killed his man. One little fellow near him once took charge

GUARD DUTY **Buffalo soldiers ride atop a stagecoach in 1869 to guard against attack by warriors or robbers. Many black troops serving in the West were Civil War veterans.**

SERGEANT'S STRIPES **African-American cavalrymen who rose to the rank of sergeant wore this full dress uniform, the same outfit worn by white cavalry sergeants.**

BATTLE FLAG Units like the First Kansas Colored Infantry, whose Civil War battles are inscribed here, included future buffalo soldiers.

NORTHERN OUTPOST A soldier reclines on a buffalo hide and another wears a buffalo robe to keep warm in this portrait of the all-black 25th Infantry Regiment taken at Fort Keogh in Montana in 1891.

of a lot of stampeded cavalry horses when Apache bullets were flying loose."

Remington's assessment was confirmed by white officers who led buffalo soldiers on the frontier, including the former Civil War hero Benjamin Grierson and the future commander of American forces during World War I, John Pershing, known as "Black Jack" after taking charge of the 10th Cavalry in 1896. By then, more than a dozen African-American soldiers had won Medals of Honor for bravery on the frontier.

Long before buffalo soldiers began patrolling the West in the late 1860s, black mountain men and prospectors were blazing trails and staking claims there. As early as 1850, nearly 1,000 African Americans had made their way to California, where many sought gold like miner Peter Brown, who called that newly organized state "the best place for black folks on the globe." Few white miners fared better than black prospector Moses Dinks, who unearthed a glittering 25-pound chunk of gold on one occasion and earned nearly $100,000 along with his mining partner.

African Americans began riding as cowboys in Texas before the Civil War. Many were born into slavery but later gained freedom and were joined by black cowhands from other states on long trails from Texas to Kansas and beyond. By one estimate, one-fourth of those who drove cattle north from Texas were African Americans. A few of them went on to become successful ranchers like Daniel Webster Wallace of Texas, or standout rodeo performers like Nat Love, who took the nickname Deadwood Dick and published a colorful account of his life.

EXODUS FROM DIXIE

For one sizable group of settlers, the West was not simply a land of opportunity but a new Canaan, where people who had labored in bondage sought deliverance. By the late 1870s, conditions for African Americans in the South had deteriorated alarmingly since the start of Reconstruction in 1865, when

DANIEL WEBSTER WALLACE
1860–1939

Most cowboys lived hard and died poor. Few saved enough of their earnings to become men of property unless they had good luck and great self-discipline. Daniel Webster Wallace (right) was blessed with both. Born a slave in East Texas in 1860, he grew up free and left his monotonous job chopping cotton at the age of 17 to herd cattle. He worked for several ranchers before he was fortunate enough to be hired by Clay Mann, a good boss who saw in him the potential to become more than just a cowpuncher. The two reached an agreement whereby Mann withheld $25 of the $30 Webster earned each month, to be used to purchase cattle that he would then graze on Mann's ranch free of charge.

The deal meant that Wallace had to forgo nearly all the pleasures that other cowboys indulged in, whether in stores or saloons. He also swallowed his pride and entered primary school as an adult to acquire basic skills in reading and arithmetic that he needed to do business. By his early 30s, he had his own ranch in West Texas, where he and his wife raised a family of four. When Wallace died at 78 and was buried there, he bequeathed to his heirs an estate worth more than a million dollars.

PRAIRIE PIONEERS The settlers pictured below in the town of Nicodemus, Kansas, were among the exodusters who answered the call of leaders such as Benjamin Singleton, who issued the poster at left for a migration he organized in 1878 before the Great Exodus of African Americans took place in 1879.

the federal government promised those freed from slavery in the former Confederate states civil rights and economic opportunity, including land grants for black homesteaders. Twelve years later, Reconstruction ended and white southern authorities—many of them former slave owners—imposed strict segregation in public places, stripped most black men of the right to vote, and left racial assaults by whites unpunished. It became increasingly difficult for blacks to farm the land except as sharecroppers, most of whom were so deeply in debt to white landowners that they were again reduced to servitude.

In 1879, urged on by leaders such as Benjamin Singleton—a former slave who had fled north to freedom before returning to Tennessee after the Civil War—more than 15,000 African Americans left the South for Kansas in a migration known as the Great Exodus. Some of those "exodusters" settled in predominantly black towns such as Nicodemus in western Kansas and took up farming, which was no easy task in that dry region. Others joined black communities around fast-growing Kansas City and Topeka and performed manual labor or domestic chores. Many needed help to get started in Kansas and were aided by Governor John St. John, who established the Freedmen's Relief Association. However difficult their circumstances, few returned to the former slave states they left behind. As the editor of the *Topeka Colored Citizen* declared in print: "It is better to starve to death in Kansas than be shot and killed in the South." ∎

Price 50 Cents

BUFFALO BILL
AND HIS ADVENTURES IN THE WEST

A STORY OF WILD ADVEN...

COVER STORIES Unlike some books, dime novels could be judged by their covers. Heroes featured on them included romanticized historical figures such as Buffalo Bill (left and below) and fictional gunmen like Twilight Charlie, shown with pistols blazing (bottom right). Heroines too were often portrayed with weapons in hand, including the sure-shooting Female Trapper (right) and the feisty cowgirl Stella, depicted fighting off villains with a branding iron (bottom left).

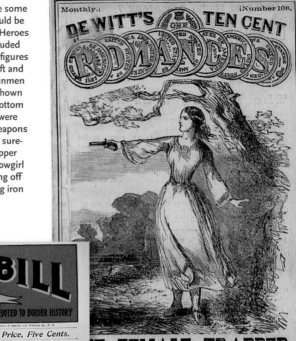

Monthly.

DE WITT'S TEN CENT ROMANCES

iNumber 108.

THE FEMALE TRAPPER.

ROB'T M. DE WITT, Publisher,
No. 33 ROSE STREET.
NEW YORK:

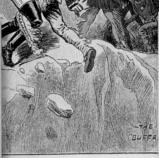

THE BUFFALO BILL STORIES

A WEEKLY PUBLICATION — DEVOTED TO BORDER HISTORY

No. 184.   Price, Five Cents.

BUFFALO BILL'S NAVAJO ALLY
or THE WAR WITH THE CAVE-DWELLERS

In the midst of the Cave-Dwellers struggled on the edge of the precipice, locked in combat, while the brave Navajo, tomahawk in hand, kept the other Indians at bay.

ROUGH RIDER
WEEKLY
THE BEST WILD WEST STORIES PUBLISHED

No. 170   NEW YORK, JULY 20, 1907.   Price, Five Cents.

KING OF THE WILD WEST'S CATTLE-WAR
or Stella's Bout with the Rival Ranchers

BY NED TAYLOR

"Keep back!" cried Stella, flourishing the red-hot iron. At the same moment the King of the Wild West landed a blow that sent the leader of the rustlers heels over head.

BEADLE'S
Dime New York Library

Vol. XXXIX.   Published Every Wednesday.   Beadle & Adams, Publishers,   Ten Cents a Copy.   No. 499.
94 William Street, N. Y., May 16, 1888. $5.00 a Year.

TWILIGHT CHARLIE THE ROAD SPORT

OR,
Sulphur Sam's Double.
A Romance of the Wild Lands of the Yampah.

BY J. C. COWDRICK,
AUTHOR OF "RAINBOW ROB," "KENTUCKY JEAN," "BLUE-GRASS BURT," "GILBERT OF GOTHAM," "THE GIANT CUPID," "BROADWAY BILLY" STORIES, ETC., ETC., ETC.

CHAPTER I.
"HANDS UP!"

IT WAS SULPHUR SAM, WHOOPING AND YELLING AS HE DASHED AWAY UP THE VALLEY AT BREAKNECK SPEED, FIRING HIS REVOLVERS AS HE WENT.

DIME NOVELS
Fictionalizing the Wild West

Nothing did more to shape the popular image of the West as a wild frontier where good ultimately triumphed over evil than dime novels, which were introduced in 1860 by an enterprising publisher named Erastus Beadle. Over the next few decades, Beadle alone issued more than 300 dime novels, and other firms churned out thousands more. They were cheap enough to be purchased by youngsters but enthralled millions of readers of all ages, many of them Easterners who never ventured beyond the Mississippi. Not all dime novels were set in the West, but mythic conflicts between cowboys and Indians or between lawmen and outlaws were among the most popular and enduring themes of this pulp fiction, which set the tone for many later Western adventure stories.

The heroes of some dime novels were fanciful versions of historical figures, including Kit Carson and William "Buffalo Bill" Cody, who served as an Army scout on the Plains in the 1860s and later won fame for the spectacular Wild West shows he produced. A dime novel published in 1882 described young Buffalo Bill confronting a band of outlaws with pistol in hand at the tender age of nine. When one of those villains "attempted to draw a weapon," the author claimed, "the boy's forefinger touched the trigger, and the outlaw fell dead at the flash, shot straight through the heart!" Dime novels extolled the adult Buffalo Bill as an Indian fighter but also portrayed him as a friend and ally of those "good" Indians who helped him tame the West and defeat "bad" Indians. Cody profited from such publicity and sometimes took credit for the imaginary feats authors attributed to him.

Although characterized as boys' fiction, dime novels also featured daring western heroines who could outride and outshoot any man who tried to get the better of them. The real Calamity Jane was born Martha Jane Cannary in Missouri in 1852 and later gained notoriety as an eccentric figure in the notorious mining town of Deadwood, South Dakota, where she sometimes appeared wearing men's clothing and once rode a bull down the street. But she was no match for the fictional Calamity Jane of dime novel fame. That fabulous figure was victimized in her youth by a villainous lecher and emerged as a tough customer who would never again be taken advantage of. Dressed in buckskin, she smoked cigars, packed a pistol, and battled incorrigible villains while consorting with other outlaws who were good men at heart, including her sweetheart Deadwood Dick.

Some adults worried that young readers would be corrupted by fiction featuring heroes and heroines with shady pasts, short tempers, and itchy trigger fingers. But most dime novels observed an informal decency code similar to that later applied to Hollywood movies in the 1930s. Calamity Jane and Deadwood Dick eventually married and had a child, but they were not allowed to live happily ever after. In the last novel he devoted to the pair, entitled *Deadwood Dick's Dust,* author Edward Wheeler condemned Dick and Jane to violent deaths and buried them side by side—a fitting conclusion for star-crossed lovers who lived beyond the pale of conventional society and its standards of behavior. ∎

FED ON PULP Portrayed on the cover of the satirical magazine *Puck,* a child wielding a knife and a pistol feeds from a bottle containing dime novels, which have transformed him into an "Infant Indian Exterminator."

THEODORE ROOSEVELT

Dude Rancher in the Badlands

In mid-1884, 25-year-old Theodore Roosevelt left his budding political career in New York City and moved to the Dakota badlands to raise cattle. Other Easterners went west as he did and became dude ranchers, seeking profit and adventure. But Roosevelt had another motive that was deeply personal. In a single day that February, he had lost both his mother and his wife, who died hours after giving birth to a daughter. "The light has gone out of my life," he wrote. Leaving the baby in his sister's care, he set out for a place far removed from New York and its sorrowful associations.

Short, thin, and bespectacled, Roosevelt donned a fringed buckskin suit that made him look like a frail eastern dude playing the part of a rugged frontiersman. But he grew into that role over time through vigorous exercise, including long rides across the badlands on his horse Manitou. As a sickly adolescent, he had steeled himself by taking up boxing. That served him well now when he was taunted by a barroom bully who addressed him as "Four Eyes" and insisted at gunpoint

T. R.'s Gun Roosevelt had this ivory-plated Colt .44 revolver monogrammed.

that he treat all present to drinks. Roosevelt knocked the man down with a blow to the jaw and took away his pistols—a feat that enhanced his reputation both locally and later nationally when he described the incident in *The Century Magazine*. Handy with guns, he also won renown as a lawman of sorts by pursuing thieves who stole his boat on the Little Missouri River and bringing them to justice.

In 1886, Roosevelt left his ranch in the future state of North Dakota and returned to New York, where he remarried and reentered public life. His western foray had strengthened him in body and spirit and helped him politically. Many Easterners viewed cowboys as ruffians, but he praised them in writing as "quiet, rather self-contained men, perfectly frank and simple," who treated strangers "with the most whole-souled hospitality." Appreciative Westerners later fought under Colonel Roosevelt as Rough Riders in Cuba during the Spanish-American War—a campaign that made him famous and propelled him to the White House. ■

East Meets West Antlers adorn Roosevelt's Elkhorn Ranch (left) near Medora in western Dakota Territory. Upon moving there from New York in 1884, he posed for the portrait opposite without his glasses, considered unbecoming for an outdoorsman. His two-year stay at the ranch within what is now Theodore Roosevelt National Park and later hunting trips made him an honorary Westerner. When he ran for a second term as president in 1904, he carried all but 3 of 19 states west of the Mississippi.

RANGE WARS AND FEUDS

Conflict in Johnson County, Wyoming, and Arizona's Pleasant Valley

Many western ranchers grazed their livestock on public land. That led to competition for good grazing areas and the right to claim unbranded cattle. Ranchers on good terms held joint roundups and divided those mavericks fairly. When cattlemen suspected neighbors of foul play, however, range wars sometimes resulted. One of the worst conflicts occurred in Wyoming, where wealthy cattle barons formed companies and amassed large herds. Many of them employed foremen to manage their ranches and settled in Cheyenne, where the exclusive Cheyenne Club became the social center for the Wyoming Stock Growers Association. Its members disdained homesteaders and small ranchers who challenged their right to monopolize the best public grazing lands. They accused those upstarts of stealing cattle and launched a vendetta known as the Johnson County War.

Nate Champion

By the late 1880s, drought and blizzards had devastated herds on the northern Plains, ruining some companies and making those big-time cattlemen who remained in business more determined than ever to crack down on small operators they suspected of rustling. In July 1889, ranchers in western Wyoming lynched two homesteaders—Ellen Watson and her partner, Jim Averell—who had been grazing a small herd of cattle along the Sweetwater River. Newspapers beholden to the cattle barons disparaged Watson as a notorious rustler and "range queen" who went by the alias "Cattle Kate." One article warned that "more hangings will follow unless there is less thieving."

That deadly incident did not bode well for other small ranchers accused of rustling—notably Nate Champion, a determined former cowboy who acquired a herd of about 200 cattle and grazed them on the fine public grasslands of Johnson County in northeastern Wyoming. Champion was a popular figure there. Many settlers resented cattle barons for branding him "king of the rustlers" and claiming that jurors in the county seat of Buffalo were coddling accused thieves and letting them off.

In 1891, prominent members of the Wyoming Stock Growers Association sent gunmen to do away with Champion and others in Johnson County they wanted dead "for the

ROUNDUP Cattle roundups like the one shown here were organized by leading members of the Wyoming Stock Growers Association, who barred upstart ranchers with small herds such as Nate Champion of Johnson County from taking part and claiming mavericks as they did. Outsiders claiming unbranded calves in the vicinity of their herds were considered rustlers, whose deeds were punishable by death.

"THE INVADERS"
JOHNSON COUNTY CATTLE WAR. TAKEN AT Ft. D.A. RUSSELL
(FRANCIS E. WARREN) MAY 4th 1892

NO.1 TOM SMITH	NO.8 A.R. POWERS	NO.15 W.C. IRVINE	NO.29 J. BARLINGS
" 2 A.B. CLARKE	" 9 A.D. ADAMSON	" 16 BOB TISDALE	" 30 M.A. McNALLY
" 3 J.N. LESLIE	" 10 C.A. CAMPBELL	" 17 JOE ELLIOTT	" 31 MIKE SHONSEY
" 4 E.W. WHITCOMB	" 11 FRANK LABERTEAUX	" 18 JOHN TISDALE	" 32 DICK ALLEN
" 5 D. BROOKE	" 12 PHIL DUFRAN	" 19 SCOTT DAVIS	" 33 FRED HESSE
" 6 W.B. WALLACE	" 13 MAJOR WOLCOTT	" 20 FRED DEBILLIER	" 34 FRANK CANTON
" 7 CHAS FORD	" 14 W.E. GUTHRIE	" 21 BEN MORRISON	" 35 Wm. LITTLE

		NO.22 W.J. CLARKE	NO.36 JEFF MYNETT
		" 23 L.H. PARKER	" 37 BOB BARLINGS
		" 24 TESCHMACHER	" 38 S. SUTHERLAND
		" 25 B.C. SCHULZE	" 39 BUCK GARRETT
		" 26 W.H. TABOR	" 40 G.R. TUCKER
		" 27 J.A. GARRETT	" 41 J.M. BENFORD
		" 28 K.A. WILSON	" 42 WILL ARMSTRONG

INVADERS FOILED After killing Nate Champion and another man, the cattlemen and hired gunmen who invaded Johnson Country in 1892 were besieged by a large posse at the TA Ranch (top). They were in danger of being overpowered when U.S. cavalrymen dispatched at the urging of Wyoming's governor, who sympathized with the invaders, arrived on the scene and took them into custody. They were escorted to Cheyenne, where they were pictured together (above) and eventually went free.

Ed Tewksbury

"I CAN'T STAND IT! I MUST BURY THEM.
THEY'LL HAVE TO KILL ME TO STOP ME."
—MARY ANN TEWKSBURY,
AFTER HER HUSBAND JOHN WAS KILLED

Tom Graham

SCORNED SHEEP Flocks like this one grazing in Wyoming were viewed by cattlemen as trespassers on their range. When the Tewksburys introduced sheep to Arizona's Pleasant Valley, their ongoing conflict with the cattle-herding Grahams turned murderous. Among the victims was Tom Graham, shown above with his accused killer, Ed Tewksbury.

good of the country." When those assassins approached his cabin at dawn on November 1, Champion drew a pistol from beneath his pillow and fought them off. During the criminal investigation that followed, two witnesses were ambushed and killed by unknown assailants. Undeterred, Champion was prepared to testify in court that a detective for the stock growers had been among his assailants. The men who plotted that attack then resolved to eliminate him as a witness and drew up an expanded death list as they prepared to invade Johnson County.

In April 1892, 50 armed men, including prominent ranchers as well as hirelings, surrounded the KC Ranch in Johnson County and fought a prolonged gun battle with Champion and Nick Ray, another small rancher, both of whom were killed. When news of that shootout reached Buffalo, much of the adult male population took up arms and went after the invaders. Trapped in the TA Ranch house by a posse of more than 200 men who were preparing to blast them out with dynamite, the invaders were saved by the arrival of cavalrymen, who escorted them back to friendly Cheyenne, where charges against them were later dismissed. Their murderous invasion shocked many people, however, and left the Wyoming Stock Growers Association in disrepute until it ceased to be a cabal of cattle barons and opened its membership to all ranchers across the state, large and small.

GRAHAM-TEWKSBURY FEUD

Some conflicts on the western range resulted from tensions between sheepherders and cattle ranchers, who complained that sheep spoiled grasslands by cropping them down to stubble. That animosity contributed to a deadly family feud in central Arizona's Pleasant Valley between the Grahams and the Tewksburys. John Tewksbury settled in the valley in 1880 with his second wife and three boys he had fathered by his first wife, an Indian woman. As they grew up, those Tewksbury boys faced scorn from white settlers and were accused of stealing cattle, as were some of the Graham boys.

The two families were already at odds when the Tewksburys began grazing sheep in the valley. The Grahams and others were intent on preserving the range for cattle only

BRANDING IRON Cattle marked with the owner's brand could be sorted out, but unbranded calves were bones of contention on the open range.

and responded by killing sheep as well as a shepherd employed by the Tewksburys. As the feud intensified in 1887, Tom Graham avenged the death of his son Bill by leading a blistering attack on the Tewksburys that left the boys' father dead outside their cabin. The shooting stopped when his wife emerged with a shovel and buried her husband and a friend who lay dead beside him, after which the raiders and the holed-up Tewksburys resumed their gunfight.

By the time the feud ended in 1892, more than 20 people had been slain. Ed Tewksbury, who had lost his two brothers in the mayhem, was practically the last man standing. Found guilty of murdering Tom Graham, his conviction was overturned on a technicality. He ended up as a lawman in Globe, Arizona, where he died of tuberculosis in 1904. ■

BIOGRAPHY

ELLA WATSON, AKA "CATTLE KATE"
1860–1889

Ellen Watson (inset), pilloried in press accounts as the notorious rustler "Cattle Kate," was long assumed to be guilty as charged by the ranchers who lynched her and her alleged partner in crime, Jim Averell, on July 21, 1889. Only recently have historians cast doubt on the accusations leveled against her. Born in 1860, Watson moved in her mid-20s to Rawlins, Wyoming. Although detractors claimed she was a prostitute who received stolen cattle in return for her services, she worked as a cook and probably obtained most if not all of her cattle legitimately.

Watson and Averell applied for a marriage license but did not marry, allowing her to claim land under the Homestead Act, as he did separately. Their adjacent lots lay near wagon trails, and they offered meals to travelers, one of whom sold her a few dozen run-down cattle for a dollar a head. By 1889, her herd had doubled in size and included calves that neighboring ranchers suspected the enterprising couple of stealing. The galling presence of homesteaders on public land that those cattlemen considered their own domain may also have driven them to commit murder. Their crime went unpunished, and journalists not only castigated Watson in print but also called for more lynchings as the vicious Johnson County War loomed. Cattlemen should not rest, wrote the editor of one journal, "until a hundred rustlers were left ornamenting the trees or telegraph poles of the territory."

THE END OF THE OPEN RANGE
Blizzards and Barbed Wire

Nature and technology combined in the late 1800s to bring to an end the time-honored practice of grazing cattle on the open range. During the bitter winter of 1886–87, hundreds of thousands of free-ranging cattle perished on the northern Plains. Some froze to death in blizzards during that "great die-up" and others died of starvation, having already grown thin on land that had been overgrazed and parched by drought. Ranchers who remained in business like Granville Stuart of Montana began fencing in their cattle, feeding them hay in winter, and building windbreaks to shield them from blizzards. As Stuart put it, "I never wanted to own again an animal that I could not feed and shelter."

Barbed wire, perfected in the 1870s, made fencing practical and affordable. Joseph Glidden of Illinois devised barbs that were less sharp than earlier versions, which wounded animals, and attached them firmly to double-twisted steel wire. He then formed a partnership with a neighbor, Isaac Ellwood, to manufacture his product and hired a gifted young salesman named John Warne Gates, who won over skeptical Texas ranchers by demonstrating how Glidden's wire could repel longhorns without injury. Production of barbed wire increased from 300 tons in 1875 to more than 40,000 tons five years later. When large ranchers began fencing public land they claimed as their own, small ranchers and homesteaders cut the wire to gain access. Conflicts over fences were common in Texas until the state legislature made fence-cutting a felony and the fencing of public land a misdemeanor.

By the end of the 19th century, most western ranches were enclosed by barbed wire, which restrained not just cows but cowboys, who now spent much of their time mending fences. The closing of the open range corralled free-roaming cowboys like E. C. "Teddy Blue" Abbott, who took part in some of the last drives north from Texas. "Just when everything was going fine, and a cowpuncher's life was a pleasant dream," he recalled, "the whole thing went Ker Plunk, and we are now a prehistoric race." ■

CUTTING CORNERS This photograph was staged to show how fence-cutters operated in Nebraska, wearing masks to conceal their identity.

WIRED UP A cowboy in Arizona herds cattle through a gateway in a barbed wire fence. Barbed wire was perfected by Joseph Glidden, who patented his product in 1874. His business partner, Isaac Ellwood, manufactured it at the plant shown in the advertisement at right.

GLIDDEN STEEL BARB WIRE

MANUFACTURED BY

I. L. ELLWOOD & CO.

AFTER THE FLOOD.

Safety to Passengers and PROPERTY.
LASTS TWICE AS LONG as any other kind of Fence.
SPARKS DO NOT SET IT ON FIRE.
Floods do not sweep it away.
Its MERITS COMMEND IT AS The BEST FENCE of the WORLD.
Pioneer Barb Fencing.

Over 150 Railway Companies USE THE GLIDDEN STEEL BARB WIRE.
More in use than of all other Kinds COMBINED.
ALL NEW STEEL.
Lighter per Rod than any other made FROM SAME SIZE WIRES
MORE BARBS PER ROD & BETTER PROTECTION
The BEST is cheapest and the GLIDDEN IS GUARANTEED WITHOUT AN EQUAL

DE KALB, ILL.

COPPER KINGDOM Soot billows from smokestacks in Butte, Montana, a town rich in copper that grew to resemble eastern industrial cities like Pittsburgh. Three copper kings dominated this area: Marcus Daly (upper left), who developed the Anaconda mine; William Clark (upper right), who made millions mining and smelting copper in Butte and pursued high office; and F. Augustus Heinze (lower right), who combined several mines to form the United Copper Company.

RISE OF THE COPPER KINGS
Multimillionaires in Montana

ontrary to the popular image of the Old West as a land of boundless vistas, fresh air, and pure water, some western mining towns developed into grimy industrial centers with polluted skies and streams, bitter labor disputes, and cutthroat competition between capitalists. In and around Butte, Montana, three industrialists known as the copper kings grew rich mining and refining that metal, which was in great demand in the late 1800s to produce copper wire that conducted electricity. Butte emerged as one of the largest and busiest towns between Minneapolis and Seattle, but along with profits for mine owners came pollution and political corruption.

Two of Montana's copper kings, Marcus Daly and William Clark, began as silver miners there. Daly and other investors purchased the Anaconda silver mine northwest of Butte in 1881 and excavated down to a depth of 600 feet, where they struck a fabulously rich vein of copper ore that made Daly's Anaconda company world famous. Clark went into the lucrative business of smelting copper, which involved roasting the ore in heaps. That process produced

thick clouds of toxic smoke laced with sulfur and arsenic that could be deadly. Clark responded to protests by claiming that the smoke killed germs and promoted public health. "It would be a great advantage to other cities," he remarked, "to have a little more smoke and business activity and less disease."

Daly was often at odds with Clark and another formidable rival, F. Augustus Heinze, who arrived in Butte as an ambitious young engineer in 1889 and went on to challenge Daly's powerful company. Heinze often prevailed in court battles against Daly, thanks to favorable rulings from a judge Heinze funded and helped reelect. While the copper kings fought among themselves, they also had to contend with mine workers who organized for better wages and working conditions and made Butte the "Gibraltar of Unionism." By 1900, those workers had enough political clout that Clark and Heinze, who had formed an alliance against Daly, granted their demand for an eight-hour workday. In return, the union supported Clark's successful bid for the U.S. Senate in a race clouded by charges that he used bribery to gain that seat. ■

MINERS AND MONARCHS Mine workers like the Anaconda crew above made about $3.50 an hour while the copper kings made fortunes.
William Clark, portrayed at top with a bundle of loot beside his rival Marcus Daly, was accused of bribing state legislators to elect him to the U.S. Senate.
The scandal increased pressure for the direct election of senators.

OKLAHOMA LAND RUSH
Boomers in Indian Territory

They called it "Harrison's Horse Race." In March 1889, President Benjamin Harrison proclaimed land unassigned to any particular tribe in Indian Territory available for settlement by any American. Troops guarded the borders as nearly 50,000 people prepared to compete for that desirable land, which lay in what is now central Oklahoma (admitted as a state in 1907) and was better suited for cultivation than the dry, western portions of Indian Territory. Some contestants would travel in rail cars, and others in wagons. But for many, the rush that began at noon on April 22 would literally be a horse race for land not easily reached by road or rail.

"At the time fixed," wrote reporter William Howard for *Harper's Weekly,* "thousands of hungry home-seekers, who had gathered from all parts of the country, and particularly from Kansas and Missouri, were arranged in line along the border, ready to lash their horses into furious speed in the race for fertile spots in the beautiful land before them . . . As the expectant home-seekers waited with restless patience, the clear, sweet notes of

HORSE RACE Riders gallop (right) to stake claims in Indian Territory, part of which became Oklahoma Territory after the first rush in April 1889. Boomers filed claims at land offices like that above in Perry and paid fees of up to $2.50 an acre. The government was still offering former Indian land to settlers in 1911, when the poster (far right) was issued.

a cavalry bugle rose and hung a moment upon the startled air. It was noon. The last barrier of savagery in the United States was broken down."

The idea that Indian Territory was savage was based not just on its reputation for harboring outlaws but on the timeworn assumption that Indians were backward and unruly. In fact, Indian Territory was home to the Five Civilized Tribes as well as other tribal groups whose communities were more orderly than some frontier towns frequented by miners or cowboys. Far from representing the triumph of civilization over savagery, the Oklahoma Land Rush that began in 1889 and continued in stages until 1893 demonstrated that the West still had wildly contested frontiers, where the race for land or riches went to the swiftest and strongest.

BOOMERS UNLEASHED

Venturesome and resourceful, land-hungry pioneers called boomers became identified with Oklahoma, and many early settlers there proudly assumed that title. But the first boomers

HUNKERED DOWN A determined boomer camps on his lot to make sure that no intruder jumps his claim. Claims were staked by driving a post into the ground with a sign or flag attached to it like the one inset, identifying the holder.

were squatters, intruding on Indian Territory in defiance of federal law. Ironically, their movement to open Indian land to white settlement was inspired in part by a Cherokee named Elias C. Boudinot, Jr., whose father had been assassinated for signing a removal treaty in 1835 opposed by the vast

BOOMTOWN Family members who arrived by wagon in 1889 stand beside their tent in the new town of Guthrie, settled by thousands within days.

majority of Cherokees. A lawyer who helped railroads gain access to Indian Territory, he argued that nearly two million acres of unassigned land there—confiscated from the Creek and Seminole tribes after the Civil War to penalize them for having backed the Confederacy—should be made available to homesteaders. In 1880, boomers led by David Payne of Kansas settled briefly at what is now Oklahoma City before being evicted as trespassers by the U.S. Cavalry. After being ousted from Indian Territory a second time, Payne was convicted in federal court in Arkansas and fined a thousand dollars by Judge Isaac Parker—a penalty he avoided because he seemingly had no assets.

Payne died in 1884, but the boomer movement gained strength as pressure mounted on tribes throughout the West to make land reserved for them available to settlers. In 1887, Senator Henry Dawes won passage of an act to allot reservation land to Indians individually—typically, 160 acres to the head of a family. The remaining land was opened for settlement and often far exceeded the total area allotted to members of the tribe. Many reformers backed the Dawes Act because they believed it would help Indians join American society as self-sufficient landholders. The law provided U.S. citizenship to those receiving allotments, but some Indians never obtained them and others were unable to make a living and hold on to them because the best acreage often went to white settlers. As a result of the Dawes Act, tribes had their reservations carved up and lost nearly two-thirds of their land.

By 1889, allotment promised to open much of Indian Territory to settlement. The government saw no reason to continue excluding boomers from the unassigned land. Before the race to claim that land began officially on April 22, some people jumped the gun and staked out prime lots in advance. Known as "sooners," they included outsiders who evaded troops patrolling the boundaries and insiders such as government agents allowed to operate within those boundaries. On April 22, when boomers arrived by train at the upstart town of Guthrie, packed so densely into the cars that some rode atop them for breathing space, they found that sooners had already claimed some of the best lots. One sooner there explained to reporter Howard that he was a deputy U.S. marshal. "I've got two lots here," he said, "and about fifty other deputies have got lots in the same way. In fact, the deputy-marshals laid out the town." They acted in violation of laws they were supposed to uphold, and their premature claims caused tempers to rise—as did intrusions by claim jumpers who took possession when the rightful owners left temporarily, ignoring stakes placed there to hold the claim. Only the fact that liquor was prohibited kept arguments from turning violent, Howard concluded: "Had whiskey been plentiful in Guthrie the disputed lots might have been watered in blood, for every man went armed with some sort of deadly weapon." ∎

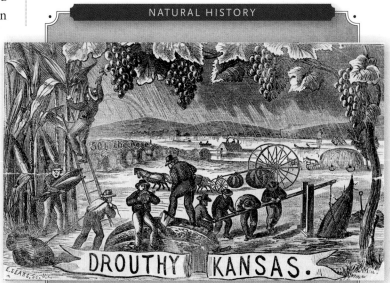

"RAIN FOLLOWS THE PLOW"

In 1880, Samuel Aughey, a science professor at the University of Nebraska, attributed a recent increase in rainfall in that state to the fact that more land was being cultivated by settlers. He theorized that plowing the ground allowed it to absorb more rainfall and that the moisture then returned to the atmosphere, producing clouds and additional precipitation. Journalists and publicists latched onto his theory and popularized the notion that "rain follows the plow." Turning "Drouthy Kansas" into a cornucopia (above) seemed ludicrous to skeptics, but railroads used similar images to entice settlers westward to areas where farming without irrigation was risky.

Unfortunately for such pioneers, their climate was determined not by cultivation but by geography. That part of the West between the Mississippi River and the 98th meridian lies north of the Gulf of Mexico, from which moisture flows on southerly winds that precede cold fronts, producing downpours. Areas beyond the 98th meridian lie north of deserts along the Mexican border and receive less rainfall. In the early 1890s, the ongoing Oklahoma Land Rush drew settlers out toward the 100th meridian and the Texas Panhandle, where wet years were often followed by severe droughts and winds that blew away topsoil. In the 1930s, that area became the core of the calamitous Dust Bowl, and proud descendants of boomers became displaced Okies.

CONCLUSION

1890–1912

AT HOME ON HORSEBACK Navajos ride through Canyon de Chelly,
the cherished heart of their homeland, in this classic photograph by Edward Curtis.
Beginning in the 1890s, Curtis set out to document the life and lasting traditions of
American Indians, taking more than 40,000 photographs over the next three decades.

CONCLUSION

THE LAST FRONTIERS
(1890–1912)

A century after it first tallied the American population in 1790, the U.S. Census Bureau surveyed the nation's progress since then, as measured by the advancing frontier of settlement. In 1790, that frontier lay just beyond the Appalachians. By 1840, it had reached the western border of Missouri. By 1890, so many places in the West had been occupied that the Census Bureau could no longer draw a clear line. "Up to and including 1880 the country had a frontier of settlement," it reported, "but at present the unsettled area has been so broken into by isolated bodies of settlement that there can hardly be said to be a frontier line." Speaking in 1893, historian Frederick Jackson Turner said that announcement by the Census Bureau signaled the end of "a great historic movement." The open frontier had shaped the American character, he argued, by offering people "a new field of opportunity, a gate of escape from the bondage of the past."

Turner's thesis was insightful and influential, but he overstated the case when he concluded that the frontier was closed. As the Census Bureau documented, large areas in the West still had population densities so low—less than two people per square mile—that they were classified as unsettled. Upheavals long associated with the open frontier continued to unfold in the 1890s, including land rushes in Oklahoma and gold rushes in the nation's largest and most remote territory, Alaska. What were once great open spaces beyond the Mississippi, however, were now fenced and plowed, and the Wild West of legend was gradually receding into memory. Some saw the taming of the West as progress. As the Census Bureau noted, between 1790 and 1890 nearly two million square miles of American soil had been "redeemed from the wilderness" by western settlers and put to "the service of man." Yet an increasing number of Americans did not want the wilderness redeemed. They wanted it preserved as it was when it served the needs of those original Americans called Indians. In 1890, Yellowstone was joined by three new national parks: Yosemite, Sequoia,

RANGE OF LIGHT Albert Bierstadt portrayed the splendor of Yosemite Valley here in 1864, the same year in which Congress enacted the Yosemite Grant, preserving the valley and the Mariposa Grove of giant sequoias as a state park in California. The pioneering conservationist John Muir, who lived for some time in a cabin he built there, campaigned to have a large area surrounding the valley preserved in 1890 as Yosemite National Park, which later absorbed the state park and assumed its present form in 1906.

and General Grant (later Kings Canyon). Two months later, a tragedy unfolded in the West that served as a sad reminder of what the nation had failed to preserve and protect—the territory and livelihood of those first Americans.

CARNAGE AT WOUNDED KNEE

Early on December 15, 1890, Lakota Sioux reservation police approached the cabin of Sitting Bull on the Standing Rock Reservation in South Dakota to arrest that renowned chief. James McLaughlin, the government agent at Standing Rock, wanted Sitting Bull jailed because he considered him the menacing "high priest" of the Ghost Dance movement. In fact, it was inspired by a Paiute named Wovoka, who after experiencing a vision during a solar eclipse prophesied that if Indians joined in the ritualistic Ghost Dance they would soon be reunited with their dead ancestors in a new world—an earthly paradise free of disease and white people. The movement he launched soon spread to the Lakota Sioux, whose once expansive domain had been whittled down to four small reservations, where much of the land was now being allotted to white settlers. Lakotas believed that their ritual would hasten the day when whites would disappear and Indians would inherit the earth. Many wore Ghost shirts that they thought had power to protect them if they were attacked for dancing in defiance of a government order prohibiting "heathenish rites" on reservations. Although Sitting Bull was initially skeptical of the movement, he backed it when he found that it gave hope to Lakotas who were hungry and dispirited. McLaughlin feared the movement would turn violent under Sitting Bull's powerful influence. Another anxious agent, Daniel Royer at the Pine Ridge Reservation, called for U.S. troops to intervene. "Indians are dancing in the snow and are wild and crazy," he warned. "We need protection now."

The dawn raid on Sitting Bull's cabin went dreadfully awry when reservation police hauled him outside and were confronted by armed supporters of the chief. A gunfight erupted that claimed the lives of Sitting Bull and seven of his followers as well as six policemen. Lakotas alarmed by his violent death then fled the Standing Rock Reservation and joined fugitives from

WOUNDED KNEE A sketch by a newspaper correspondent shows the situation on the morning of December 29, 1890, as troopers of the Seventh Cavalry commanded by Col. James Forsyth (misidentified here as "General Foresythe") prepared to disarm Lakotas led by Chief Big Foot, camped near Wounded Knee Creek. After the shooting started, the artillery battery shown at right opened fire on the Indians.

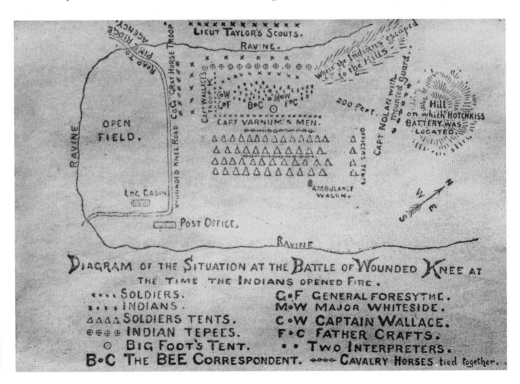

Buriel of the Dead at the Battle of Wounded Knee S.D.
NorthWestern Photo Co
Chadron Neb

BITTER AFTERMATH Soldiers look on as victims of the Wounded Knee massacre are buried in a common grave (top). Some of those killed wore Ghost shirts like the one above, which they hoped would help protect them.

the nearby Cheyenne River Reservation, led by a chief named Big Foot. Together, they made their way south toward the Pine Ridge Reservation, where Red Cloud—a former war leader who had renounced hostilities—was trying to resolve the dispute between the government and the Ghost Dance followers. On December 28, soldiers of Custer's old regiment, the Seventh Cavalry, overtook Big Foot and his party, consisting of some 350 men, women, and children. The chief agreed that he and his people would accompany the soldiers to their camp on Wounded Knee Creek.

Col. James Forsyth of the Seventh Cavalry had orders to disarm Big Foot's followers, who feared that they would be targeted for embracing the Ghost Dance, as Sitting Bull was. Tensions ran high on the morning of the December 29 as 500 soldiers surrounded the Lakotas and began disarming the 100 or so warriors in their midst. A soldier seized the weapon of a deaf man who had not heeded his order to surrender the rifle, and it went off. Men on both sides then opened fire. More than 60 Americans fell dead or wounded in the chaotic fighting, many of them hit by friendly fire. What began as a battle soon degenerated into a massacre. Forsyth's men poured

artillery fire into the Lakota camp and chased down people who fled. "We tried to run," said one woman who survived the mayhem, "but they shot us like we were buffalo." Those wearing Ghost shirts found them no protection against the bullets. Precisely how many were killed is unknown, but the bodies of 150 Lakotas, including 44 women and 18 children, were retrieved afterward in a snowstorm and buried in a mass grave. "Something else died there in the bloody mud, and was buried in the blizzard," said the Lakota holy man Black Elk, who had joined the ill-fated Ghost Dance movement. "A people's dream died there."

Wounded Knee was the last major clash of arms between U.S. troops and Indians. There were occasional confrontations in years to come, but for most Indians the battle was no longer a military one against the United States but a struggle to gain recognition and rights as Americans while maintaining their tribal identity. Not until the mid-20th century did they secure the right to vote in all states. Public acknowledgment that they were Native Americans—full-fledged citizens of the U.S. as well as people native to North America with ancient ties to the continent—took even longer to achieve.

BUFFALO BILL'S WILD WEST

In 1893, Chicago belatedly celebrated the 400th anniversary of the arrival of Columbus in America by hosting the World's Columbian Exposition at the White City, a showpiece whose handsome classical buildings were not made to last but dazzled visitors. Some 25 million people passed through the gates before the exposition closed in October. It was a great American attraction—and one with rich commercial potential for that shrewd showman Buffalo Bill Cody, who staged his Wild West show nearby and drew three million spectators that summer. In keeping with the international flavor of the exposition, he included in his show an extravaganza entitled the Congress of Rough Riders of the World, featuring dashing equestrians from around the globe, including Russian Cossacks, Argentinean gauchos, Mexican vaqueros—and, of course, American cowboys and Indians, who figured prominently in all of Buffalo Bill's productions. One poster for the show gave the cowboys top billing and called them "the real Rough Riders of the World whose daring exploits have made

their very names synonymous with deeds of bravery." Impressed by Buffalo Bill's showmanship, Theodore Roosevelt later assembled his own troop of Rough Riders—western cowboys and eastern dudes recruited to fight in the Spanish-American War—and rode to fame with them in Cuba in 1898.

Born in Iowa in 1846, William Cody rode for the Pony Express in his teens before enlisting to fight for the Union. After the war, he earned his nickname by hunting buffalo to feed men building the Union Pacific Railroad, and then served as a scout for the Fifth Cavalry in campaigns against Plains Indians. That was an impressive résumé for a man destined to become a legend, but he did not achieve fame by sticking to the facts. In 1869, he met Edward Judson, who wrote numerous dime novels under the pen name Ned Buntline and who proceeded to fictionalize Buffalo Bill's career. Far from objecting to Judson's puffery, Cody took cues from the novelist and touted his service as an Army scout, claiming that he killed Chief Tall Bull of the Cheyenne in battle at Summit Springs in Colorado Territory and made off with his horse. Official records

MASTER OF CEREMONIES
Surrounded by his cast, Buffalo Bill Cody sits near the center of this picture behind several Indian children. The Indians he hired as performers sang and danced in tribal fashion but also appeared as wild, menacing figures in skits Cody staged. "I liked the part of the show we made," recalled Black Elk of the Lakota, "but not the part the Wasichus [whites] made."

make no mention of him at that battle, which he later portrayed heroically in his show. In fact, it was a brutal contest that claimed the lives of Cheyenne women and children.

Cody did not achieve stardom and success simply by glorifying himself and other white scouts, soldiers, or cowboys as Indian fighters. He understood that while some people on the frontier viewed Indians as mortal enemies, the public at large regarded them with mixed feelings, including fear, fascination, and even admiration, as evidenced by the respect Americans paid to renowned Indian foes who no longer posed a threat, such as Tecumseh, who after his death in battle had several towns named after him. Cody had enough rapport with Indians to persuade a number of them to join his Wild West show, including Sitting Bull, who agreed to appear in 1885 for $50 a week and a handsome signing bonus. Like other Indians in the show, Sitting Bull needed the money to support his family and welcomed the chance to escape the reservation and see the world. Cody knew better than to include him in acts where Indians staged phony attacks and were then thrashed by cowboys. Sitting Bull simply appeared on horseback in the arena to the astonishment of spectators, some of whom booed or hissed while he sat there impassively, retaining as much dignity as he could when put on display.

Cody's promotional genius led him to avoid what was truly wild and brutal in the West— where Wounded Knee was one of many massacres perpetrated by whites or Indians—and produce shows that had just enough simulated violence and menace to excite viewers without

BUFFALO BILL'S WILD WEST
AND CONGRESS OF ROUGH RIDERS OF THE WORLD.

A COMPANY OF WILD WEST COWBOYS. THE REAL ROUGH RIDERS OF THE WORLD WHOSE DARING EXPLOITS HAVE MADE THEIR VERY NAMES SYNONYMOUS WITH DEEDS OF BRAVERY.

COL. W. F. CODY
BUFFALO BILL
WILL APPEAR
AT EVERY PERFORMANCE

alarming them. The formula for that fictional Wild West, where good was sure to triumph over evil, had been concocted by Ned Buntline and other dime novelists, and Cody made it all the more vivid and compelling by enacting it in the arena. Wild West patrons raised on the dime novel exploits of the fictional Calamity Jane found a more admirable and respectable female sharpshooter in the person of Annie Oakley, who starred in Buffalo Bill's productions for many years. Unlike her sometime competitor in the show, the brash "California Girl" Lillian Smith—who was heard to boast on one occasion that Annie was "done for"—Oakley was demure and ladylike and later went to great lengths to defend her reputation against slanderous stories in the press.

Buffalo Bill's stirring but sanitized version of the Wild West influenced Western movies, which were among the first motion pictures produced in America when that technology was refined around 1900. His suspenseful acts, in which dire threats posed by Indians or outlaws were foiled in the nick of time by heroes on horseback, served as models for Western films

ROUGH RIDERS Buffalo Bill appears as a dignified figure on horseback beside cavorting cowboys in this poster for a show that combined his usual Wild West acts with his "Congress of Rough Riders of the World."

for decades to come. However fanciful, the shoot-'em-ups that Cody staged and Hollywood perpetuated reflected harsh realities that eluded scholars like Frederick Jackson Turner, who delivered his famous address on the American frontier in Chicago in July 1893 while Buffalo Bill and his Rough Riders were wowing crowds nearby. Turner portrayed the open frontier as a safety valve that allowed people to escape from populous areas where opportunities were scarce, but for many pioneers there was little safety and no escaping conflict with Indians or other settlers. Turner envisioned the West as "free land," but the cost of transforming Indian country into American territory went far beyond what American officials paid tribal leaders for their land. The price was often paid in blood, and in that sense those Wild West gunfights came closer to the truth than Turner's idealized view of the frontier, which was still kicking when he wrote its obituary.

RUSH TO ALASKA

Purchased from Russia for $7 million in 1867 at the urging of Secretary of State William Seward, Alaska shed its unwarranted reputation as Seward's Folly three decades later when gold strikes on either side of its border with Canada galvanized the territory and doubled its population within a few years. The great rush north began in 1897 when prospectors returned from Alaska by ship to Seattle and San Francisco with bulging sacks of gold found along the Klondike River in Yukon Territory. Some people made plans to leave for the goldfields on the next available steamer north. Others hoped to "mine the miners" by selling supplies to fortune hunters.

Supplying prospectors was especially lucrative during this gold rush because miners had to haul to the remote Klondike almost everything they needed to function there for months on end and survive its brutal winter. Before leaving San Francisco for Alaska, prospector William Haskell and his partner bought 800 pounds of flour, 300 pounds of bacon, and 200 pounds of beans, among other rations and equipment, amounting to 3,200 pounds of supplies. Haskell's partner had been up north before and knew that those goods would be scarce and costly in Alaska and virtually nonexistent in the Klondike. The amount they purchased was not excessive. To keep prospectors from starving, Royal Canadian Mounted Police patrolling the Alaska-Yukon border required that each miner destined for the Klondike carry more than 1,000 pounds of food.

Hauling such loads from the Alaska ports of Skagway or Dyea over steep mountain trails leading to the Klondike was a herculean task. Some prospectors hired Tlingit Indians as bearers. Others used dogsleds or horse carts. Many pulled sleds themselves or carried supplies on their backs, which meant making the climb repeatedly before crossing the border. Large numbers of fortune hunters lost heart and turned back before entering Yukon Territory. Nearly 100,000 people set out for the Klondike during the rush. No more than 40,000 reached their destination, and only about 4,000 of those returned with any appreciable amount of gold. Most of the promising claims had been staked by the time the rush reached its peak.

Some of those who failed to reach the Klondike found other opportunities in Alaska, including

GLITTERING PROSPECTS The cover of this Klondike journal features a warmly clad prospector flanked by huge gold nuggets and predicts a spectacular haul of $40 million by miners there in 1898. The actual figure was closer to $10 million.

employment in the boomtown of Skagway, which had more than 15,000 inhabitants by 1898, many of whom were transients. A Canadian policeman who visited Skagway called it "about the roughest place in the world," a reputation for which one outlaw in particular, Jefferson "Soapy" Smith, deserved considerable credit. A con man who refined his craft running crooked gambling operations in Denver and other western towns, he became Skagway's criminal kingpin, whose underlings specialized in fleecing fortune hunters. Concerned that the town's unsavory reputation would drive prospectors away to the rival port of Dyea, residents formed a vigilance committee in 1898 and gathered to take action against the gang after several of them cheated a prospector out of a small fortune in gold dust. Informed of the meeting, Smith approached with

HEAVY GOING Lured by glowing press accounts like the one at top, prospectors bound for the Yukon harness sled dogs to haul their supplies up Alaska's Chilkoot Pass as fortune hunters ascend the slope ahead of them (above). Some discouraged miners turned back and tried their luck gambling in Dyea or Skagway.

Look forward, women, always; utterly cast away
    The memory of hate and struggle and bitterness;
Bonds may endure for a night, but freedom comes with the day,
    And the free must remember nothing less.

Forget the strife; remember those who strove—
    The first defeated women, gallant and few,
Who gave us hope, as a mother gives us love,
    Forget them not, and this remember, too:

How at the later call to come forth and unite,
    Women untaught, uncounseled, alone and apart,
Rank upon rank came forth in unguessed might,
    Each one answering the call of her own wise heart.

They came from toil and want, from leisure and ease,
    Those who knew only life, and learned women of fame,
Girls and the mothers of girls, and the mothers of these,
    No one knew whence or how, but they came, they ca

SHEDDING LIGHT Liberty carries her torch eastward from the 11 western states where women have secured the right to vote to less enlightened states in this illustration published in 1915, five years before the 19th Amendment assured voting rights for women nationwide.

rifle in hand and died in a shootout with a guard posted at the door, thus earning distinction as one of the last notorious frontier figures to bite the dust.

By 1899, the gold frenzy was beginning to dissipate in the Klondike even as it intensified at faraway Nome, Alaska, near the Bering Strait, where gold was found right on the beach. Thousands of prospectors pitched their tents "within a few feet of where the surf is breaking," wrote one correspondent. Millions of dollars' worth in gold were extracted there just a few hundred miles from Russia, which had sold Alaska short. Unlike the great California gold rush, however, the rush to Alaska did not suddenly propel that territory to statehood. Although its population rose

The faces of some were stern, and some were gay,
And some were pale with the terror of unreal dangers;
But their hearts knew this: that hereafter come what may,
Women to women would never again be strangers.

Alice Duer Miller.

BY HY MAYER

to 64,000 in 1900, that was barely above the threshold of 60,000 required for statehood under the Northwest Ordinance of 1787, which applied only to territories in today's Midwest. Elsewhere, there was no specific population requirement for statehood, but Alaska remained the least populous American territory in 1900 and would have to wait more than 50 years to be admitted as a state. Nonetheless, the gold frenzy brought something vital to Alaska that the California gold rush lacked—women. As many as 10 percent of those who entered Alaska in the late 1890s were women, and lots of them went prospecting. Trudging up Chilkoot Pass on his way to the Klondike, Haskell saw women bearing heavy loads who "seemed to show a fortitude superior to the men," sometimes encouraging husbands who were losing heart and insisting that they continue on.

SUFFRAGE AND STATEHOOD

When the 20th century dawned, a nation that took great pride in its democratic principles contained only four states where women could vote, all of them in the West—Wyoming, Colorado, Utah, and Idaho. Wyoming was the pioneer, having granted women that right a year after it was organized as territory in 1868. One reason for doing so was to encourage women to settle in Wyoming, where men outnumbered them six to one. Without more women, mothers, and children, the territory had dim prospects for developing and achieving statehood. William Bright, who introduced the bill giving women the vote, was offended that the newly adopted 15th Amendment extended voting rights to black men in Wyoming and other territories while offering no such guarantee to white women, including his wife, Julia, who influenced his position. Mixed motives led the all-male legislature to support Bright's bill, but once enacted it drew thousands of women into the political process and gained strong support. Before approving Wyoming's application for statehood in 1890, the U.S. Congress proposed that it conform with other states by eliminating woman

IN NEW TERRITORY Women line up to vote in Wyoming. The first American territory to grant women that right, Wyoming later became the first state to do so when it entered the Union in 1890.

suffrage. Wyoming's leaders replied that they would remain out of the Union for 100 years rather than disenfranchise women there.

Utah, one of the few Far West territories with nearly as many women as men, was quick to follow Wyoming's lead, but elsewhere suffragists had to campaign long and hard to win the vote. In the Northwest, Abigail Scott Duniway of Oregon joined forces with the legendary Susan B. Anthony to press their case. Anthony told legislators in Washington Territory that enfranchising women would produce "the most gratifying of results—the immigration of a large number of good women to the territory." Washington did so in 1883, but its supreme court later overruled

LAST OF THE 48 At right, President Howard Taft sits among dignitaries at a signing ceremony in February 1912 that admitted Arizona as the 48th state. New Mexico entered the Union a month earlier, more than a decade after its application for statehood stalled in the Senate. On the cover of *Puck* (opposite), illustrator Rose O'Neill portrayed New Mexico then as a supplicant in Mexican attire, seeking admission from an elegant Lady Liberty of lighter complexion representing Anglo-American society.

that decision by the legislature. Duniway faced an even bigger challenge in Oregon, where suffrage for women had to be approved not just by the legislature but by the all-male electorate. Because the suffrage movement overlapped with the women's temperance movement, Duniway found it hard to win over men who liked their liquor. She insisted that suffrage and temperance were separate causes, and though accused of "selling out to whiskey" ultimately won her campaign in Oregon.

In 1893, Colorado became the first state to approve woman suffrage by popular vote. Crucial support there came from the Populist Party, which arose in the West and championed reforms that were later adopted nationally, including the direct election of U.S. senators—originally chosen by state legislators—and voting rights for women. The leading role that Westerners played in making America a true land of liberty demonstrated that the frontier was indeed a place where people could "escape from the bondage of the past," in Turner's words, and build a new and better world. Before the Civil War, people in California and Kansas had rejected slavery and set the nation on the arduous path to emancipation. Later, Westerners pioneered the process of extending property rights and voting rights to fully half the nation's population.

If there was any one moment when the Old West gave way to the new, it came in 1912 when the nation's oldest territory, New Mexico, was admitted as a state along with Arizona, completing the map of the 48 contiguous states. Admission for New Mexico had been delayed for some time, not for lack of population but because many of its residents were Hispanics with ancestral ties to Spanish colonists or Pueblo people whose communities predated the Spanish colonial era. There was resistance in Washington, D.C., to admitting a state with so many non–Anglo Americans and two official languages, English and Spanish. By embracing New Mexico, the nation crossed a cultural frontier and renewed its commitment to recognizing all people native to this country as Americans, including those whose ancestors had inhabited the West long before the United States of America arose and laid claim to it. ∎

VOL. L. No. 1294.

PUCK BUILDING, New York, December 18th, 1901.

Copyright, 1901, by Keppler & Schwarzmann.

PRICE TEN CENTS.

"What fools these Mortals be!"

Puck

Entered at N. Y. P. O. as Second-class Mail Matter.

NEW MEXICO

STATEHOOD

THE NEXT CANDIDATE FOR STATEHOOD.

WHAT BECAME OF THEM

These biographical sketches of significant figures mentioned during the course of this book follow them to the conclusion of their life's story.

DANIEL BOONE
NOVEMBER 2, 1734–SEPTEMBER 26, 1820

After blazing the Wilderness Road through Cumberland Gap in 1775, Boone founded Fort Boonesborough in Kentucky, settled with his family there, and served as a militia captain, defending that fortified settlement and two others in the area against attacks by Indians. In 1776, his daughter Jemima was among three girls seized by Shawnee and Cherokee raiders. Boone led a party in pursuit, tracked down the Indian camp, and rescued Jemima and the two other captives—an exploit later fictionalized in James Fenimore Cooper's novel *The Last of the Mohicans*. Boone himself was captured by Shawnees in 1778 and impressed one of their chiefs, who took him in until he escaped four months later. In 1799, having fallen into debt and lost his property, he left Kentucky with family members for Missouri, within Spanish-held Louisiana Territory, and received a land grant, which was later nullified when the United States took charge of the area. Boone lived with relatives and explored the area. He petitioned Congress to restore his land, much of which he later sold to pay old debts in Kentucky. A pioneer of two states, he died soon after Missouri entered the Union in 1820.

BLACK HAWK
1767–OCTOBER 3, 1838

After surrendering to U.S. troops in 1832, Black Hawk was incarcerated at Jefferson Barracks in St. Louis. He was then escorted east and met President Andrew Jackson in Washington before being confined briefly at Fort Monroe in Virginia. Secretary of War Lewis Cass released Black Hawk in 1833 and had him taken on a tour of major American cities, where crowds turned out to see the famous war leader. Rejoining his family among the Sauk tribe in Iowa, he was placed under the authority of his longtime rival, Chief Keokuk, and was left powerless. Black Hawk dictated his autobiography through an interpreter and lived quietly at his home along the Des Moines River. "I was once a great warrior," he said shortly before he died in 1838. "I am now poor." He was not allowed to rest in peace. His grave was robbed, and his remains ended up in a museum.

WILLIAM CLARK
AUGUST 1, 1770–SEPTEMBER 1, 1838

Bolstered by the fame of his historic expedition to the Pacific, William Clark went on to a distinguished career in government. In 1807, President Thomas Jefferson placed him in charge of Indian affairs in the Louisiana Territory, where he also served as brigadier general of the militia. He married Julia Hancock, who bore him a son they named Meriwether Lewis Clark in honor of his dear friend and co-leader. Clark was governor of Missouri Territory from 1813 until it achieved statehood in 1820. He remained a leading figure in the West thereafter as superintendent of Indian affairs at St. Louis. Clark acted with greater respect and consideration for Indians than most American officials who dealt with them, but he arranged for the removal of various tribes living in Missouri and east of the Mississippi to the future Kansas Territory, where many were displaced by white settlers after his death. In 2001, President Bill Clinton promoted Clark posthumously from lieutenant to captain, the same rank held by Meriwether Lewis.

MERIWETHER LEWIS
AUGUST 18, 1774–OCTOBER 11, 1809

Meriwether Lewis struggled to find his way after returning from his transcontinental journey in 1806. Appointed governor of Louisiana Territory by President Jefferson, he quarreled with William Bates, the territorial secretary, and struggled to satisfy the often conflicting demands of settlers, traders, and tribes in that sprawling new American domain. In 1809, he fell into a deep depression amid political pressures, financial troubles, marital rejections, and problems arranging publication of the expedition journals. He began drinking heavily and twice attempted suicide. On October 10, while on his way back to Washington, he stopped overnight at a tavern in Tennessee. Shots rang out in his room, and he died the following morning of bullet wounds to the head and chest. Some have speculated that he was murdered, but most historians believe he took his own life. As Jefferson wrote a few years after his death, Lewis "did the deed which plunged his friends into affliction and deprived his country of one of her most valued citizens."

KIT CARSON
DECEMBER 24, 1809–MAY 23, 1868

Following the Mexican War, Carson spent much of the last two decades of his life alternately trying to keep peace with Indians and fighting them. In 1853, after driving a flock of sheep to California and making a handsome profit there, he returned to New Mexico Territory and began serving as an Indian agent. "I frequently visit the Indians," he stated around that time, "speak to them of the advantages of peace, and exert my influence to keep them satisfied with the proceedings of those placed in power over them." Yet peace seldom lasted long in New Mexico, where raids by Apaches and Navajos led to retaliatory expeditions in which Carson sometimes took part. During the Civil War, he campaigned strenuously against those tribes as well as against Comanches and Kiowas in Texas and was promoted from colonel to brigadier general in the Union Army. In 1866, he commanded Fort Garland in Colorado Territory before resigning because of ill health. His last public service was to help negotiate a treaty with the Ute, concluded not long after he died in 1868.

JOHN C. FRÉMONT
JANUARY 21, 1813–JULY 13, 1890

Touted as the "Pathfinder" for his expeditions across the West, Frémont suffered a serious setback in 1847 when Brig. Gen. Stephen Kearny replaced him as governor of American-occupied California and charged him with insubordination and mutiny. A court martial found him guilty. President James Polk then granted him clemency, but he resigned from the Army and entered politics in the new state of California, which sent him to the U.S. Senate in 1851. After losing to Democrat James Buchanan as the Republican Party's first presidential nominee in 1856, Frémont returned to duty as a Union general in 1861. Removed from command in Missouri by President Lincoln, he challenged Lincoln for the Republican nomination in 1864 before withdrawing to avoid splitting the party. He later served as the territorial governor of Arizona from 1878 to 1881, but reckless railroad business ventures cost him his wealth. Only the resourcefulness of his wife, Jessie Benton Frémont, kept him from dying totally destitute in 1890.

GRENVILLE DODGE
APRIL 12, 1831–JANUARY 3, 1916

While serving as chief engineer of the Union Pacific Railroad in the late 1860s, Dodge was elected to Congress, representing his home district in Iowa and dealing with railroad legislation and Indian policy. In 1869, when the transcontinental railroad was completed, Dodge left Congress and the Union Pacific but remained involved with railroads. Having purchased shares in Crédit Mobilier, the shady construction company set up by Union Pacific directors, he was called to testify before a congressional committee investigating the scandal that erupted in 1872 but evaded the summons. Unlike some who became notorious for schemes they devised to finance railroads, he maintained his reputation as a builder of them. Under his supervision, thousands of miles of tracks were laid from the Gulf of Mexico to the Rockies, and he later engineered railroads in Cuba and across Siberia, as well as a tunnel through the Alps. Not until he was in his late 70s did declining health slow him down. He died at his home in Council Bluffs, Iowa, in 1916.

JOHN WESLEY POWELL
MARCH 24, 1834–SEPTEMBER 23, 1902

Powell's celebrated venture down the Colorado River in 1869 launched him on two remarkable careers. As an explorer and geologist, he went on to become director of the U.S. Geological Survey. He also became an eager ethnologist, who studied tribal cultures sympathetically and dealt closely with Indians. Investigating the fate of three missing men who left his 1869 expedition, Powell returned west in 1870 and met with Shivwits, a band of Paiutes, who admitted killing the men in the mistaken belief they were hostile. Powell demanded no punishment and came away with a better understanding of those Indians. "We will be friends," they said to him in parting, "and when you come we will be glad." In 1873, the U.S. Indian commissioner sent him to assess the "conditions and wants" of Great Basin tribes, whose rich cultural traditions he documented with the help of a photographer. At his urging, Congress in 1879 established the Bureau of Ethnology, which Powell directed for the rest his life, devoting full attention to it after resigning as head of the Survey in 1894.

ABIGAIL SCOTT DUNIWAY
OCTOBER 22, 1834–OCTOBER 11, 1915

Born in Illinois, Abigail Scott began her career as an author by keeping a journal of her family's trek west on the Oregon Trail in 1852, during which her mother died of cholera. A year later in Oregon, she wed Benjamin Duniway, who became disabled in an accident in 1862. To support him and their children, she taught school and wrote articles and novels. In 1871, she founded a weekly in Portland called *The New Northwest*, advocating women's rights. She began speaking and campaigning as a suffragist, and in 1884 became vice president of the National Woman Suffrage Association. In 1887, she moved to Idaho, where she helped women win voting rights in 1896. Returning to Portland, she launched a new weekly, *The Pacific Empire*, in which she serialized several of her novels. Duniway achieved a long-sought goal when her suffrage referendum finally won approval in Oregon in 1912. She became the first woman in her county to register to vote, and died three years later after completing her autobiography, *Path Breaking*.

JOHN MUIR
APRIL 21, 1838–DECEMBER 24, 1914

John Muir and the Sierra Club he oversaw from its inception in 1892 viewed the establishment of Yosemite National Park in 1890 as just one step toward preserving precious wilderness areas in California and elsewhere in the nation. The spectacular Yosemite Valley remained under California's jurisdiction, and Muir worried that the state would yield to pressure from those seeking to develop the area and exploit its resources. He found an ally in President Theodore Roosevelt, a fellow conservationist who camped with Muir in 1903 and agreed that Yosemite Valley should be part of the national park, thus shielding it from commercial development. When Roosevelt signed a bill to that effect in 1906, Muir achieved a heartening victory. But he and the Sierra Club suffered a sad defeat in 1913 when Congress allowed a dam to be built that immersed Hetch Hetchy Valley, located within the national park and comparable to Yosemite Valley in grandeur. That loss shadowed the last year of Muir's life, but he would be remembered as the "father of our national parks."

BUFFALO BILL
FEBRUARY 26, 1846–JANUARY 10, 1917

Awarded the Medal of Honor in 1872 for gallantry in action against Indians as an Army scout, William Cody entered show business that same year by portraying himself on stage. Featured in several dime novels, he published an autobiography in 1879. He returned west periodically after launching his acting career, serving briefly as an Army scout after the Battle of the Little Bighorn and escorting wealthy men on hunting expeditions. In 1883, he began staging the Wild West shows that made him world-famous. After Sitting Bull left his cast and embraced the Ghost Dance movement in 1890, Cody was asked by Maj. Gen. Nelson Miles to "secure the person of Sitting Bull" and place him in military custody. Cody set out with gifts to persuade the chief to yield but was prevented by Indian agent James McLaughlin from interceding in the crisis that led to Sitting Bull's death and the Wounded Knee Massacre. Cody later went bankrupt and lost control of his show but continued performing until he was 70. He remained an iconic figure to millions when he died in 1917.

QUANAH PARKER
CIRCA 1848–FEBRUARY 23, 1911

When he surrendered in 1875 and settled on the reservation, Quanah Parker was leader of one Comanche band, the Quahada. Over the next 15 years, his influence increased until he became the first ever principal chief of the Comanche. Along the way, he had to contend with staunch traditionalists like the medicine man Isa-tai, who opposed his plan to lease tribal land to surrounding ranchers. Indians on the reservation approved the deal, and the leases helped them survive, if not thrive. Quanah retained his tribal identity by keeping his long braids and refusing to adopt monogamy or Christianity, but he opposed the Ghost Dance movement that convulsed the Lakota Sioux reservations in 1890. When federal authorities prepared to apply the Dawes Act and carve up the reservation, he bargained hard with them and preserved nearly a half million acres of tribal land. As befit a man who straddled two worlds, he went to his grave in 1911 wearing full Comanche regalia like his father, Chief Peta Nocona, and was laid to rest beside his mother, Cynthia Ann Parker.

DOC HOLLIDAY
AUGUST 14, 1851–NOVEMBER 8, 1887

John Henry "Doc" Holliday absconded to Colorado with Wyatt Earp in 1882 after helping him avenge the attacks on his brothers. While visiting Denver that spring, Holliday was arrested and faced extradition to Arizona on charges of murdering Frank Stilwell and others killed by Wyatt's posse. Bat Masterson, a friend and ally of Holliday and Earp, appealed to Colorado governor Frederick Pitkin, warning that Holliday would be killed by lawless "cowboys" in Arizona before he could stand trial. Pitkin denied extradition, citing another warrant for Holliday in Colorado that Masterson had contrived. Holliday never appeared in court, but he was sentenced to slow death by a natural cause—tuberculosis. He took drugs and drank heavily, but his hand was still steady enough in 1884 to stop a man who came after him in Leadville, Colorado, by shooting him in the arm. Despite his grim reputation, Holliday had committed few verified homicides when he died at a sanatorium in Glenwood Springs, Colorado, three years later.

WYATT EARP
MARCH 19, 1848–JANUARY 13, 1929

After Wyatt Earp and his unauthorized posse killed those he suspected of murdering his brother Morgan and shooting his brother Virgil in Tombstone, he sought refuge from prosecution in Arizona by catching a train to Colorado in 1882. Late that year, he rejoined his common-law wife, former actress Josephine "Sadie" Marcus, in California. They traveled widely as he tried mining in Idaho, gambling in San Francisco—where he refereed a prizefight in a way that many considered crooked—saloon-keeping in Alaska, and consulting for Western movies in Hollywood late in life. Disturbed by lurid stories in the press of his days in Tombstone, he tried to improve his image and reap some profit by contracting with journalist Stuart Lake to write his biography. That book, published two years after Earp's death, was highly fictionalized but helped establish him as a folk hero and a legendary figure in films. Among the actors who portrayed him over the decades were Henry Fonda, James Stewart, Burt Lancaster, James Garner, Kurt Russell, and Kevin Costner.

PAT GARRETT

JUNE 5, 1850–FEBRUARY 29, 1908

Billy the Kid still had numerous admirers among New Mexicans when Sheriff Pat Garrett tracked him down and killed him in 1881. Garrett received some plaudits in the press, but citizens of Lincoln County ousted him in the next election. In 1884, he lost another race for the New Mexico state senate. He relied later on appointments, first as sheriff of Doña Ana County in the 1890s and then as a customs agent in El Paso, Texas. He owed that job to President Theodore Roosevelt, who admired him but did not reappoint him. Returning to his ranch in New Mexico after his stint in customs, Garrett found himself on the brink of bankruptcy. To ease his financial troubles, he leased part of his land to Wayne Brazel. When Garrett tried to sell his ranch, Brazel refused to leave. Brazel shot and killed Garrett on February 29, 1908. The evidence indicated that he was murdered. But in a final insult to the memory of the man who brought down Billy the Kid, Brazel got off by pleading self-defense.

ANNIE OAKLEY

AUGUST 13, 1860–NOVEMBER 3, 1926

After surviving a train accident in 1901, Annie Oakley left Buffalo Bill's Wild West show. She recovered and regained her shooting skills, only to suffer another shock in 1903 when she was slandered by a story portraying her as a cocaine addict and a thief, an account widely reprinted after it first appeared in Chicago newspapers run by William Randolph Hearst. It was a case of mistaken identity, and she filed more than 50 separate lawsuits against newspapers to uphold her reputation, prevailing in all but one of them. During World War I, she and her husband, fellow sharpshooter Frank Butler, toured Army camps, wowing recruits with their skills. In 1921, she was injured in an automobile accident and had to wear a steel brace but could still hit targets with uncanny precision. When she died five years later at the age of 66, the "Little Sure Shot" who had dazzled Sitting Bull four decades earlier was remembered fondly as "America's Sweetheart."

FOLLOWING PAGES: Loggers and family members gather around a giant sequoia felled in California's Converse Basin in 1901. Located outside what was then General Grant National Park (now Kings Canyon National Park), Converse Basin was extensively logged until it was protected within Sequoia National Forest in the 1930s, preserving some of the largest trees in the world.

Included here are good books that served as sources for this book and a short, selective list of informative websites on western history, of which there are many.

BOOKS

Ambrose, Stephen E. *Nothing Like It in the World: The Men Who Built the Transcontinental Railroad, 1836–1869.* New York: Simon & Schuster, 2000.

——. *Undaunted Courage: Meriwether Lewis, Thomas Jefferson, and the Opening of the American West.* New York: Touchstone, 1996.

Athearn, Robert G. *William Tecumseh Sherman and the Settlement of the West.* Norman: University of Oklahoma Press, 1995.

Billington, Ray Allen, and Martin Ridge. *Westward Expansion: A History of the American Frontier.* Albuquerque: University of New Mexico Press, 2001.

Carson, Kit. *Kit Carson's Autobiography.* Edited by Milo Milton Quaife. Lincoln: University of Nebraska Press, 1996.

Chaffin, Tom. *Pathfinder: John Charles Frémont and the Course of American Empire.* New York: Hill and Wang, 2002.

Clappe, Louise. *The Shirley Letters from California Mines in 1851–52.* San Francisco: Thomas C. Russell, 1922.

Corbett, Christopher. *Orphans Preferred: The Twisted Truth and Lasting Legend of the Pony Express.* New York: Broadway Books, 2003.

Custer, Elizabeth B. *"Boots and Saddles" or, Life in Dakota with General Custer.* Norman: University of Oklahoma Press, 1961.

Dary, David. *Cowboy Culture: A Saga of Five Centuries.* Lawrence: University Press of Kansas, 1989.

——. *The Santa Fe Trail: Its History, Legends, and Lore.* New York: Alfred A. Knopf, 2000.

——. *Seeking Pleasure in the Old West.* New York: Alfred A Knopf, 1995.

Davis, John W. *Wyoming Range War: The Infamous Invasion of Johnson County.* Norman: University of Oklahoma Press, 2010.

Davis, William C. *Three Roads to the Alamo: The Lives and Fortunes of David Crockett, James Bowie, and William Barret Travis.* New York: HarperCollins, 1998.

Denton, Sally. *Passion and Principle: John and Jessie Frémont, the Couple Whose Power, Politics, and Love Shaped Nineteenth-Century America.* New York: Bloomsbury, 2007.

Dykstra, Robert R. *The Cattle Towns.* Lincoln: University of Nebraska Press, 1983.

Goetzmann, William H. *Exploration and Empire: The Explorer and the Scientist in the Winning of the American West.* New York: W. W. Norton, 1966.

Goetzmann, William H., and Glyndwr Williams. *The Atlas of North American Exploration: From the Norse Voyages to the Race for the Poles.* New York: Prentice Hall, 1992.

Gregg, Josiah. *Commerce of the Prairies.* Edited by Max L. Moorhead. Norman: University of Oklahoma Press, 1990.

Greenberg, Amy S. *A Wicked War: Polk, Clay, Lincoln, and the 1846 U.S. Invasion of Mexico.* New York: Vintage Books, 2012.

Greever, William S. *The Bonanza West: The Story of the Western Mining Rushes, 1848–1900.* Norman: University of Oklahoma Press, 1963.

Gwynne, S. C. *Empire of the Summer Moon: Quanah Parker and the Rise and Fall of the Comanches, the Most Powerful Indian Tribe in American History.* New York: Scribner, 2010.

Hämäläinen, Pekka. *The Comanche Empire.* New Haven: Yale University Press, 2008.

Haskell, William B. *Two Years in the Klondike and Alaskan Gold-Fields, 1896–1898: A Thrilling Narrative of Life in the Gold Mines and Camps.* Fairbanks: University of Alaska Press, 1998.

Holliday, J. S. *The World Rushed In: The California Gold Rush Experience.* Norman: University of Oklahoma Press, 2002.

Hyslop, Stephen G. *Bound for Santa Fe: The Road to New Mexico and the American Conquest, 1806–1848.* Norman: University of Oklahoma Press, 2002.

——. *Contest for California: From Spanish Colonization to the American Conquest.* Arthur H. Clark and University of Oklahoma Press, 2012.

James, Ronald M. *The Roar and the Silence: A History of Virginia City and the Comstock Lode.* Reno: University of Nevada Press, 1998.

Josephy, Alvin M., Jr., and the Editors of Time-Life Books. *War on the Frontier: The Trans-Mississippi West.* Alexandria, Va.: Time-Life Books, 1986.

Katz, William Loren. *The Black West.* New York: Harlem Moon/Broadway Books, 2005.

Lamar, Howard R., ed. *The New Encyclopedia of the American West.* New Haven: Yale University Press, 1998.

Lavender, David. *Bent's Fort.* New York: Doubleday, 1954.

——. *Westward Vision: The Story of the Oregon Trail.* Lincoln: University of Nebraska Press, 1985.

Leckie, Robert. *From Sea to Shining Sea: From the War of 1812 to the Mexican War, the Saga of America's Expansion.* New York: Harper Perennial, 1993.

Limerick, Patricia Nelson. *The Legacy of Conquest: The Unbroken Past of the American West.* New York: W. W. Norton, 1987.

Magoffin, Susan Shelby. *Down the Santa Fe Trail and into Mexico.* Edited by Stella M. Drumm. New Haven: Yale University Press, 1962.

Mattes, Merrill J. *The Great Platte River Road: The Covered Wagon Mainline via Fort Kearny to Fort Laramie.* Lincoln: University of Nebraska Press, 1987.

McCracken, Harold. *George Catlin and the Old Frontier.* New York: Dial Press, 1959.

McCullough, David. *Mornings on Horseback.* New York: Simon & Schuster, 1981.

Miller, Alfred Jacob. *Braves and Buffalo: Plains Indian Life in 1837.* Toronto: University of Toronto Press, 1973.

Owens, Robert M. *Mr. Jefferson's Hammer: William Henry Harrison and the Origins of American Indian Policy.* Norman: University of Oklahoma Press, 2007.

Parkman, Francis. *The Oregon Trail.* Edited by E. N. Feltskog. Lincoln: University of Nebraska Press, 1994.

Remini, Robert V. *Andrew Jackson and the Course of American Empire, 1767–1821.* New York: Harper & Row, 1977.

———. *Andrew Jackson and the Course of American Freedom, 1822–1832.* New York: Harper & Row, 1981.

———. *Andrew Jackson and the Course of American Democracy, 1833–1845.* New York: Harper & Row, 1984.

Roberts, Randy, and James S. Olson. *A Line in the Sand: The Alamo in Blood and Memory.* New York: Touchstone, 2001.

Ronda, James P. *Lewis and Clark among the Indians.* Lincoln: University of Nebraska Press, 1984.

Saban, Edwin L. *Kit Carson Days, 1809–1868.* Lincoln: University of Nebraska Press, 1995.

Sandburg, Carl. *Abraham Lincoln: The Prairie Years and the War Years.* New York: Harcourt, 1982.

Schlissel, Lillian. *Women's Diaries of the Westward Journey.* New York: Schocken Books, 2004.

Sherman, William T. *Recollections of California, 1846–1861.* Oakland: Biobooks, 1945.

Shirley, Glenn. *Belle Starr and Her Times: The Literature, the Facts, and the Legends.* Norman: University of Oklahoma Press, 1982.

Siringo, Charles. *A Texas Cow Boy or, Fifteen Years on the Hurricane Deck of a Spanish Pony.* Chicago: M. Umbdenstock, 1885.

Smith, Jean Edward. *Grant.* New York: Simon & Schuster, 2001.

Sprague, Marshall. *So Vast, So Beautiful a Land: Louisiana and the Purchase.* Boston: Little, Brown, 1974.

Starita, Joe. *The Dull Knifes of Pine Ridge: A Lakota Odyssey.* New York: Berkley Books, 1995.

Starr, Kevin. *California: A History.* New York: Modern Library, 2005.

Stewart, George R. *The California Trail.* Lincoln: University of Nebraska Press, 1983.

Stiles, T. J. *Jesse James: Last Rebel of the Civil War.* New York: Alfred A. Knopf, 2002.

Tefertiller, Casey. *Wyatt Earp: The Life behind the Legend.* New York: MJF Books, 1997.

Townsend, John Kirk. *Narrative of a Journey across the Rocky Mountains to the Columbia River.* Edited by R. G. Thwaite. Lincoln: University of Nebraska Press, 1978.

Twain, Mark. *Roughing It.* New York: Oxford University Press, 1996.

Utley, Robert M. *Billy the Kid: A Short and Violent Life.* Lincoln: University of Nebraska Press, 1989.

———. *The Indian Frontier, 1846–1890.* Albuquerque: University of New Mexico Press, 2003.

———. *The Lance and the Shield: The Life and Times of Sitting Bull.* New York: Henry Holt, 1993.

———. *A Life Wild and Perilous: Mountain Men and the Path to the Pacific.* New York: Henry Holt, 1997.

Victor, Frances Fuller. *The River of the West: Life and Adventure in the Rocky Mountains and Oregon.* Hartford: R. W. Bliss, 1870.

Wallace, Anthony F. C. *Jefferson and the Indians: The Tragic Fate of the First Americans.* Cambridge: Harvard University Press, 1999.

Weber, David J. *The Mexican Frontier, 1821–1846: The American Southwest under Mexico.* Albuquerque: University of New Mexico Press, 1982.

———. *The Spanish Frontier in North America.* New Haven: Yale University Press, 1996.

White, Richard. *Railroaded: The Transcontinentals and the Making of Modern America.* New York: W. W. Norton, 2011

WESTERN HISTORICAL WEBSITES

Encyclopedia of Arkansas History and Culture: www.encyclopedia ofarkansas.net/

Encyclopedia of the Great Plains: http://plainshumanities.unl.edu /encyclopedia/

Encyclopedia of Louisiana: www.knowla.org/

Encyclopedia of Oklahoma History and Culture: www.okhistory.org /publications/encyclopediaonline

Encyclopedia of Wyoming History: www.wyohistory.org /encyclopedia

Kansas History Web Sites: www.kansashistory.us/

Library of Congress, "Early California History: An Overview": http://memory.loc.gov/ammem/cbhtml/cbintro.html

Library of Congress, "Prairie Settlement: Nebraska Photographs and Family Letters, 1862–1912": http://memory.loc.gov:8081/ammem /award98/nbhihtml/pshome.html

New Mexico History: www.newmexicohistory.org/

Online Encyclopedia of Washington State History: www.history link.org/

Online Nevada Encyclopedia: http://onlinenevada.org/

Oregon History Project: www.ohs.org/education/oregonhistory /index.cfm

PBS, *The West:* www.pbs.org/weta/thewest/program/episodes/

Texas State Historical Association: www.tshaonline.org

LC = Library of Congress Prints and Photographs Division
NPS = National Park Service

FRONT COVER: Charles Phelps Cushing/ClassicStock/The Image Works **BACK COVER:** (background) The Granger Collection, NYC; (L to R) Chicago History Museum/Bridgeman Images, Yale Collection of Western Americana/Beinecke Library, Archive of Modern Conflict Toronto, De Agostini Picture Library/Bridgeman Images **FRONT MATTER:** 1, Smithsonian American Art Museum, Washington, DC/Art Resource, NY; 2–3, The Oregon Trail, 1869 (oil on canvas), Bierstadt, Albert (1830–1902)/Butler Institute of American Art, Youngstown, OH, USA/Gift of Joseph G. Butler III 1946/Bridgeman Images; 4, Texas Rangers armed with revolvers and Winchester rifles, 1890 (b/w photo), American Photographer (19th century)/Private Collection/Peter Newark Western Americana/Bridgeman Images **INTRODUCTION:** 6, Everett Collection Inc./Alamy; 6–7, The Granger Collection, NYC; 7, The Treaty of Mortefontaine, 30th September 1800 (pen & ink on paper), French School (19th century)/Archives du Ministere des Affaires Etrangeres, Paris, France/Archives Charmet/Bridgeman Images; 8, GraphicaArtis/Corbis; 9, INTERFOTO/Alamy; 10–11, The Mariners' Museum, Newport News, VA; 12, W. Langdon Kihn/National Geographic Creative; 13 (UP), Album/Tolo Balaguer/Newscom; 13 (LO), Father Serra Celebrates Mass at Monterey, 1876 (oil on canvas), Trousset, Leon (1838–1917)/California Historical Society Collections at the Autry/Bridgeman Images; 14, STC 22790, Houghton Library, Harvard University; 15, William Penn's Treaty With the Indians in November 1683, 1771–72 (oil on canvas), West, Benjamin (1738–1820)/Pennsylvania Academy of the Fine Arts, Philadelphia, USA/Bridgeman Images; 16–17, The Shooting of General Braddock at Fort Duquesne, Pittsburgh, 1755 (oil on canvas), Deming, Edwin Willard (1860–1942)/State Historical Society of Wisconsin, Madison, USA/Bridgeman Images; 18, Pontiac (1720–69) incites other tribes to fight British troops in 1763 (colored engraving), American School (18th century)/Private Collection/Peter Newark American Pictures/Bridgeman Images; 19, Daniel Boone escorting settlers through the Cumberland Gap, 1851–52 (oil on canvas), Bingham, George Caleb (1811–79)/Washington University, St. Louis, USA/Bridgeman Images; 20, The Granger Collection, NYC; 21, The Granger Collection, NYC **CHAPTER ONE:** 22–3, LC, #09855; 24 (LE), General Andrew Jackson at the Battle of New Orleans (oil on canvas), Chappel, Alonzo (1828–87)/© Chicago History Museum, USA/Bridgeman Images; 24 (RT), The Texas Collection, Baylor University, Waco, Texas; 25 (LE), The Granger Collection, NYC; 25 (RT), Courtesy Walker Country Treasures/Sam Houston Memorial Museum Images Collection; 26, Buffalo Bill Center of the West/The Art Archive at Art Resource, NY; 28–9, Library of Congress, Geography and Map Division; 29 (UP-both), Courtesy of Independence National Historical Park; 29 (LO), Smithsonian Institution/Corbis; 30 (UP), Library of Congress, #g0019; 30 (LO), The Granger Collection, NYC; 31 (UP), Sacagawea with Lewis and Clark during their expedition of 1804–06 (color litho), Wyeth, Newell Convers (1882–1945)/Private Collection/Peter Newark American Picture/Bridgeman Images; 31 (LO), The Granger Collection, NYC; 32, Library of Congress, Geography and Map Division; 33 (UP), Courtesy of Independence National Historical Park; 33 (LO), The Granger Collection, NYC; 34, Photo © Christie's Images/Bridgeman Images; 34–5, The University of Texas at Arlington Library Special Collections; 35, The Granger Collection, NYC; 36–7, LC, #01891; 37 (UP), National Portrait Gallery, Smithsonian Institution; gift of Mrs. Herbert Lee Pratt, Jr.; 37 (LO), Special Collections, Toronto Public Library; 38, General Andrew Jackson at the Battle of New Orleans (oil on canvas), Chappel, Alonzo (1828–87)/© Chicago History Museum, USA/Bridgeman Images; 39 (UP), Wellcome Library, London; 39 (LO), Alabama Department of Archives and History, Montgomery, Alabama; 40 (UP), The Granger Collection, NYC; 40 (LO), flickr/Antique Military Rifles - https://creativecommons.org/licenses/by-sa/2.0/legalcode; 41 (UP), The Granger Collection, NYC; 41 (LO), LC, #01838; 42, The Granger Collection, NYC; 42–3, Schalkwijk/Art Resource, NY; 43, The Granger Collection, NYC; 44, MPI/Getty Images; 44–5, Report of Lieut. J. W. Abert, of His Examination of New Mexico, in the Years 1846–'47. Washington, 1848, Courtesy The Beinecke Rare Book and Manuscript Library; 46, North Wind Picture Archives/The Image Works; 47 (UP), Courtesy Aureo y Calicó; 47 (LO), LC, #LC-USZ62-69690001; 48–9, Fur traders in boat on Missouri by George Caleb Bingham (1811–79), oil on canvas, 74x93 cm, 1845/De Agostini Picture Library/Bridgeman Images; 50 (UP), Missouri History Museum, St. Louis; 50 (CTR), LC; 50 (LO), Oregon Historical Society, #aa006128; 51 (LE), Everett Collection Inc./Alamy; 51 (RT), Jedediah Smith (1799–1831) being attacked by a grizzly bear (color litho), American School (19th century)/Private Collection/Peter Newark American Pictures/Bridgeman Images; 52, Everett D. Graff Collection, American Heritage Center, University of Wyoming; 53, The Granger Collection, NYC; 54, Alfred Jacob Miller (American, 1810–1874), The Trapper's Bride, 1850, oil on canvas, Joslyn Art Museum, Omaha, Nebraska, Museum purchase, 1963.612; 55 (UP), Oregon Historical Society, #aa006086; 55 (LO), Yale Collection of Western Americana, Beinecke Rare Book and Manuscript Library; 56, The Walters Art Museum, Baltimore, #37.2556; 56–7, The Walters Art Museum, #37.1940.177; 58–9, Friends of the Governor's Mansion, Austin; 59 (UP), Prints and Photographs Collection, Texas State Library and Archives Commission, #1977/166-1; 59 (LO), Portrait of Antonio López de Santa Ana (1794–1876), c.1858 (oil on linen), L'Ouvrier, Paul (fl.1858)/© Collection of the New-York Historical Society, USA/Bridgeman Images; 60, The Granger Collection, NYC; 61 (UP), The San Jacinto Museum of History, S. Seymour Thomas; 61 (LO), The State Preservation Board, Austin, Texas; 62, LC, #3g03156; 62–3, The Granger Collection, NYC; 63, Clements Library, University of Michigan; 64 (UP), Portrait of Black Hawk (1767–1838) by Homer Henderson c.1870 (oil on canvas), King, Charles Bird (1785–1862) (after)/© Chicago History Museum, USA/Bridgeman Images; 64 (LO), George Catlin, Defeat and Capture of Black Hawk, from the Collection of Gilcrease Museum, Tulsa, Oklahoma; 65 (UP), National Portrait Gallery, Smithsonian Institution/Art Resource, NY; 65 (LO), State Archives of Florida, Florida Memory, http://floridamemory.com/items/show/31651; 66 (UP), Smithsonian Institution/Corbis; 66 (LO), The Buffalo Hunt (oil on canvas), Catlin, George (1796–1872)/Smithsonian Institution, Washington DC, USA/Bridgeman Images; 67, Portrait of Osceola (1804–38) (oil on canvas), Catlin, George (1796–1872)/Private Collection/Bridgeman Images; 68–9, MPI/Getty Images; 69, Time Life Pictures/Getty Images; 70 (UP), With permission of the Royal Ontario Museum © ROM; 70 (CTR LE), Narcissa Whitman (1808–47) (litho) (see also 268168), American School (19th century)/Private Collection/Peter Newark American Pictures/Bridgeman Images; 70 (CTR RT), Marcus Whitman (1802–47) (color litho) (see also 268169), American School (19th century)/Private Collection/Peter Newark American Pictures/Bridgeman Images; 70 (LO), Denver Public Library, Western Art Collection, #WHJ-10644; 71 (UP), Mary Evans/Pharcide/The Image Works; 71 (LO), Oregon Historical Society Research Library, #bb000025; 72–3, North Wind Picture Archives; 73 (LE), The Granger Collection, NYC; 73 (RT), National Portrait Gallery, Smithsonian Institution/Art Resource, NY; 74 (UP), Courtesy iCollector.com; 74 (LO), The Art Archive/F&A Archive/Art Resource, NY; 75 (UP), Courtesy College of the Siskiyous Library, Mount Shasta Collection; 75 (CTR), The Art Archive/Art Resource, NY; 75 (LO), The University of Texas Arlington Library, Special Collections; 76 (UP), The Granger Collection, NYC; 76 (LO), U.S. National Archives; 77, LC, #3g06742 **CHAPTER TWO:** 78–9, California History Room, California State Library, Sacramento, California; 80 (LE), LC, #3g02957; 80 (RT), Isaac I Stevens, September 1862 (engraving), American School (19th century) (after)/Private Collection/© Look and Learn/Bridgeman Images; 81 (UP), John D. Jenkins, www.SparkMuseum.com; 81 (LO), LC, #3a50931; 82, Oakland Museum of California, All Rights Reserved; 84–5, LC, #02525; 85, The Granger Collection, NYC; 86, The Granger Collection, NYC; 87, Photo of object in the collection of The New Mexico History Museum by Jim Steinhart of TravelPhotoBase.com; 88 (UP), LC, #3c09945; 88 (LO), The University of Texas at Arlington Library Special Collections; 89 (UP), Yale Collection of Western Americana, Beinecke Rare Book and Manuscript Library; 89 (LO), Bent's Old Fort National Historic Site, Colorado, a reconstructed 1840s adobe fur trading post on the mountain branch of the Santa Fe Trail/Omniphoto/UIG/Bridgeman Images; 90, Mel Shaw/MelShawStudios.com; 91 (LE), George Eastman House/Getty Images; 91 (RT), 000-742-0019, William A. Keleher Pictorial Collection, Center for Southwest Research, University Libraries, University of New Mexico; 92 (UP), Library of Congress; 92 (LO), Dorothy Sloan-Rare Books, Inc.; 93, Library of Congress, Geography and Map Division; 94, Courtesy of the California History Room, California State Library, Sacramento, California; 94–5, The Granger Collection, NYC; 95, Chip Clark, National Museum of Natural History, Smithsonian Institution; 96, Courtesy of the California History Room, California State Library, Sacramento, California; 97, Mystic Seaport; 98, LC, #04937; 99 (BOTH), The Granger Collection, NYC; 100, World History/TopFoto/The Image Works; 101, Archive of Modern Conflict Toronto; 102 (UP LE), The Granger Collection, NYC; 102 (UP RT), Richard Cummins/Getty Images; 102 (LO), Courtesy of the California History Room, California State Library, Sacramento, California;

104–105, MPI/Getty Images; 106–107, C. C. A. Christensen (1831–1912), Winter Quarters, c.1878, tempera on muslin, 76 3/4 x 113 3/4 inches. Brigham Young University Museum of Art, gift of the grandchildren of C. C. A. Christensen, 1970; 107 (UP), Brigham Young, age 49, © Intellectual Reserve, Inc.; 107 (LO), Corbis; 108, The Granger Collection, NYC; 109 (UP), Salt Lake City in the 1860s by C. W. Carter © Intellectual Reserve, Inc.; 109 (LO), Irina Tischenko/Shutterstock; 110, The Beinecke Rare Book and Manuscript Library; 110–11, Art Resource, NY; 112–13, LC, #03028; 113, Corbis; 114 (UP), SuperStock/Getty Images; 114 (LO), National Postal Museum, Curatorial Photographic Collection; 115 (UP), LC, #04481; 115 (LO), Photo used with permission from Wells Fargo Bank, N.A.; 116–17, Fort Laramie, 1858–60 (w/c on paper), Miller, Alfred Jacob (1810–74)/© Walters Art Museum, Baltimore, USA/Bridgeman Images; 118 (UP), Everett Collection, Inc.; 118 (LO LE), Texas Rangers badge (metal), American School/Private Collection/Peter Newark American Pictures/Bridgeman Images; 118 (LO CTR), Courtesy of Special Collections, Fine Arts Library, Harvard University; 118 (LO RT), Picture courtesy of Heritage Auctions, www.HA.com.119 (LE), Colt "Walker" model .44-caliber revolver of 1847 (wood & metal), American School (19th century)/Private Collection/Peter Newark American Pictures/Bridgeman Images; 119 (RT), Denver Public Library, Western History Collection, #X-33655; 120, Museum of History and Industry; 121 (UP), LC, #02650; 121 (CTR), David Rumsey Map Collection/www.davidrumsey.com; 121 (LO), Museum of History and Industry/Corbis; 122, Library of Congress, Geography and Map Division; 123 (UP), LC, #LC-USZ62-44752001; 123 (LO), The Granger Collection, NYC; 124–25, North Wind Picture Archives/Alamy; 125, INTERFOTO/Alamy; 126, Special Collections Department, University of Nevada, Reno, Libraries; 127 (UP), The Western Nevada Historic Photo Collection; 127 (LO), Washington State Historical Society, Tacoma; 128 (UP), akg-images/The Image Works; 128 (LO), LC, #3b38367; 128–29, Library of Congress, Geography and Map Division; 130 (UP), Dred Scott, c.1857 (oil on canvas), American School (19th century)/© Collection of the New-York Historical Society, USA/Bridgeman Images; 130 (LO), Engraving attributed to N. Orr published in Joshua Reed Giddings' 1858 history, The Exiles of Florida, courtesy www.johnhorse.com; 131 (UP), Kansas State Historical Society; 131 (LO), Western Reserve Historical Society, Cleveland, Ohio; 132–33, A postman of the American Pony Express being attacked by Native Americans (colored engraving), French School (19th century)/Bibliotheque Nationale, Paris, France/Archives Charmet/Bridgeman Images; 133, National Postal Museum, Smithsonian Institution; 134 (LE), Underwood Archives/Getty Images; 134 (RT), National Postal Museum, Smithsonian Institution; 134–35, Library of Congress, Geography and Map Division; 135, LC, #3c27508 **CHAPTER THREE:** 136–37, Yale Collection of Western Americana, Beinecke Rare Book and Manuscript Library; 138 (LE), Little Crow, 1863 (oil on canvas), Cross, Henry H. (1837–1918)/Minneapolis Institute of Arts, MN, USA/The Julia B. Bigelow Fund/Bridgeman Images; 138 (CTR), Don Troiani/Corbis; 138 (RT), Kansas State Historical Society; 139 (LE), Directors of the Union Pacific Railroad in a private rail car during construction of the line, 1868 (b/w photo), Russell, Andrew Joseph (1830–1902)/Private Collection/Peter Newark American Pictures/Bridgeman Images; 139 (RT), The Granger Collection, NYC; 140, Train by River, the Route to California, lithograph, Currier & Ives, 1871, Currier, N. (1813–88) and Ives, J. M. (1824–95)/Private Collection/J. T. Vintage/Bridgeman Images; 142 (UP), LC, #05992; 142 (LO), LC, #07417; 142–43, Battle of Glorieta Pass by Roy Andersen, PECO 30848, in the collection of Pecos National Historical Park, Pecos, New Mexico. Courtesy of the NPS; 143, Photo of object in the collection of New Mexico History Museum by Jim Steinhart of TravelPhotoBase.com; 144, The Historic New Orleans Collection, acc. no. 1979.123; 145 (UP), LC, #3c22438; 145 (LO), U.S. National Archives; 146 (UP), Kansas State Historical Society; 146–47, North Wind Picture Archives/The Image Works; 147, Kansas State Historical Society; 148 (BOTH), Courtesy of Wilson's Creek National Battlefield; 149 (UP), Wisconsin Historical Society, WHS-1909; 149 (LO), MPI/Getty Images; 150 (UP LE), Courtesy of Wilson's Creek National Battlefield; 150 (UP RT), John Ross (1790–1866) (color litho), American School (19th century)/Private Collection/Peter Newark American Pictures/Bridgeman Images; 150 (LO), LC, #129295p; 150–51, Smithsonian American Art Museum, Washington, DC/Art Resource, NY; 152, Denver Public Library, Western History Collection, #X-32438; 152–53, LC, #3g02995; 154 (UP), Oklahoma Historical Society; 154 (LO), The Granger Collection, NYC; 155 (UP), Corbis; 155 (LO), DEA Picture Library/Getty Images; 156, Corbis; 157 (UP), Courtesy of the Palace of the Governors Photo Archives (NMHM/DCA), #007151; 157 (LO), U.S. National Archives; 158 (UP), Courtesy The

Mark Twain House & Museum; 158 (LO), TopFoto/The Image Works; 159, Corbis; 160–61, University of Nevada, Reno, Libraries; 161, The Granger Collection, NYC; 162, Tarker/Corbis; 163, U.S. National Archives; 164–65, LC, #3b35947; 165, Idaho State Historical Society, #455-29; 166, LC, #1s00618; 166–67, Yale Collection of Western Americana, Beinecke Rare Book and Manuscript Library; 167, The Granger Collection, NYC; 168 (UP), LC, #3b48647; 168 (LO), LC, #05485; 169, Last Spike, Union Pacific Railway, Promontory Point, Utah, May 10th, 1869 (oil on canvas), Hill, Thomas (1829–1908)/Private Collection/Bridgeman Images; 170–71, Pajaro Valley Historical Association; 172–73, Library of Congress; 173, Yale Collection of Western Americana, Beinecke Rare Book and Manuscript Library; 174 (UP), Kansas State Historical Society; 174 (LO), The Granger Collection, NYC; 175, Mary Evans/Library of Congress/age fotostock; 176, NDSU Archives, likely taken by Job V. Harrison; 177, Library of Congress; 178 (UP), U.S. National Archives; 178 (LO), LC, #3c04167; 179, Buyenlarge/Getty Images; 180, LC, #02625u; 180–81, www.TexasMapStore.com; 182 (UP), Cattle Drive 1, c.1877 (oil on canvas), Walker, James (1818–89)/California Historical Society Collections at the Autry/Gift of Mr. and Mrs. Reginald F. Walker/Bridgeman Images; 182 (LO), Grant-Kohrs Ranch National Historic Site, GRKO 17419, Courtesy NPS Museum Management Program; 183, Jim Richardson/National Geographic Creative; 184, DeGoyler Library, SMU; 185 (UP), North Wind Picture Archives/The Image Works; 185 (LO), Corbis; 186 (Hat), Buffalo Bill Center of the West, Cody, Wyoming; 186 (Chaps), Grant-Kohrs Ranch National Historic Site, GRKO 545, Courtesy NPS Museum Management Program; 186 (Lariat), Buffalo Bill Center of the West, Cody, Wyoming; 186 (Saddle), Grant-Kohrs Ranch National Historic Site, GRKO 1570, Courtesy NPS Museum Management Program; 186 (Spurs), Grant-Kohrs Ranch National Historic Site, GRKO 17511, Courtesy NPS Museum Management Program; 187 (UP), The Granger Collection, NYC; 187 (LO), Photo circa 1890 in the public domain - http://commons.wikimedia.org/wiki/File:Charles_A_Siringo.jpg; 188 (UP), Grand Canyon National Park Museum Collection, #17227; 188 (LO), North Wind Picture Archives; 189, The Granger Collection, NYC; 190, LC, #3b37380; 190–91, U.S. National Archives **CHAPTER FOUR:** 192–93, Yale Collection of Western Americana, Beinecke Rare Book and Manuscript Library; 194 (UP LE), LC, #4a32155; 194 (UP RT), Eli Maier/Shutterstock; 194 (LO), The Granger Collection, NYC; 195 (LE), LC, #03110; 195 (CTR), Buffalo Bill Center of the West, Cody, Wyoming; 195 (RT), Train Passengers shooting Buffalo for sport, c.1870 (color litho), American School (19th century)/Private Collection/Peter Newark American Pictures/Bridgeman Images; 196, Comanchee Village (color litho), Catlin, George (1796–1872) (after)/Private Collection/Bridgeman Images; 198, The Granger Collection, NYC; 199, LC, #LC-USZ62-92580001; 200, Bettmann/Corbis; 201 (UP), Hugh Talman, National Museum of American History, Smithsonian Institution; 201 (LO), Moccasins and gaiters, Plains Indians, c.1820 (leather & beads), American/Private Collection/Photo © Boltin Picture Library/Bridgeman Images; 202 (UP), LC, #35235; 202 (LO), The Granger Collection, NYC; 203, Richard Throssel Collection, American Heritage Center, University of Wyoming; 204–205, Burton Historical Collection, Detroit Public Library; 205, Buffalo Bill Center of the West, Cody, Wyoming, Gift of Anne T. Black; 206–207, Kim Wiggins; 208, DeGoyler Library, SMU; 209, Quanah Parker, Comanche Indian Chief, 1915 (photo)/Universal History Archive/UIG/Bridgeman Images; 210 (BOTH), Yale Collection of Western Americana, Beinecke Rare Book and Manuscript Library; 211 (UP), LC, #05076; 211 (LO), DeGoyler Library, SMU; 212–13, The New-York Historical Society/Getty Images; 213, The Granger Collection, NYC; 214–15, General Custer's last stand at the Battle of Little Bighorn, June 25, 1876. Native American Wars, United States, 19th century/De Agostini Picture Library/Bridgeman Images; 215 (LE), LC, #03110; 215 (RT), LC, #3c11147; 216 (UP), LC, #3b02596; 216 (LO), U.S. National Archives; 217 (UP), Sioux Chiefs on Horseback in full War Regalia 1905 (photo)/Universal History Archive/UIG/Bridgeman Images; 217 (LO), Ann Ronan Pictures/Print Collector/Getty Images; 218, Courtesy of the Bancroft Library, University of California, Berkeley, #I0045128; 219, LC, #03130; 220–21, David Rumsey Map Collection, www.davidrumsey.com; 222 (UP), Buffalo Bill Center of the West, Cody, Wyoming, Gift of Dr. Harold McCracken; 222 (LO), Interior of Red Cloud's House, 1891 (b/w photo), Morledge, Clarence Grant (1865–1948)/Denver Public Library, Western History Collection/Bridgeman Images; 223, LC, #02515; 224, Buffalo Bill Center of the West, Cody, Wyoming, Adolf Spohr Collection, Gift of Larry Sheerin; 224–25, National Anthropological Archives, Smithsonian Institution, #NAA INV 06824700; 225, Corbis; 226, Buffalo Bill Center of the West, Cody, Wyoming, Gift of Olin Corporation,

NATIONAL GEOGRAPHIC
THE OLD WEST
STEPHEN G. HYSLOP

PUBLISHED BY THE NATIONAL GEOGRAPHIC SOCIETY

GARY E. KNELL, President and Chief Executive Officer

JOHN M. FAHEY, Chairman of the Board

DECLAN MOORE, Chief Media Officer

CHRIS JOHNS, Chief Content Officer

PREPARED BY THE BOOK DIVISION

HECTOR SIERRA, Senior Vice President and General Manager

LISA THOMAS, Senior Vice President and Editorial Director

JONATHAN HALLING, Creative Director

MARIANNE R. KOSZORUS, Design Director

R. GARY COLBERT, Production Director

JENNIFER A. THORNTON, Director of Managing Editorial

SUSAN S. BLAIR, Director of Photography

MEREDITH C. WILCOX, Director, Administration and
    Rights Clearance

STAFF FOR THIS BOOK

SUSAN STRAIGHT, Editor

CAROL FARRAR NORTON, Art Director

ULIANA BAZAR, Photo Editor

ZACHARY GALASI, Contributing Writer

CARL MEHLER, Director of Maps

MARSHALL KIKER, Associate Managing Editor

MIKE O'CONNOR, Production Editor

MIKE HORENSTEIN, Production Manager

CONSTANCE ROELLIG, Rights Clearance Specialist

KATIE OLSEN, Design Production Specialist

NICOLE MILLER, Design Production Assistant

RACHEL FAULISE, Manager, Production Services

The National Geographic Society is one of the world's largest nonprofit scientific and educational organizations. Founded in 1888 to "increase and diffuse geographic knowledge," the Society's mission is to inspire people to care about the planet. It reaches more than 400 million people worldwide each month through its official journal, *National Geographic,* and other magazines; National Geographic Channel; television documentaries; music; radio; films; books; DVDs; maps; exhibitions; live events; school publishing programs; interactive media; and merchandise. National Geographic has funded more than 10,000 scientific research, conservation and exploration projects and supports an education program promoting geographic literacy. For more information, visit www.nationalgeographic.com.

For more information, please call 1-800-NGS LINE (647-5463) or write to the following address:

National Geographic Society
1145 17th Street N.W.
Washington, D.C. 20036-4688 U.S.A.

Your purchase supports our nonprofit work and makes you part of our global community. Thank you for sharing our belief in the power of science, exploration and storytelling to change the world. To activate your member benefits, complete your free membership profile at natgeo.com/joinnow.

Visit us online at www.nationalgeographic.com/books

For information about special discounts for bulk purchases, please contact National Geographic Books Special Sales: ngspecsales@ngs.org

For rights or permissions inquiries, please contact National Geographic Books Subsidiary Rights: ngbookrights@ngs.org

ISBN: 978-1-4262-1555-1
ISBN: 978-1-4262-1556-8 (deluxe)

Printed in the United States of America

15/QGT-CML/1

XANFI

XANFI